Date Due

Why
Lawyers
Derail
Justice

John C. Anderson

WHY LAWYERS DERAIL JUSTICE

Probing the Roots of Legal Injustices

The Pennsylvania State University Press
University Park, Pennsylvania

Library of Congress Cataloging-in-Publication Data

Anderson, John C. (John Charles), 1954–
    Why lawyers derail justice : probing the roots of legal injustices
/ John C. Anderson.
        p.   cm.
    Includes bibliographical references and index.
    ISBN 0-271-01842-9 (cloth : acid-free paper)
    ISBN 0-271-01843-7 (paper : acid-free paper)
    1. Justice, Administration of—United States.   2. Practice of law—United
States.   3. Judicial error—United States.   4. Law reform—United States.
5. Justice.   I. Title.
KF384.A85   1999
347.73'12—dc21   98-16936
                                                                                        CIP

It is the policy of The Pennsylvania State University Press to use acid-free paper for
the first printing of all clothbound books. Publications on uncoated stock satisfy the
minimum requirements of American National Standard for Information Sciences—Permanence of Paper for Printed Library Materials, ANSI Z39.48-1992.

Dedicated to my wife, Marcia; our two sons, Albert and Ian; Victor and Mary Lepisto; Walter and Alice Cochrane; Albert and Ida Foster; Louise, Charles, June, Paul, and Joan Anderson; and Mary, Bobby, Michael, and Daniel Ashley.

"If I were asked where I place the American aristocracy, I should reply without hesitation that it is not among the rich, who are united by no common tie, but that it occupies the judicial bench and the bar. The more we reflect upon all that occurs in the United States, the more we shall be persuaded that the lawyers, as a body, form the most powerful, if not the only, counterpoise to the democratic element."
    —Alexis de Tocqueville, *Democracy in America,* chapter 16

Contents

Contents

Acknowledgments

This book developed out of a dissertation project for the School of Philosophy at Catholic University, Washington, D.C. I am especially grateful to my dissertation adviser, Professor Daniel Dahlstrom, now teaching philosophy at Boston University, for his encouragement, patience, insights, criticisms, and, yes, *epieikeia,* during many a difficult period. The book would not have been written true to its own spirit without his support and encouragement. As members of my dissertation committee, Dean Jude Dougherty and Russell Hittinger likewise provided constructive criticisms and encouragement. Many other members of the Catholic University philosophy faculty inspired this effort with their scholarly example and dedication to truth.

Professor Daniel Robinson of Georgetown University provided highly useful comments and criticisms that helped me to shape this into a better book. Professor Hadley Arkes's open-minded engagement with my argument was equally challenging and encouraging; his input inspired further insights about the nature of natural justice and the polity. I owe a few examples in the climax of Chapter 4 to Professor Arkes, examples with which I hope to make it easier for readers to understand the workings of epieikeia. As different as all of these scholars are in their orientation, their engagement with my work and the problem posed was very heartening and inspiring.

This book would never have seen the light of day were it not for Sandy Thatcher of Penn State Press. I recognize a common thread in many of his authors in their quest to recover some of the same political virtues touched on in the present book, without which our legal system and our democratic notions become mere pretenses.

Of course, the encouragement and assistance of all these people does not at all necessarily indicate any endorsement of the positions advanced in this book. Their support indicates merely an intellectual honesty that has recognized the importance of letting my admittedly provocative and novel view of law and jurisprudence be fully heard and debated.

Finally, a special acknowledgment is due to all my family members, who endured my asocial behavior during holidays and vacations while I worked on this manuscript, writing about the importance of human sociability. My wife, father, and brother provided especially useful criticisms, which I have incorporated into my argument.

Prelude

Then came there two women, that were harlots, unto the king, and
stood before him. And the one woman said, O my lord, I and this
woman dwell in one house; and I was delivered of a child with her in
the house. And it came to pass, the third day after that I was delivered, that this woman was delivered also: and we were together;
there was no stranger with us in the house, save we two in the house.
And this woman's child died in the night; because she overlaid it.
And she arose at midnight, and took my son from beside me, while
thine handmaid slept, and laid it in her bosom, and laid her dead
child in my bosom. And when I rose in the morning to give my child
suck, behold, it was dead; but when I had considered it in the morning, behold, it was not my son which I did bear. And the other
woman said. Nay: but the living is my son, and the dead is thy son.
And this said, No: but the dead is thy son, and the living is my son.
Thus they spake before the king. Then said the king, The one saith
This is my son that liveth, and thy son is the dead: and the other
saith, Nay: but thy son is the dead, and my son is the living. And the
king said, Bring me a sword. And they brought a sword before the
king. And the king said, Divide the living child in two, and give half
to the one, and half to the other. Then spake the woman whose the
living child was unto the king, for her bowels yearned upon her son,
and she said, O my lord, give her the living child, and in no wise slay
it. But the other said, Let it be neither mine nor thine, but divide it.
Then the king answered and said, Give her the living child, and in
no wise slay it: she is the mother thereof. And all Israel heard of the
judgment which the king had judged: and they feared the king: for
they saw that the wisdom of God was in him, to do judgment.[1]

The story from the Old Testament of Solomon's wisdom in rendering legal
judgment is incomprehensible in a contemporary legal framework or theory of jurisprudence. While the positions of the disputants (the two mothers) are recognizable in a contemporary setting, Solomon's judgment cannot be readily simplified into a universalizable formula, rule, or legal
opinion that could serve as a precedent. Legislature, executive, and judge
are combined in one figure who rules by decree. His power is absolute and

has the potential to be arbitrary. Yet he is wise in the use of this power, as illustrated by his specific adjudication in this story.

If a contemporary judge were to act as Solomon did, he would at least be criticized, and maybe even removed from office for abusing his authority. But a court that wrested a child against her will from the only home she had ever known was somehow not considered *legally* arbitrary.[2] In the *Claussen* case, the Michigan Supreme Court caused a three-year-old to be forcibly handed over to virtual strangers, who happened to be her biological parents but had abandoned her to adoption at birth. The Michigan Supreme Court issued a lengthy, reasoned opinion based on jurisdictional arguments to justify this result.

How is it that the result in the *Claussen* case typically raises distress only among lay persons but is dispassionately discussed by most professional lawyers as the only possible outcome? Can it be assumed so readily that "law" is truly a limitation on what is inherently arbitrary in any exercise of official power—or is law, as such, more a disguise for what is arbitrary? Were the judges in the Michigan Supreme Court truly confronted with no choice other than to treat the interest of the child as secondary to the jurisdictional legal issue?

Aside from the greater regard for abstract legal issues in the *Claussen* case, which had a lengthy legal opinion and involved protracted litigation over a three-year period, how might contemporary jurisprudential theory legitimately and convincingly distinguish the judgment of Solomon from the *Claussen* case? Why has no such attempt been made? Why is such an obvious question not even considered in contemporary jurisprudence? Is there really so much that sets Solomon's circumstances apart from contemporary adjudications?

Some might dismiss the story of Solomon's judgment as simply anachronistic. Still, it may be worthwhile to pause and consider whether the historical distance of Solomon's decision from contemporary society truly disposes of its relevance for us. Was Solomon's adjudication wise? Is it possible to articulate a contemporary theory of jurisprudence that would adequately explain why Solomon's decision was wise or appropriate in his own circumstances, and why it would or would not be so in contemporary circumstances as well? If he were to be considered wise in his own circumstances and unwise in contemporary circumstances, is there any legitimate basis for these different assessments?

The story of Solomon's judgment prompts a further question: has something been lost in the process of displacing such wise men as Solomon within the complex bodies of law that are such a part of contemporary society and without which much of contemporary society would be unthinkable? Is it sufficient to rely solely on a system of laws for justice, or does a system of laws not also need a Solomon to render it just?

Even more significantly, if individuals such as Solomon do not need sophisticated legal systems to be just, what need do we have for such legal systems? Is Solomon's judgment really so incomprehensible in a contemporary setting? More important, should contemporary theories of jurisprudence attempt to recapture something of its essence in their considerations of ways to reform the legal system to render it more just? Is something gained or lost by evaluating the contemporary legal system through an uncritical acceptance of the demarcation between legislative, judicial and executive?

At the root of the following analysis of legal injustices is the conviction that the story of Solomon's wisdom is vital to an examination of contemporary jurisprudence, and, in particular, to diagnosing flaws in jurisprudential theory.

Notes

1. This passage is the well-recognized story from 1 Kings 3:16–28 Authorized (King James) Version, concerning the wisdom of Solomon.

2. *Claussen*, 502 N.W.2d 649 (Mich. 1993).

1

The Split Between Legal Language and Common Sense

A split is generally acknowledged to exist between the ordinary language and opinions of lay persons and those of so-called experts, that is, lawyers and professors, on the notion of law and justice. The academic experts, including jurisprudential philosophers, typically focus on the question: What is law? Or, more precisely, on the question: What may properly be deemed to fall within the realm of law?

Debate about these questions centers on whether law includes (1) merely the laws enacted by legislators, or (2) also judge-made law, or (3) also certain shared principles embodied in the language games or customs of the legal elite (that is, customary practices of judges and maybe lawyers), or (4) also a so-called natural law (ranging from Lon Fuller's procedural concerns on the art of law to a substantive notion of natural law).

This debate is carried on as though it exhausted the range of possibilities and as though the exclusive concern with the debated issues were appropriate and unassailable.[1] This debate, not surprisingly, mirrors the practice and orientation of the other category of experts in the realm of law—the practicing lawyers. Lawyers typically present themselves as experts in determining what the law is in any particular area or factual circumstances—for a fee. By extension (and this may appear unremarkable), lawyers do not regard themselves as experts in determining what justice is—only the question of what law is concerns them.

Indeed, the working assumption behind the practice of law is that mere adherence to the proper legal procedures will assure that justice, whatever it is, will be done. When an injustice occurs, this is merely due to some deficiency in the procedures or legal rules as applied to the facts (for example, procedural due process). Generally implicit (though occasionally explicit) in this working assumption is the notion that focusing on legal procedures has the advantage of appearing objective, something that a more overt consideration of justice may lack. Competing views of justice are often disputed indirectly through the advocacy of different procedural rules, thereby concealing what is really at stake in a legal controversy.

In contrast to the experts, the lay person is typically concerned about the law in terms of its relation to justice, rather than about the question of what law is. The lay person may disagree with other lay persons about what is just in a particular case, but more often than not, there is a common core of agreement about what generally is or is not just among ordinary persons—particularly in ongoing relationships between persons who know each other and live and work together. The legal system is often an alien world to be avoided by most, even in today's highly litigious society.

Most people are too busy trying to survive and get along with each other, and they lack the resources or time to get involved in the legal system. Moreover, if lay persons want to find out what the law is on a particular matter, they go to a lawyer, if they can afford one, hoping that the lawyer is skilled and lucky enough to find the right verbal formula expressing the legal procedure that brings about the result most advantageous to their needs.

Often, the presumption is that the ordinary understanding of what is going on is deficient, and that the expert's technical language completely comprehends the problem. I abandon and contest this presumption favoring the expert in my examination of legal injustices.

One goal of this study is to show that confining jurisprudence to the question of what law is serves the parochial interest of lawyers, without being of benefit to the well-being or justice of society. When real, tangible examples of legal injustice are made the starting points of an examination of jurisprudence, it becomes evident that the traditional problems and technical language of the experts actually conceal the real problem of law in relation to justice. There is a striking disconnection between jurisprudential and ethical theory on the one hand and the actual experiences of persons on the other. This disconnection is best revealed by focusing attention on the full range of injustices inflicted under the color of law—ranging from the obvious examples of slavery and the Holocaust to more controversial examples arising out of our own "democratic" legal system.

In addition, this disconnection is often obscured when some abstract notions of justice form the starting point of ethical inquiries. This is because such abstract notions of justice are imperfect and incomplete because of the very nature of the subject matter of justice.

On the other hand, so-called notions of legal justice give the illusion of greater objectivity and concreteness, because they obscure and ignore this complexity. By merely playing word games about what law is, one need never confront the real problems of the relation of law to justice. Only by contrasting legal reasoning, in theory and practice, against the actual facts in a case can one come to grips with the real problem of determining justice concretely. In effect, this means first identifying concrete instances of injustice.

It is an undeniable fact of human history that many injustices are often justified in the name of justice. Accordingly, any theory of justice ought to be carefully scrutinized for ambiguities and confusions that might contribute to its misuse as a justification for acting unjustly. Indeed, the use of theories of legal interpretation, or jurisprudential legalism, to justify unjust legal results is one of the principal foils of this analysis of legal injustices.

For our purposes, jurisprudential legalism is the label applied to the following cluster of concepts shared in part by contending contemporary schools of jurisprudence. They are concepts that, I argue, are at the root of many legal injustices: an excessive egalitarianism; an undue emphasis on universalizability, coherence, and predictability; the identification of the community with the nation state or its legal institutions; an overemphasis on impartiality; a preoccupation with rights, duties, and rules; the public duty/private duty distinction; the notion that laws may be interpreted within a single, universal interpretation; and the tendency to regard legal interpretation as the central problem of jurisprudence.

In addition, I challenge the traditional notion of jurisprudential legalism that jurisprudence is properly confined to questions of adjudication, to the exclusion of any consideration of the effect of a legal system and its interpretations within the broader community from which it ultimately obtains its legitimacy and meaning. Jurisprudential legalism, in its most extreme versions, is often manifested in what I shall refer to as the legalist fallacy, a fallacy that is rooted in the neglect or outright rejection of any teleological framework for law and morals.

As such, the legalist fallacy is exemplified in both law and morals in two *instances*: (1) when one holds that law and the legal system are in and of themselves somehow inherently good or just, or that the legal system does not (or need not) have justice as its end, (2) when the legal text or the interpretation of universalizable legal or ethical rules is emphasized to the exclusion of the consideration of what is a just end or result in particular circumstances, or to the exclusion of properly recognizing the degree to which justice is grounded in (and constrained by) human sociability.

I have found it instructive to appropriate certain features of Aristotle's ethical and political philosophy in order to better illuminate the defects of the legalist fallacy, or jurisprudential legalism, and to counterpose what I believe to constitute a better approach to jurisprudential problems. The absence of a developed jurisprudence in Aristotle, in terms of the types of questions that have been the preoccupation of most contemporary jurisprudential thought, frees up the inquiry to explore foundational questions obscured by contemporary preoccupations.[2] There is no preoccupation with defining law with any degree of precision in Aristotle. There is no notion of the practice of law being confined to an exclusive professional class in Aristotle. There is no notion of a complete and rigid separation of legal and moral questions into unrelated preserves. The absence of these distinctions opens the door to exploring, in the fullest sense, just what Aristotle meant by his notion of *epieikeia,* sometimes translated as "equity."

The notion of epieikeia, as used in my analysis of legal injustices, is distinct from legal-based notions of equity as fairness, insofar as epieikeia does not focus on the degree to which a desired outcome conforms to the egalitarian principle of treating everyone the same. Moreover, epieikeia is flexible, restrained, merciful, and forgiving, rather than legalistic: epieikeia is less concerned with insisting upon its legal rights or with articulating a legal justification of a particular action that may be universalized; it has more to do with the justice of a particular action, as applied to a specific person in particular circumstances wherein its concept of justice connotes some partiality or continuing social connection with that person.

It is in this sense that the legalist fallacy and epieikeia are mirror images: (1) the legalist fallacy emphasizes a universal rule rather than particular ends and typically engages in abstractions in a presumably impartial manner; therefore, it often regards justice independently of any social connections between persons; (2) epieikeia emphasizes particular ends as exceptions to a universal rule, and, more important, interacts with persons with restraint and mercy—even when law does not require this restraint.

The legalist fallacy essentially ignores the exception (a particular end) in favor of a rule or principle that can be universalized, irrespective of the social connections that exist (or ought to exist) between persons. In contrast, the essence of epieikeia is to make exceptions, while mindful of the social connections of all involved persons; and this is the grounding of its mercy and restraint. Accordingly, the restraint and flexibility of epieikeia limits the scope of "law's empire," whereas the legalist fallacy motivates the almost limitless expansion of law's empire. The suppression of any glimmerings of epieikeia serves the interests of lawyers very well.

It is very important to bear in mind that there are two very distinct senses of *universal* at issue in my discussion of epieikeia. With respect to the interpretation of laws with an eye to their value as precedents—that is, with respect to their universalizability as abstract rules—epieikeia has to be seen as a departure from universal considerations. With respect to the particular circumstances for which the exercise of the virtue of epieikeia requires a departure from a universal rule, there is only one just and correct result, and that is the outcome that epieikeia demands.

The outcome is an *action* or *decree,* not an *abstract principle* that may be replicated in the manner of a legal precedent. In other words, there can never arise a body of law based on principles or rules of epieikeia without risking the perversion of the very notion of epieikeia. But the necessity underlying this action or decree is universal, because it is necessary—if the exact circumstances were replicated, the same action or decree would be required.

The problem arises when the two very different senses of *universal* are collapsed together. The notions of universalizable rules or legal precedents can be reduced to a body of law and principles of legal interpretation, which can be learned in the same manner as mathematical principles are learned by young persons. But discerning the particular just outcome as an exception to a universal rule in particular circumstances is a species of wisdom (not knowledge) that can only be cultivated by virtuous persons with experience in living together justly. The former can be taught in law schools. The latter can result only from living a life of virtue. "In politics, it is impossible that all things should be precisely set down in writing; for enactments must be universal, but actions are concerned with particulars."[3]

Accordingly, I argue that there has been a displacement and confusion of epieikeia with legalisms, such as procedural due process, the various legal rules of equity arising out of equitable jurisdiction, impartiality, and equality, none of which, in the end, can ever temper the inherent injustice of the law in the same way that epieikeia can. Indeed epieikeia remains hidden, because these legal and moral notions conceal, in the procedural formula of the lawyer and the contemporary preoccupation with equality and freedom, the true nature of justice.

This confusion may lend support to the prerogatives of lawyers, as does the jurisprudential presumption that the split between ordinary language and jurisprudence shows the deficiencies of ordinary language, rather than the reverse. The thrust of my analysis of legal injustices, however, is that a legal theory that does not sustain the ordinary understanding of law and justice is fundamentally flawed. The subject matter of natural justice, as the object of practical wisdom and as exemplified in the political virtue of epieikeia, cannot be reduced exclusively to legalistic terms, as if law were completely impartial and indifferent to the well-being and ends of natural human associations.

Using the flexibility, mercy, restraint, and particularity of epieikeia as my touchstone, in this chapter I briefly sketch a number of contemporary paradigms of legal injustice within the framework of five major categories:

1. Legal injustices arising from manipulation, misuse, or expansion of the criminal law

2. Injustices arising from formalism and impartiality
3. Injustices arising from law's expansion into the private sector
4. Inflexibility, moral neutrality, and harshness of legalistic egalitarianism
5. Legalistic morality

As these examples show, I propose a radically different paradigm. I ask only that the reader temporarily suspend deference to the traditions of jurisprudential legalism in reviewing these examples, until having fully considered the following chapters.

1. Legal Injustices Arising from Manipulation, Misuse, or Expansion of the Criminal Law

1.1. Guilty Acquitted or Innocent Convicted, with Due Process.

The claim that the acquittal of a guilty person of a crime in one set of circumstances before an adjudicative body somehow assures the acquittal of an innocent person of a different crime in a different set of circumstances before another adjudicative body is a common illustration of the legalist fallacy that has almost become a cliché. In other words, the legalist fallacy presupposes that a particular injustice is required in order to fashion a legal rule that will work efficiently or justly in hypothetical circumstances not being adjudicated.

But innocent persons are far too often erroneously convicted of crimes in adjudicative proceedings where all recognized rules of due process have been complied with—just as often as guilty persons are let free because of due process. Fashioning a rule pertaining to due process, or correcting a different injustice than that being adjudicated, has nothing to do with rendering justice in the particular circumstances.[4]

1.2. Evidentiary Rules Inadequate Where Juries Are Unjust.

The notion that persons who lack communal or associative bonds (or who, even, are hostile or racist toward each other) can somehow impartially adjudicate whether a member of one community injured a member of the other community merely through legal procedures, sequestered juries, the legal rules of evidence on hearsay and burdens of proof, and jury instructions is another common illustration of the legalist fallacy. This example assumes that justice is reducible to an abstract body of rules that may be given meaning independent of the social context in which a teleological framework of justice is grounded.

Justice is a social good and cannot be adequately defined by abstractions and rules divorced from the social bonds that are the end of justice and necessarily presupposed by it. The absence of natural social bonds cannot be artificially corrected through a fabricated set of rules and procedures that presuppose the presence of social bonds and community for their very functioning.[5]

1.3. Immunities of Prosecutors for Misconduct.

The notion that certain officials must be privileged to the extent of being immune (more or less) for misconduct while engaged in their official duties, in order to protect government officials from litigious harassment when they are acting properly in the performance of their official duties in other circumstances is one of the more extreme versions of the legalist fallacy, sometimes referred to as sovereign immunity.[6] But the very ability of the legal system to function at all requires certain minimal levels of natural justice and restraints by most citizens.

If sovereign immunity in all its manifestations (whether "absolute" or "qualified") is all that restrains the mass of society from pursuing meritless litigation against an official, that society is not much of a community at all, but more like the mythical Hobbesian "state of nature," a notion that I emphatically reject. Moreover, if an official will only perform his duty when his actions are insulated from accountability by sovereign immunity, that official is nothing but a coward and a bully who ought not to be entrusted with such power.

1.4. Entrapment of Citizens in Order to Prosecute.

In our legal system, the doctrine of entrapment permits *officials* or their *agents* to induce a person to commit a crime in order to prosecute that person. (However, if a private person were to induce another person to commit a crime, that in itself would be a crime.) Entrapment is thought necessary because of the inability of police, to otherwise obtain convictions of criminals, because of strict adherence to procedural and evidentiary obstacles.

This corruption of the system sometimes leads to even greater police abuses, such as when an agent provocateur commits other more serious crimes while attempting to induce a morally weak person to commit a lesser crime.[7] The only concern of our courts with regard to entrapment is whether or not there was a so-called predisposition to commit the crime, under the assumption that entrapping persons who are supposedly predisposed is meritorious.[8] Aside from the difficulty in distinguishing between entrapped persons who were predisposed to commit the crime and persons who were entrapped without any so-called predisposition, the very idea that officials should be inducing morally weak persons to commit crimes, rather than preventing crimes, is about as unnatural as parents tricking their children to do wrong so that they can punish them.[9]

1.5. Targeting People First, Then Fitting Criminal Statute to Their Conduct.

When there are too many laws or when the complexity and scope of laws requires professional specialists to interpret them, it becomes possible for people to violate laws without any injury to others and without knowing that they have violated a law. Prosecutors can take advantage of this situation by targeting a person for prosecution and then looking for some technical point in the law that that person may have unwittingly violated. Thus the definition of criminality turns exclusively on the creative interpretation of legal texts, as exemplified in the manipulation of the mail-fraud statute against Senator Alphonse D'Amato's brother and in the Racketeering in Criminal Organizations (RICO) statutes against Michael Milken.[10]

1.6. Merciless Prosecutors.

Under the "rule of law," so-called prosecutorial discretion has been so narrowly conceived that teenagers engaging in consensual sex and who were ultimately married are criminally prosecuted for statutory rape and compelled to register as "dangerous sexual predators." On the other hand, child molesters, kidnappers, and murderers are released from prison because they have "paid their legal dues" by serving their time.[11]

1.7. Innocent Persons Remain in Prison in Interests of "Finality."

As a result of the weakening of the writ of habeas corpus in the federal courts, some state legislatures have limited presumably "frivolous" prisoner appeals of their convictions with rigid rules providing for time limits on the use of newly discovered exonerating evidence. It is difficult to fathom just what might be frivolous about exonerating evidence, unless the alleged evidence does not really exonerate.

The apparent inability of judges to factually distinguish meritorious from frivolous postconviction appeals by failing to deny clearly frivolous appeals has been replaced with a rigid rule denying even meritorious appeals after a certain time limit has expired. As a result, an Oregon couple wrongly convicted of murder was held in prison in 1995—even after the prosecution admitted their error in the light of evidence uncovered after the deadline.[12]

1.8. Harshness of Egalitarian-Motivated Criminal-Sentencing Guidelines Designed to Limit Discretion.

The Federal Sentencing Guidelines, 18 U.S. Code, sections 991 et seq., were recently enacted to assure that criminal defendants be treated more uniformly. This was effected by replacing the sentencing discretion traditionally used by judges to lengthen or shorten sentences with a complex body of rules that establish numerically weighted criteria to be considered when imposing sentences. Prosecutors and defense counsel have responded to the guidelines with creative ingenuity, since the time served is greatly affected by the mere changing of a few words in a criminal charge. The result is that criminal defendants committing the same offense can end up serving widely disparate sentences, depending on the competence of their defense counsel and the creativity and caseload of their opposing prosecutor.

Some judges resign in disgust at the harshness and severity of the sentences they are forced to impose under the guidelines; certain segments of the public accuse the guidelines' drafters of bias, because of statistical disparities in sentences between different classifications of criminal defendants. These segments of the public also propose changes in the weights and criteria to reduce this disparity. However, the majority of opinion supports continuation of the guidelines, because the criteria and weights are uniform (nondiscretionary) and therefore thought to be fair.[13]

1.9. Life Imprisonment for Nonviolent, First-Time Drug Crime.

In *Harmelin v. Michigan,* 115 L.Ed.2d 836 (1991), the Supreme Court majority held that the sentencing of a first-time nonviolent drug offender to life imprisonment without possibility of parole under state law (not federal guidelines) was not "cruel and unusual punishment," because that was the sentence required by the law enacted by the state legislature. The majority further reasoned that only if such a sentence were imposed through the discretionary act of a judge would it constitute an arbitrary act of cruel and unusual punishment. The court dissenters argued that the sentence was cruel and unusual, because it was not uniform with other state laws and with federal law; virtually every other state and federal law would have imposed a sentence of less than a few years. Based on the minority argument, presumably the sentence would not have been cruel and unusual punishment if it had been uniform with every other state sentencing law.

1.10. Regulators Manipulating Definition of *Wetland* to Criminalize Property Improvements.

Persons who have improved property—if it happens to be classified as a wetland by the Army Corps of Engineers—without obtaining a permit from the Corps have been criminally prosecuted and imprisoned. A property may be classified as a wetland even if it is dry 350 days a year, and even if it has not previously been deemed a wetland. Thus, criminality is exclusively a function of interpretation of a text, such that an act that is not criminal on one day becomes criminal the following day, based on a change in a legal definition of *wetland*.[14]

1.11. Legal Incentives for Fabricated Child Sex-Abuse Charges.

In 1974 Congress enacted a law, the Mondale Child-Abuse Prevention and Treatment Act, to deal with the real problem of underreporting and coverup of child abuse, by providing incentives for reporting child abuse through matching federal funds to state programs established for the identification, prosecution, and treatment of child abuse.[15] The law provides funding to states that enact statutes giving qualified immunity from prosecution to any person making an accusation of sexual abuse, even if it is false, with a presumption that the person made the accusation in good faith.

Within this framework, some juries, prosecutors, and judges have had difficulty in distinguishing between real cases of sexual abuse of children from cases arising from therapists manipulating children to fabricate sex-abuse allegations. In each questionable case, the therapist(s) conducted repeated unsupervised and unmonitored sessions where they made suggestions that sexual abuse had occurred, suggestions initially denied by the children. After prolonged exposure to repeated therapy sessions, after sustained local press coverage suggesting that abuse had occurred, and after exchanging stories between children, the children finally alleged sexual abuse.[16]

1.12. More Nonviolent Than Violent Criminals in Prison, Arising from Expansion of Criminal Laws.

Prosecutorial enforcement priorities (and judicial outcomes) do not always accord with natural notions of justice, reflected in the fact that violent crimes are often punished more leniently than nonviolent crimes, in the United States.

Crimes of violence against women are often prosecuted less severely and result in lighter punishments than other violent crimes.[17] Kidnappers of children and other sexual predators are not necessarily locked away for life, except in a few states.[18] There are numerous examples of violent criminals being released after serving their sentences (or after being paroled with reduced sentences), only to commit more violent crimes upon their release.[19] Some have estimated that the time served by convicted murderers in the United States averages only six years, and that only 100,000 of about 900,000 murderers in the United States are currently incarcerated.[20] But the state and federal prison population in 1992 was triple that of 1980. Moreover, the United States has the dubious distinction of leading the world in the percentage of its population held in prison. This is, in part, due to the war on drugs.[21]

1.13. Imprisonment for Self-Defense from Violent Criminal Because of Gun Control.

In *Commonwealth v. Lindsay,* Massachusetts's highest court affirmed the conviction and imprisonment of a person who had shot a person knifing him— for the second time—even though the court acknowledged that "it is possible that the defendant is alive today only because he carried the gun that day for protection."[22]

1.14. Abused Spouse Murdered Because of Gun Control.

In Cheektowaga, New York, the police confiscated a handgun from Mrs. Polly Przybyl when they responded to her call for help against the efforts of her violent, former husband to break into the house. Consequently, Mrs. Przybyl's former husband returned with a shotgun and killed her. The handgun was subject to local gun-control ordinances, but the shotgun was not.[23]

1.15. Wife's Jointly Owned Car Forfeited to State for Husband's Use of It with Prostitute.

In *Bennis v. Michigan,* the Supreme Court upheld the state's confiscation of an automobile used by a husband with a prostitute, even though the wife had a joint-property interest in the vehicle and had not known that it was being used for prostitution.[24] In effect, the Supreme Court was unable to distinguish what natural justice would recognize as the wife's property interest from her husband's—when the state had a claim.

1.16. Justification of Excessive Force Based on Rules of Engagement.

In the Senate hearings on Ruby Ridge (where federal agents shot the wife and nine-year-old son of Randy Weaver, who had failed to appear at a court hearing for alleged gun violations), the focus was on the so-called rules of engagement and whether different rules of engagement would have prevented federal agents from using excessive force. But the federal sharpshooters themselves emphasized that their actions were justified (and that they would do it again) even under different rules of engagement.

The notion that mere modified rules of engagement could somehow safeguard and preclude misconduct by officials in other circumstances, or that the rules of engagement somehow excuse the agents at Ruby Ridge for using excessive force, epitomizes the legalist fallacy.[25]

2. Injustices Arising from Formalism and Impartiality

2.1. Foiled Mugger Sues Police for Damages.

In *McCummings v. New York City Transit Authority,* the court affirmed a jury award of $4.3 million to a subway mugger against the New York City Transit Authority because the mugger was injured by a Transit policeman shooting him.[26] The shooting foiled the subway mugger's attempt to rob an elderly man.

In affirming the award, New York's highest court reasoned that in a civil-negligence action, it had to view the controverted factual issues (where the plaintiff-mugger contradicted the police and the victim's account) in the light most favorable to the plaintiff. This meant that the court had to assume that the transit officer did not actually see a mugging, even though, in a separate criminal action for the incident, the mugger pleaded guilty to second-degree attempted robbery.

2.2. Sterilization of the Retarded with Due Process.

In *Carrie Buck v. J. H. Bell,* the forcible sterilization of an allegedly mentally disabled person was held to be constitutional because she had been afforded "procedural due process" and "equal protection"; that is, the procedures prescribed in the state statute authorizing her sterilization had been strictly followed. There is an often unrecognized distinction between natural justice and procedural due process or equal protection, which are insufficient and inadequate surrogates for justice.[27]

2.3. Legal Issues, Not Equity, Subject to Appellate Review.

In the *Claussen* case, the Supreme Court refused certiorari. The notion that it is beneath the Supreme Court to act in the interests of mercy and justice because of crowded court dockets, and the notion that only rarefied legal issues are worthy of their attention (not the life of a mere child) epitomizes the legalist fallacy. The fear is that if an exception were to be made to deal with a supposedly nonlegal issue, the Court would be overwhelmed with other cases. Thus, an exception is not made out of fear of what could happen in other circumstances. Originally, separate courts of equity in medieval England ostensibly performed this function, and this, indeed, is often the naive lay person's erroneous conception of the Supreme Court's role. But the concept of equity has been transmuted over time into just another set of legal rules and reduced to the principle of equality.[28]

2.4. Child Removed Against Will from Adoptive Home to Home of Original Parent.

In another example of the legalist fallacy, the highest court in Illinois held that a three-year-old child who was attached to his adoptive parents had to be forcibly returned to the biological parents, who had initially abandoned him. The Illinois court based its disregard of the child's best interests on the need to fashion a general rule that would not encourage baby snatching in hypothetical circumstances that were not at issue in the facts before the court.[29]

2.5. Abortion Permitted Because Fetus Not a "Person" for Purposes of Fourteenth Amendment.

The way in which legal argumentation distorts, confuses, and hides what is really at stake from the standpoint of natural justice is exemplified in *Roe v. Wade,* where the Supreme Court held that states had no legitimate interest in protecting the fetus from abortion through the second trimester of pregnancy.[30] The court's holding was principally based on the notion that a fetus was not a "person," for the purposes of the protections of the Fourteenth Amendment, given the court's historical analysis of the liberal abortion practices in the nineteenth century contemporaneous with the adoption of the Fourteenth Amendment.

Meanwhile, the issue is about as polarized as the pre–Civil War slavery debate, with a majority of the public appearing somewhat muddled on the issue. The majority favors *Roe v. Wade* without really understanding the extent to which it permits abortions (throughout the entire pregnancy for any reason), and yet opposes unrestricted abortion on demand.

2.6. Fugitive Slave Returned to Master Because Slave Not a "Person" for Purposes of Constitution.

Similar legal distortions of natural justice occurred in *Dred Scott v. Sandford*. In that case, the Supreme Court held that a fugitive slave lacked standing to sue to protect his freedom from slavery in the courts, based on a historical analysis of who was numbered among the citizens of the United States when the Constitution was first adopted. The court based this on the historical fact that slaves were not considered citizens at the time of the initial ratification of the Constitution.[31]

2.7. Using a Law for the Protection of Employee Benefits to Deny Health Care to Insured Employee.

In *Corcoran v. United Healthcare, Inc.*, a fetus died because a claims administrator of an employer's health-insurance plan denied coverage for the extended hospitalization recommended by the attending physician to a mother in a high-risk pregnancy.[32] The mother sued the health plan and the claims administrator for a wrongful-death action. If the mother had been covered by health insurance purchased by her as an individual rather than by her employer, she would have had a viable claim under state law. However, because she had a health-insurance plan provided by her employer, it was subject to a federal law governing employer benefit plans, and this law preempted her state law claim.

The federal law was originally enacted with the primary focus of assuring the soundness of employer pension and retirement plans, and it provided no comparable remedy for an action like hers, against an employer health plan. The reason for this was that Congress had not anticipated the use of medical utilization review procedures in employee benefit plans when it had enacted the Employee Retirement Income Security Act (ERISA) in 1974. In a classic case exemplifying the absence of epieikeia, the court was well aware that this was an omission or oversight in the law, and yet it refused to render justice in the case before it.

2.8. Impartial Medical Utilization Review Panels Second-Guess Personal Physicians.

As much as ordinary persons purport to favor equality "in general," they really want to be treated specially (and not with mere equality): with due regard for their own particular circumstances. A good test of such sentiments concerns the attitude a person has toward the recent practice by insurers of having "medical utilization review panels" second-guess the medical decisions of the doctor who is actually treating a family member, for the purpose of reducing the costs of medical treatment.

Few persons that I know would want medical decisions regarding themselves or any of their loved ones to be subject to such impersonal decision making. Yet they lack the vocabulary for articulating just precisely why they feel that such an approach is unjust. The infamous medical utilization review panels are among the most egalitarian institutions in our society. Yet, whether imposed by a government bureaucracy or by the private bureaucracies of insurance companies, such an approach epitomizes the absence of epieikeia and the notion of natural justice as developed in my examination of legal injustices.[33]

2.9. Mean-Spirited Inflexibility of Welfare and Its Focus on "Welfare Cheaters."

Governmental institutions seem to be as demeaning and inflexible in their dispensation of benefits as they are coercive in collecting the revenues to pay for them. This illiberal attitude is reflected in the elaborate and complex rules for assuring that only qualified persons obtain benefits, and in the periodic characterization of deviations from these complex and often ambiguous rules as indicative of "medicare fraud"[34] or "welfare cheaters." What sometimes would involve discretion, flexibility, and true liberality under private charitable giving is labeled as fraud.[35]

2.10. Using Literal Wording of Law Intended to Protect Employee Stock Ownership Plan (ESOP) Beneficiaries to Financially Ruin ESOP Beneficiaries.

In *Zabolotny v. Commissioner*,[36] a law (which we will call the Prohibited Transaction statute) enacted by Congress to protect beneficiaries of retirement plans from poor investments resulting from conflicts of interest was literally interpreted and rigidly applied by the IRS and Tax Court to injure the beneficiaries of an ESOP.

A husband and wife who owned farm land in North Dakota where oil was discovered leased mineral rights to Gulf Oil Corporation in return for royalties. The farmers incorporated their farming operation on the land and established an ESOP for themselves as the farm's employees. The farmers then sold their initial interest in the land to the ESOP in exchange for payments to be received from a joint and survivor annuity established by the ESOP for their benefit, as the *sole* beneficiaries. In this case, the investment in the land by the ESOP technically violated the Prohibited Transaction statute but was actually a very sound and highly profitable investment. Yet the IRS and Tax Court applied the law in a manner that injured the ESOP and its beneficiaries through draconian penalties that would have financially destroyed the plan and its beneficiaries, even though this approach was completely incompatible with the intent of the statute.

3. Injustices Arising from Law's Expansion into Private Sector

3.1. Corporate Employers Less Likely to Make Exceptions to Help Individual Employees, as Result of Expansion of Employee Benefit Law.

With the growth of both federal regulation of employee benefits and the specialized legal community of "employee benefits specialists" who interpret these arcane regulations, the discretion of what were once humane and employee-oriented employers to provide benefits in unique circumstances to rank-and-file workers has been severely limited. For example, a surviving spouse of an IBM employee receives a $340-a-month pension, rather than a pension of almost $1,800 a month, solely because her husband died of a heart attack four months short of thirty years' employment with the company.[37] Legal practitioners usually advise corporate personnel departments to limit their discretion with codified policies as a method of limiting their potential liability in litigation.[38]

3.2. Legal Reform Movement from Status to Contract Favors Stronger Party in Employment or Marital Relationship.

The terminable-at-will doctrine of employment law is analogous to no-fault divorce laws, insofar as the long-term nature of the relationship is viewed largely as a matter of contractual convenience and utility. The party with the greatest bargaining power or persuasive skills takes advantage of the weaker party under either approach, and this so-called atomistic freedom of contract is viewed by many as an advance over the supposedly more primitive status- or property-based view of the relationship.

It is my view in this study, however, that this contractual view of human association is at the root of many injustices. Further, it is inferior to viewing human associations as involving a more complex web of shared goods that are either tacitly or explicitly understood to exist between the parties (and that are often relied upon by the weaker party).[39]

3.3. Employees' Interests Legally Subordinated to Those of Corporate Shareholders.

The notion that a corporate manager is acting in accordance with the highest fiduciary standards when he or she is ostensibly concerned with maximizing shareholder value, even to the detriment of the employees and their families, as well as to the customers and suppliers of that corporation, is another common illustration of the legalist fallacy. In this example, an artificial legal-property right—that of the shareholder—is given meaning outside of the social framework that a teleological notion of justice presupposes.

But the bonds of human association are prior to all legal rights, including those of property. Otherwise, a long-term employee's status is analogous to that of a slave or alien in an ancient Greek polity, with citizenship restricted to shareholders.[40]

3.4. Law's Expansionism Through Sex-Harassment Law.

Since the Supreme Court's *Meritor Savings Bank v. Vinson* (1986) promulgation of a subjective legal standard for sex-harassment claims—"it is 'sex harassment' if a 'reasonable' accuser thinks it is"—many contemporary legal and academic theorists have had difficulties in effectively distinguishing violent rape, date rape, and egregious forms of sexual harassment from false or silly accusations of rape or sex harassment (for example, a six-year-old boy kissing a little girl). I contend that it is possible to make these distinctions.[41] Also, false sex-harassment claims have sometimes been used to derail the careers of fellow employees within corporations.[42]

When a sex-harassment claim is alleged, the sole issue should be: Did sex harassment occur? This question should not involve the abstract impact of the particular case on other sex-harassment claims, another common version of the legalist fallacy—sacrificing particular justice to our desire to make a point: that sex harassment is bad.

3.5. Discouraging Gifts to Family Members Assures Larger Social Role for Government.

A perverse consequence of the estate and gift tax not often remarked upon, in this age of egalitarianism, is the way in which such taxes inhibit parents from passing on wealth to the natural objects of their bounty, their children. Giving through public and private bureaucracies displaces this most natural and direct type of giving. In fact, giving to someone to whom one has any social connection is discouraged by this perverse arrangement. In this way, persons are made subjects of the government.

In a similar manner, children are less likely to care directly for their parents, a very natural and healthy approach to living in pre–twentieth century society. Caring for the elderly is, supposedly, a state responsibility through Social Security (which is really an intergenerational tax program) and Medicaid. Instead of being cared for by one's children, one becomes older alone and ultimately dies in some warehouse for the aged. Artificial legal arrangements with bureaucracies (both private and public) are now favored over family and community arrangements.[43]

3.6. Zoning Regulations Are Modern Sumptuary Laws.

So long as zoning regulations regulate land use without overtly implicating the antidiscrimination laws, they effectively act to separate the economic classes into distinct communities, just as sumptuary laws in the middle ages segregated classes in terms of clothing. In this way, the problems of the poor are more easily relegated to the national government and are not effectively dealt with at the community level.

Although everyone knows that this is the result of zoning regulations, this result is possible because the legal text and its supporting rationale are given a greater ontological weight than the real, practical effects of these laws.[44] However, zoning regulations are about the only effective means, under the current legal regime, of keeping nude dancing nightclubs out of middle-class residential neighborhoods, a laudable effect.[45]

4. Inflexibility, Moral Neutrality, and Harshness of Legalistic Egalitarianism

4.1. Inflexibility of Affirmative Action Yields Paradoxical Results.

The notion that affirmative action is a legal remedy required to correct historical wrongs against African Americans, rather than limiting such a remedy to specific instances of real discrimination against a particular African American, is a perfect illustration of the legalist fallacy. Having a more easily administered, universal rule favoring adjudications that find discrimination even where it does not exist is preferred over particularized adjudications.

If an exception is made, to find nondiscrimination in a case where, in fact, there has not been any real discrimination, the fear of some aggressive proponents of affirmative action is that it will be harder for them to obtain a remedy for illegal discrimination when it does, in fact, occur. Accordingly, a particular injustice in the case being adjudicated is justified, based on the need to fashion a sufficiently general legal rule to cover some other hypothetical circumstance not being immediately adjudicated.[46]

In this way, upper-middle-class, protected minorities who are technically entitled to affirmative action are often its prime beneficiaries, even as lower-class groups who are most in need of it are often not technically covered by this entitlement. More important, while legal enforcement of the civil-rights laws has a very important role, the problem of unjust racial or sexual barriers cannot be completely remedied through litigation: at some point, this problem requires that people of different backgrounds voluntarily behave justly with each other, without the threat of coercive legal rules poisoning every aspect of the relationship.

4.2. Inflexible Separation of Church and State Sometimes Censors Religion.

It is unconstitutional for students to pray in public schools in clergy-led prayer, yet, for a time in New York, gay activists were allowed to proselytize a permissive view of sex to elementary schoolchildren, contrary to the wishes of their parents.[47]

4.3. Egalitarian Threats to Religious Freedom: "Religious-Harassment" Law.

The Equal Employment Opportunity Commission (EEOC) proposed "religious-harassment" guidelines for the work place (later withdrawn) that would have outlawed private employers from allowing employees to attend lunchtime Bible studies, say grace before company-sponsored dinners, sing carols at company Christmas parties, or post a photo of the wailing wall in the office.[48]

4.4. Legalistic Egalitarianism Fails to Distinguish Between KKK Crosses and Religious Symbols.

The American Civil Liberties Union (ACLU) has successfully sued to allow Ku Klux Klan crosses to be displayed next to holiday nativity scenes and menorahs.[49]

4.5. Inflexible Expansion of Disabilities Law at Risk to Public Health and Safety.

The Americans with Disabilities Act (ADA) has been interpreted by the EEOC and courts to prohibit discrimination against persons with contagious illnesses, even in circumstances where failure to discriminate posed substantial risks to public health and safety (such as in hospitals and restaurants).[50] Here again, the problem is not necessarily with the ADA or its purposes, but with its rigid and inflexible interpretation in a legalistic culture unacquainted with the restraints of epieikeia.

4.6. Egalitarianism's Threats to Free Speech.

Many contemporary legal and academic theorists have exhibited difficulties in determining when speech may be limited because it offends or discriminates against a particular group presumed to merit special legal protections against real or imagined insulting speech.[51]

4.7. Elitism, Complexity, and Harshness of Theoretically Egalitarian Tax Code.

The ostensible aims of the income-tax, estate-tax, and gift-tax systems are to (1) raise revenues, and (2) redistribute wealth more fairly.

The manner in which wealth is redistributed through the tax laws is primarily a function of access to political power (and expertise in the tax code) and, theoretically, a function of egalitarian notions of fairness.[52] This situation results in a complex tax code requiring (1) specialists, (2) an intrusive enforcement bureaucracy (with extraordinary police powers to ruin taxpayers financially and even imprison them), and (3) paid informers.

Any failure to comply with this complex system can result in draconian IRS penalties, of which there are currently more than 150.[53] Penalties and interest can soon outpace in magnitude any deficiency that was the basis for imposing the penalties in the first place.[54] Paradoxically, the complexity associated with a fair code fosters an elitist, self-contained community of lawyers, accountants, actuaries, and other specialists who largely talk to each other and move back and forth in a revolving door between the IRS and the private-sector economy.[55]

The essential difference between a tax evader who is legal and a criminal under the tax code exclusively turns on this community's interpretations of the complex and ambiguous provisions that make up the Internal Revenue Code and its regulations. For criminality to turn exclusively on the interpretation by a self-contained community of tax specialists of texts that are ambiguous, continually changing, and complex has the effect of making prosecutions under the tax code appear arbitrary.[56]

5. Legalistic Morality

5.1. Reduction of Ethical Behavior to Legal Behavior.

The legalist fallacy is even exemplified in contexts where no legal rules apply and morality is infected by legalisms, such as the case when mere compliance with so-called ethical rules is the sum total (or essence) of ethics. The proliferation of business ethics and legal ethics courses, ethics consultants, and professional ethical codes with hair-splitting dissections of rules shows how this perversion of morality pervades our culture. This makes ethics the unique realm of professional experts in rules—ethicists and lawyers. But most persons somehow know right from wrong without consulting experts or codifications of rules to cover every possible contingency.[57]

5.2. Prosecution of Holocaust Rescuer for Violation of Immigration Laws, and Failure of Jury to Nullify.

The notion that jury nullification is always unjust is belied by the case in which a government official in Switzerland was criminally prosecuted for fraud and violation of immigration laws that he was entrusted with enforcing.

Paul Grueninger broke laws by rescuing Jews from the Holocaust. In this particular case, there was no jury nullification, but rather the jury believed that failure to convict this official for violation of the immigration laws would somehow send a message that it was permissible to disobey the law in other circumstances. Again, an exception to a legal rule was not made based on hypothetical circumstances that were not being adjudicated.[58]

Notes

1. See summary of representative jurisprudential thinkers at the beginning of Chapter 2. For a strikingly different view, see Bernard Yack, *The Problems of a Political Animal: Community, Justice, and Conflict in Aristotelian Political Thought* (Berkeley and Los Angeles: University of California Press, 1993), 178. Iredell Jenkins, in *Social Order and the Limits of Law* (Princeton: Princeton University Press, 1980), 380–81, emphasizes the "supplemental" role played by law as an "instrument of order and justice," a role that is "heavily dependent on other [social] institutions," and a role that is undermined as law becomes more pervasive and expansive.

2. My characterization of Aristotle's notion of law as involving a somewhat different emphasis from contemporary preoccupations—at least as far as his major ethical and political writings are concerned—is not intended to underestimate what he tried to do in his *Athenaion Politeia*.

3. Aristotle, *Politics* II.8., 1269a10–12. For a fuller explication of this distinction, I refer the reader to the sections 3.2 and 3.3 in Chapter 4 of this book, where I discuss the citations to Aristotle and recent scholarship on this matter in greater detail.

4. See, for example, *Escobedo v. Illinois*, 378 U.S. 478 (1964); *Miranda v. Arizona*, 384 U.S. 436 (1966). This particular fallacy was much in evidence among many pundits during various television commentaries in the discussions immediately contemporaneous with the O. J. Simpson acquittal. For examples of innocent persons convicted with due process, see notes 12 and 16.

5. See *Batson v. Kentucky*, 476 U.S. 79 (1986): prosecutors barred from using peremptory challenges to exclude African Americans from a jury that will try an African American defendant. See also Greg Seigle, "D.C. Man Convicted in Hill Aide's Murder; Jury in 2d Trial Takes Just 3 1/2 Hours," *Washington Times*, 7 September 1994, A1, A10; Stephen J. Adler, "Lawyer's Poker: Stacking the Marcos Jury," *Wall Street Journal*, 14 September 1994, B1, B12. For a standard introduction to the rules of evidence, see Edward W. Cleary et al., *McCormick on Evidence*, 3d ed. (St. Paul, Minn.: West Publishing Co., 1984).

6. *Burns v. Reed*, 111 S.Ct. 1934, 1938 (1991): "It is 'better to leave unredressed the wrongs done by dishonest officers than to subject those who try to do their duty to the constant dread of retaliation.'" In *Burns*, a mother was wrongly charged with the attempted murder of her two sons, who had been shot by someone while they were sleeping. The charge was based on an alleged "confession" obtained from her while she was under hypnosis. She unsuccessfully attempted to sue the prosecutor for his misconduct.

7. *United States v. Jennifer Skarie*, No. 91-50007, 1992 U.S.App. LEXIS 16884 (9th Cir., July 28, 1992); James Bovard, *Lost Rights: The Destruction of American Liberty* (New York: St. Martin's Press, 1994), 247.

8. *Jacobson v. United States*, 112 S.Ct. 1535 (1992).

9. Plato's notion that part of the education of children would somehow involve testing the durability of their virtue while drunk is, obviously, contrary to the argument expressed herein against entrapment. On the other hand, consistent with the criticism of entrapment offered here, Montesquieu argued that education in the virtues was least compatible with despotic governments and was most required and desirable in democracies. Fear and ignorance are the tools of despotisms, whereas true democracies are based on the type of citizen virtue that self-consciously obeys the laws out of respect for the laws. Where law has largely replaced morality as a curb on inappropriate behavior, as, apparently, is the case in contemporary society, despotic tools such as entrapment become comprehensible. See Montesquieu, *The Spirit of the Laws*, trans. Thomas Nugent (New York: Hafner Press, 1949), 29–34.

10. *United States v. D'Amato*, 39 F.3d 1249 (2d Cir. 1994). Jonathan R. Macey, "The '80s Villain, Vindicated," *Wall Street Journal*, 18 July 1995, A12. For further discussion of *United States v. D'Amato*, see pages 171–75.

11. Roberto Suro, "Town Faults Law, Not Boy, in Sex Case," *Washington Post*, 11 May 1997, A1.

12. See "Evidence Clears Two; The Law Doesn't: Limits on Evidence Appeals Keep an Oregon Couple in Prison." *New York Times*, 26 November 1995, A28. See also, for example, *Commonwealth v. Amirault*, 677 N.E.2d 652, 665, 424 Mass. 618 (1997). J. Fried, for majority: "Once the regular procedures have run their course the presumption tilts heavily toward finality." J. O'Conner, dissenting: "Our desire for finality should not eclipse our concern that in our courts justice not miscarry."

13. See commentary by the Federal Sentencing Commission in preface to Title 18, Federal Sentencing Guidelines (1995), 6–10. See also Mary Pat Flaherty and Joan Biskupic, "Rules Of-

ten Impose Toughest Penalties on Poor, Minorities: Justice by the Numbers," *Washington Post,* 9 October 1996, A1, A27–28.

14. See, for example, Bovard, *Lost Rights,* 34; Jonathan Tolman, "A Sign of the Times," *Wall Street Journal,* 20 September 1994, A22.

15. 42 U.S.C. Section 5106a; Richard A. Gardner, "Modern Witch Hunt: Child Abuse Charges," *Wall Street Journal,* 22 February 1993, A10.

16. See, for example, *Michaels v. New Jersey,* 625 A.2d 489, 510–11 (N.J.Super.A.D. 1993). See also Eugene L. Meyer, "Poisoned Memories: Danny Smith Was Tried for Child Abuse. Then His Daughter Had Second Thoughts." *Washington Post,* 27 May 1994, D1, D4.

17. William Hamilton, "Crimes of Passion Spark Intense Debate," *Washington Post,* 14 August 1994, A3.

18. Television interview on *Larry King Live,* CNN, 16 November 1994, with Mike Gibson of Operation Outlook, John Walsh, and the mother of Melissa Brannen. The judicial outcome was far from certain in the Melissa Brannen case. See, for example, *Hughes v. Commonwealth,* 16 Va.App. 576, 431 S.E.2d 906 (1993), ordering a new trial of Brannen's abductor and murderer, based on a highly legalistic evidentiary ruling overturning the jury's conviction. *Rehearing en banc,* 18 Va.App. 510, 446 S.E.2d 451 (1994), affirming the conviction and reversing the panel.

19. See, for example, *People v. Purvis,* 52 Cal.2d 871, 346 P.2d 22 (1959); *People v. Gilbert,* 63 Cal.2d 690, 408 P.2d 365 (1965); *People v. Peete,* 28 Cal.2d 306 (1946).

20. Peter Carlson, "The Magazine Reader: Murder in the First Degree," *Washington Post,* 16 September 1997, E1, E8.

21. Bovard, *Lost Rights,* 213.

22. *Commonwealth v. Lindsay,* 489 N.E. 2d, 666, 669 (Mass. 1986).

23. Samuel Francis, "The News You Won't Be Hearing from the Anti-Gun Lobby," *Washington Times,* 1 November 1994, A19.

24. *Bennis v. Michigan,* 116 S.Ct. 994 (1996).

25. Sen. Hrg. No. 104–799, Hearings Before the Subcommittee on Terrorism, Technology, and Government Information of the Senate Judiciary Committee, *The Federal Raid On Ruby Ridge, ID,* 6–8, 12, 14–15, 19–22, 26 September; 13, 18–19 October 1995 (Washington, D.C., 1997).

26. *McCummings v. New York City Transit Authority,* 81 N.Y.2d 923, 613 N.E.2d 559 (1993).

27. *Carrie Buck v. J. H. Bell,* 274 U.S. 200 (1927).

28. 28 U.S.C. Sections 1251, 1254, 1257 (Supreme Court jurisdiction), and Sections 1291 and 1292 (grounds for federal-court appellate jurisdiction). See, for example, Robert L. Stern et al., *Supreme Court Practice,* 7th ed. (Washington, D.C.: Bureau of National Affairs, 1993), 162–221 ("Factors Motivating the Exercise of the Court's Certiorari Jurisdiction"); *Claussen,* 502 N.W.2d 649 (Mich. 1993), *cert. denied* (1993). See also Spencer W. Symons, *Pomeroy's Equity Jurisprudence,* 5th ed. (Union, N.J.: The Lawbook Exchange, 1994).

29. See Edward Walsh, "Illinois Court Backs Biological Parents," *Washington Post,* 14 July 1994, A3.

30. *Roe v. Wade,* 410 U.S. 113, 157–58 (1973).

31. *Dred Scott v. Sandford,* 60 U.S. (19 How.) 393 (1856).

32. *Corcoran v. United Healthcare, Inc.,* 15 E.B.C. 1793, 1805 (5th Cir. 1992).

33. See, for example, "Summary Plan Description, Blue Cross and Blue Shield Service Benefit Plan: A Managed Fee-for-Service Plan with a Preferred Provider Organization and a Point of Service Product Administered by the Blue Cross and Blue Shield Association" (1998), 42–43, discussing the precertification requirement. Avram Goldstein, "Lawmakers Rethink Managed Care Appeals Process," *Washington Post,* 6 December 1997, B4.

34. See, for example, George Anders and Laurie McGinley, "Surgical Strike, a New Brand of Crime Now Stirs the Feds: Health-Care Fraud," *Wall Street Journal,* 6 May 1997, A1.

35. Barbara Vobejda and Judith Havemann, "Welfare Clients Already Work Off the Books," *Washington Post,* 3 November 1997, A1.

36. *Zabolotny v. Commissioner,* 7 F.3d 774 (8th Cir. 1993).

37. As noted in an article by Laurie Hays, "A Matter of Time: Widow Sues IBM over Death Benefits," *Wall Street Journal,* 6 July 1995, A1.

38. This advice is generally based on *Firestone v. Bruch,* 489 U.S. 101 (1989), and its progeny, all ERISA cases.

39. See, for example, Henry N. Butler, "The Contractual Theory of the Corporation," *George Mason University Law Review* 11 (Summer 1989): 99–123. See also Mary Ann Glendon's comparison of the more laissez-faire and individualistic Anglo-American legal system with the French and German systems. *Abortion and Divorce in Western Law: American Failures, European Challenges* (Cambridge: Harvard University Press, 1987), 132–33: "For example, French and German law quite early worked out limitations on the power of an employer to fire an at-will employee for any or no reason. Under the French and German civil codes, a married property owner was not free to disinherit his children, or even make large gifts to the detriment of the family. One might mention, too, the legal duty to rescue, so typical in civil law systems, and so indigestible to Anglo-American law."

40. It is somewhat ironical that the narrow vision of corporate responsibility is based on the "equitable" principles of the law of trusts, a circumstance that says much about how notions of equity have changed from the Aristotelian notion of epieikeia. See, for example, Adolph A. Berle Jr., "Corporate Powers as Powers in Trust," *Harvard Law Review* 44 (1931): 1049–74; and Berle, "For Whom Are Corporate Managers Trustees? A Note," *Harvard Law Review* 45 (1932): 1365–72. Marianne M. Jennings criticizes the notion of corporations' owing broader duties than to the shareholder in "Trendy Causes Are No Substitute for Ethics," *Wall Street Journal,* 1 December 1997, A22. For examples of broader notions of corporate responsibility to employees and community, see E. Merrick Dodd, "For Whom Are Corporate Managers Trustees?" *Harvard Law Review* 45 (1932): 1145–63; Lawrence E. Mitchell, ed., *Progressive Corporate Law* (Boulder, Colo.: Westview, 1995).

41. See, for example, Meg Greenfield, "Sexual Harasser?" *Washington Post,* 30 September 1996, A23; Suzanne Fields, "Even Among Academics, Bad Taste Is Not a Crime," *Washington Times,* 17 October 1994, A19.

42. John Green, "Canned: When a Beer Company Executive Tried to Discuss a Racy 'Seinfeld' Episode with a Female Co-Worker, He Was Fired. But He Got the Last Laugh." *Washington Post,* 5 October 1997, F1.

43. See Alexis de Tocqueville, "Memoir on Pauperism," trans. Seymour Drescher, *Public Interest* 70 (Winter 1983): 102; Bruce Ingersoll, "Old Order: GOP's Plans to Curtail Government Benefits Bring No Pain to Amish," *Wall Street Journal,* 22 December 1995, A1: "In Arthur, Ill., an alms fund substitutes for Medicaid, farming is subsidy-free."

44. See *Belle Terre v. Borass,* 416 U.S. 1 (1974), for an example of a town ordinance that restricted housing in a certain area to families, excluding accommodations of more than two unrelated persons.

45. See *Young v. American Mini Theatres,* 427 U.S. 50 (1976).

46. This aspect of the legalist fallacy is epitomized by the recent settlement of the Piscataway, N.J., case, where a civil-rights coalition paid off a white schoolteacher whose case was pending before the Supreme Court and who had been fired because she was white, in the name of achieving greater diversity. The civil-rights groups feared that the facts, in this particular case, were so unfavorable to retaining an affirmative-action legal framework that the Supreme Court might gut affirmative action in other contexts. Yet the case was vigorously litigated for seven years before reaching the Supreme Court and was only settled because of this fear.

The affirmative-action legal framework, and not what was just in the particular case, governed their litigation strategy from the beginning to the end of this case. See James K. Glassman, "Buying Off Justice," *Washington Post*, 25 November 1997, A19 (discussing *Piscataway Township Board of Education v. Taxman*, 91 F.3d 1597 [3d Cir. 1996]).

47. *Lee v. Weisman*, 112 S.Ct. 2649 (1992); Dennis Farney, "Shaky Ground: Gay Rights Confront Determined Resistance from Some Moderates," *Wall Street Journal*, 7 October 1994, A1: "A push for 'sexual parity' fuels a backlash begun by the religious right." Nat Henthoff, "A Zero for Jesus in a Public School," *Washington Post*, 26 January 1996, A23: "When papers on witchcraft, black magic, and spiritualism are approved, how could one on the life of Christ be banned?"

48. Richard B. Schmitt, "EEOC May Pit Church vs. State at Work," *Wall Street Journal*, 8 June 1994, B8; 58 Fed. Reg. 51266 (1 Oct. 1993): EEOC Proposed Regulations on Religious Harassment; later withdrawn.

49. *Capital Square Review and Advisory Bd. v. Knights of the Ku Klux Klan*, 132 L.Ed.2d 650 (1995).

50. James Bovard, "Disabilities Law, Health Hazard," *Wall Street Journal*, 23 March 1994, A14.

51. See Ronald Dworkin, "Reply to Catherine MacKinnon," *New York Review of Books*, 3 March 1994, 48; Richard Bernstein, *Dictatorship of Virtue* (New York: St. Martin's Press, 1994); Heather MacDonald, "Free Housing Yes, Free Speech No," *Wall Street Journal*, 8 August 1994, A12; Nat Henthoff, "'I Would Prefer Not To': The Man Who Refused to Go to Sexual-Harassment Prevention Class," *Washington Post*, 24 September 1994, A27; *R.A.V. v. City of St. Paul, Minnesota*, 505 U.S. 377 (1992).

52. Milton Friedman, "Why a Flat Tax Is Not Politically Feasible," *Wall Street Journal*, 30 March 1995, A14.

53. See 26 United States Code Sections 6651 et. seq.

54. See 26 United States Code Section 6601; see also Bovard, *Lost Rights*, 266.

55. See "IRS Battles Colgate on Tax Deal," *Wall Street Journal*, 3 May 1996, A4, for an example of this revolving door.

56. Abuse of power is inherent in such a tax system. See Sen. Hrg. No. 105–190, Hearings Before the Senate Finance Committee, *Practices and Procedures of the Internal Revenue Service*, 23–25 September, 1997 (Washington, D.C., 1997); Albert B. Crenshaw, "Beleaguered IRS Announces Steps to Curb Abuses," *Washington Post*, 26 September 1997, A13; Stephen Barr, "In Tax Offices, Performance Goals Sounded Like Quotas: Program Led to Overzealous Enforcement," *Washington Post*, 26 September 1997, A13; Michael Hirsh, "Inside the IRS: Lawless, Abusive, and Out of Control," *Newsweek*, 13 October 1997, 33–39.

57. Meg Greenfield, "Right and Wrong in Washington: Why Do Our Officials Need Specialists to Tell the Difference?" *Washington Post*, 6 February 1995, A19: "Having all those ethics boards is not the same as having ethics." See also ABA Model Rules for Professional Responsibility (1980); and Fred C. Zacharias, "Specificity in Professional Responsibility Codes: Theory, Practice, and the Paradigm of Prosecutorial Ethics," *Notre Dame Law Review* 69 (1993): 223–309.

58. Peter Gimbel, "A Swiss Who Bent Rules to Save Jews Is Refused a Pardon: Treatment of Paul Grueninger Reflects Europe's Turmoil over World War II Legacy," *Wall Street Journal*, 3 June 1994, A1.

2
Dworkin's Interpretive "Community"

As the conditions of men become equal among a people, individuals seem of less and society of greater importance; or rather every citizen, being assimilated to all the rest, is lost in the crowd, and nothing stands conspicuous but the great and imposing image of the people at large. This naturally gives the men of democratic periods a lofty opinion of the privileges of society and a very humble notion of the rights of individuals; they are ready to admit that the interests of the former are everything and those of the latter nothing. They are willing to acknowledge that the power which represents the community has far more information and wisdom than any of the members of that community; and that it is the duty, as well as the right, of that power to guide as well as to govern each private citizen. . . .

Every central power, which follows its natural tendencies, courts and encourages the principle of equality; for equality singularly facilitates, extends, and secures the influence of a central power. . . .

The foremost or indeed the sole condition required in order to succeed in centralizing the supreme power in a democratic community is to love equality, or to get men to believe you love it. Thus the science of despotism, which was once so complex, is simplified, and reduced, as it were, to a single principle.[1]

One important reason for examining Dworkin's jurisprudence and political philosophy is the enormous influence it enjoys in the legal community. This very influence makes his thought particularly relevant to understanding the breakdowns in the legal system that I identified in Chapter 1. Indeed, Dworkin does accurately describe and reflect the way in which most lawyers and judges actually think in their practice of law. Whether law should actually be practiced in this way is another matter and is the issue considered in this chapter.[2]

The breakdowns in the legal system identified in Chapter 1 are due, to a considerable extent, to the legal system as described and as justified by Dworkin. To the extent that his argument for the legitimacy of the legal system that fosters or at least countenances these breakdowns is flawed, there is all the less reason to confine oneself within the current legal system and its presuppositions when speculating about reforms. Therefore this chapter presents a critical examination of Dworkin's jurisprudence, for the purpose of clearing the foundations for a new way of examining the legal system.

However, before broadening the analytical framework to encompass an assessment of how well Dworkin's jurisprudence deals with the legal injustices identified in Chapter 1, I will first attempt to orient the reader within the context of Dworkin's jurisprudence. For Dworkin law is interpretation,[3] and the legitimacy of a legal interpretation is established through "testing" its "fit" against the ways in which judges (and lawyers) interpret the law in practice.[4]

Accordingly, the plausibility of Dworkin on his own terms (rather than the terms of our problem of legal injustices) can best be understood from the limited standpoint of the opinions and practices of the legal community, and from a positivist standpoint (which he apparently conceives as his principal rival). It is important to recognize the extent to which Dworkin retains much of the positivist orientation, terminology, presuppositions, method, and choice of problems, even as he distinguishes himself from some of their positions. Dworkin's method of fit (discussed below) presupposes the positivist approach that the question of law is a factual-historical question concerning the decisions of legislators and judges, and not an ontological or moral question that would challenge those decisions beyond the coherence or fit of a particular decision with other decisions.

As I will show, the only truly central difference between traditional positivists and Dworkin is his insistence on adding "principles," such as that of equality, to the legal rules accepted by positivists. Since the principle of equality is already largely enacted in statutes and judicial interpretations of the Constitution, this is not such a radical difference. And, as a result of this small difference from traditional positivists, Dworkin would accordingly give judges less discretion in deciding cases, since he claims that his extralegal principle of equality (among others) fills in any so-called "gaps in the law."

1. The Positivist, Natural Law, and Realist Framework

At this point, I will outline a brief historical sketch of the positivist and realist positions in contemporary jurisprudence, as well as (secondarily) certain selected natural law positions. With the exception of Iredell Jenkins, the positions of other thinkers who emphasize the importance of the social order relative to law are not outlined here, particularly since the questions raised by their work do not neatly fit within the framework of debate chosen by natural law and positivist thinkers.

This sketch is made for the limited purposes of providing readers with an understanding of how the contemporary jurisprudential framework overlaps (and differs) from that envisioned by Dworkin. Since the framework of my inquiry is specifically outside of the mainstream debate between positivists and natural law thinkers, it is very important not to pigeonhole me within any of their categories of analysis. I accept and reject different positions from both the positivists and natural lawyers, and I consider most of their debate to be beside the point.

To the extent that my criticisms of Dworkin might appear to superficially overlap criticisms made of him from the standpoints of natural law, critical legal studies, or realist philosophy, it is important to understand that my criticisms are deduced from very different premises and, accordingly, might have to be taken in a different sense. This sketch is not intended to be complete or exhaustive, but is merely provided to give some context for an understanding of this chapter. I will view positivism and realism (and, secondarily, natural law thinkers) from the vantage point of only three questions, which are not altogether distinct (depending upon who is framing the questions), and which do not exhaust the range of problems considered by these different schools of thought:

1. What is law for the purposes of jurisprudential inquiry? Is law merely the expression of the will of the sovereign authority (or the dominant groups in a society), or must law be defined to exclude bands of robbers or regimes like the Nazi state from the domain of what may properly be called law?
2. May the application of law be described and evaluated purely in formalistic (or procedural) terms without regard to substantive ends? That is, is adjudication separate from lawmaking? Is the finding of equitable remedies or "legal fictions" a mere question of judicial discretion (that is, is it merely a question of filling in legislative gaps in the law)?

   Are there no gaps in the law at all? Is this question on the adequacy of formalism merely a question concerning whether legal reasoning is deductive (that is, whether law is complete and without gaps)? Or is there a broader question at stake here?
3. What is justice and how does justice relate to law, if at all? What is (or ought to be) the relation between law and morals (or justice) for the purposes of jurisprudence? Is it possible or appropriate to attempt to merely describe law without also evaluating law against some notion of perfection? Are morals (or justice) lawlike? Is it appropriate to describe justice and morals in legal terms as moral laws or rules?

In answering the first and third questions, the most extreme version of positivism would appear to be Thrasymachus's "might makes right" argument in Plato's *Republic*. In contrast, Thomas Aquinas articulates the traditional natural law position that a human law not in accord with natural law is a perversion of law and lacks the force of law.[5] Aquinas reasons that natural law is the same (universal) with regard to general principles of practical reason to which all men are naturally inclined, to the extent that they use their reason.[6] However, Aquinas also reasons that the application of the practical reason of natural law to matters of detail is not necessarily universal.[7]

As for the second question, Aquinas recognizes a role for equity as an exception to harsh enforcement of the positive law.[8] However, he limits its role as much as possible to competent judges with jurisdiction for equitable matters and does not encourage its invocation by just anyone.[9] Moreover, he argues that it is better to be regulated by laws as much as possible, rather than by judges.[10]

Thomas Hobbes emphasizes that the civil laws (that is, the positive laws) are the commands of the sovereign, and that these are always in accord with the laws of nature.[11] Hobbes locates (and effectively limits) the domain of natural law in the anarchic state of nature (the war of all against all) hypothesized by him to precede the stability and peace brought about by government.[12] The natural law for Hobbes is merely the right to self-preservation in this anarchic, prepolitical state of nature.[13] Accordingly, Hobbes is commonly identified as an early precursor to legal positivism. For Hobbes, insofar as law is the expression of the will of the sovereign who makes the laws, judges must be obedient to the sovereign lawmaker when they interpret the law (that is, judges must not legislate).[14] Moreover, only the judges to whom the sovereign has given jurisdiction may properly interpret laws.[15] Finally, the morality of an action is not a private matter, but determined solely by the civil (that is, positive) law.[16]

Presupposing a formalist position in response to the second question, Jeremy Bentham answered the first question by viewing law as properly confined to statutes and as excluding the common law.[17] Bentham seriously entertained the notion that it was possible to formulate a complete body of laws at the purely legislative level that would somehow preclude illegitimate judicial lawmaking in the manner of the common law judges (that is, any interpretation would be transparent). Bentham wanted to minimize the kind of judicial discretion that had been exercised by the common law judges: in his view, it had been arbitrarily exercised.[18] Accordingly, under Bentham's scheme, legislation would be based upon his utilitarian formula of the greatest good for the greatest number.

Bentham's utilitarian principle, in some form or another, has retained considerable influence and is sometimes referred to as consequentialism, for the notion that one ought to select a course of action pursuant to a rule with the idea of achieving the greatest overall good. Modern self-styled jurisprudential pragmatists, such as Richard Posner (a judge), owe much to Bentham for their economic approach to law, where justice is defined as avoiding waste and where noneconomic, moral values are excluded.[19]

The legalist fallacy is an example of consequentialism applied by judges when they fashion legal holdings based on an examination of the "types of decision which 'would have to be given' in other cases if a certain decision is given in the case before them."[20] The Uniform Federal Criminal Sentencing Guidelines, enacted to assure greater uniformity and equality in sentences (discussed at greater length later in this chapter and in Chapter 4) probably represent a very good contemporary example of the force of Bentham's ideas to this day. Of course, in practice, the operation of these rules has been criticized as excessively harsh and overly complex, giving greater opportunities for police and prosecutors to manipulate the rules against certain criminals who are too poor to have adequate counsel.[21]

It is to John Austin that we owe what I consider to be the unfortunate practice of positivists' framing their debate with natural law thinkers in terms, primarily, of the first question. When the debate between positivism and natural law thought is reduced to the first question only, natural law thinking superficially (and superficially only) appears trivial. Austin puts it very simply: "The existence of law is one thing; its merit or demerit is another. Whether it be or be not is one enquiry; whether it be or be not conformable to an assumed standard, is a different enquiry."[22]

Austin restricted the positive law to the "commands" of the "sovereign" and excluded "international law" from the domain of law, calling it "positive international morality." Although later positivists (such as Hart) argue otherwise, it is to Austin's choice of problems and exclusive emphasis on the first question—the status of law as distinct from its relation to justice—that we owe the resilience of the formalist orientation within positivist and mainstream legal thought, exemplified in the very practice of most lawyers.

As much as positivists might be concerned about contaminating law with moral considerations through the operation of natural law, Immanuel Kant is a natural law thinker who illustrates the dangers of infecting morality with legalisms. To the extent that Kant distinguishes between the moral law in the domain of ethics and the positive law expressive of the will of the legislator, the traditional characterization of him as a natural law thinker is appropriate. However, Kant defines justice in legalistic terms as a "right" or as an "authorization to use coercion."[23] Kant also argues that equity is not appropriate in courts of law, which should strictly comply with the letter of the law.[24] His notion of the type of freedom required for moral action, based on his categorical imperative, is key to understanding his legalistic notion of justice.

Kant uses legal metaphors and analogies to describe and illustrate the application of his categorical imperative, which emphasizes an impartial, rule-based morality.[25] Only through the "self-legislative" willing to act in conformity with a maxim that might be universalizable as a "moral law" without exception can a "rational being" assure that it is acting with the freedom required for categorically necessary moral action.[26] The injustices that conceivably can result from misapplications of the categorical imperative are the topic of Chapter 3.[27]

Oliver Wendell Holmes is commonly credited with starting the realist school in America, largely from a positivist launching pad. He viewed the role of a judge as following (or reflecting) the movement of power in society, thereby rejecting a moral grounding for law.[28] The ability to correctly predict what a judge or group of judges would do constituted law for Holmes, rather than a moral evaluation of what they ought to do. In this regard, it should be remembered that Holmes authored one of the examples of legal injustices in Chapter 1—the sterilization case (*Buck v. Bell*)—and that the social Darwinist "survival of the fittest" notions probably influenced his thinking to a great degree. Holmes argued that one ought to look at law from the perspective of the bad man: if one does bad things, certain bad things will happen (such as fines, imprisonment, or damages). Thus it is fine if one breaches a contract: one will just have to pay damages when this occurs (assuming that a sheriff can seize or attach one's assets once the other party obtains a judgment for that breach).

But Holmes's entire approach fails to account for why a legal system even exists or works at all, which is the customary adherence to legal and nonlegal (moral) norms by most people (who are not bad). A society of completely bad men would not be a society or have laws at all.[29] Therefore, if his approach is realistic, realism will have to take on a new meaning. However, upon closer examination of the writings of two later American realists, as much as Holmes is claimed by them as a forebear, there are very important distinctions between their positions and his.

For example, Roscoe Pound makes unabashed appeals to the importance of justice, and he appeals to Aristotle's notion of equity as necessarily operating in the application of law.[30] He traces the eighteenth-century separation of powers notion to dissatisfaction with the "personal" nature of the administration of justice under an equitable regime, but then he rejects such "mechanical" attempts at interpretation.[31] Indeed, Pound emphasizes the importance of equity, which he identifies largely with judicial or executive discretion, as a means of bringing (largely undefined) moral considerations of justice to bear on the application of law. "Almost *all* of the problems of jurisprudence come down to a fundamental one of *rule* and *discretion,* of administration of justice by law and administration of justice by the more or less trained intuition of experienced magistrates" (emphases added).[32]

Pound is closer in spirit to my inquiry than any of the other realists. However, the absence of a developed theory of justice in Pound carries with it the risk that his notion of discretion is not as close to epieikeia as I interpret it to be.

Jerome Frank invoked Holmes as a paragon of realist thought.[33] He primarily embarked on a descriptive project to show that the law was not as certain, rational, or determinate as commonly assumed.[34] He argued that judges did not merely interpret laws, but that they also made laws, and that it was proper for them to do so.[35] He defended the notion of "legal fictions" against Bentham's denunciations as indispensable to the development of law in furtherance of "social needs".[36] Frank defined law as the decision of a court on a specific set of facts, specifying that prior to such a decision, the opinion of lawyers on the law that might be applied constituted informed guesses.[37]

To define law without reference to the way it has been applied, according to Frank, is meaningless nonsense. Frank debunked the notion that is is only judges who determine the law, with the jury confined to fact finding, arguing that juries also determine what law to apply to the facts—often ignoring a judge's instructions on what the law requires.[38] Frank did not go so far as Pound, in recognizing that his rejection of formalism carried implicit within it the notion of morals or justice affecting the application of law.

Hans Kelsen argues that the "coercive order" of robber bands (such as the Barbary pirates) constitutes law so long as it is effectively asserted over a defined territory that could constitute a nation state.[39] Indeed, the nation state is the "personification" of the legal order in Kelsen.[40] For Kelsen, justice is not the criterion that distinguishes the lawfulness of one coercive order from another.[41] Moreover, just as legal orders are subject to change, so is the content of morality.[42] In other words, for Kelsen, morality does not have a universal and necessary grounding. Jurisprudence cannot supply any single correct interpretation of a legal norm; rather, such interpretation, which fills so-called gaps in the law, is a "law-creating" function that can only be performed by a "law-applying organ."[43]

H.L.A. Hart defends the positivist positions of Bentham and Austin concerning the first question (what is law) from realist criticisms of formalism, by arguing that Bentham and Austin were not really formalists. He lays the

bane of formalism at the doorstep of his favorite natural law straw man—
William Blackstone.[44] Hart does this by narrowing the realist criticism to an
issue of law's completeness: whether there are gaps in the law requiring clarification (the so-called penumbra question of meaning, where a statute is
not clear and transparent).[45] He then properly (in my view) argues that a
formalist criticism in no way affects the outcome of the issue of whether an
unjust law is really a law.[46]

However, I do not believe that Hart fairly disposes of the charge of formalism against Bentham and Austin by merely shifting the charge onto Blackstone. As properly pointed out by Roberto Mangabeira Unger, formalism is
not merely a narrow question about whether law is a complete framework
from which correct answers can be deduced—that is, it is not merely a question about the existence of gaps in the law and the degree of appropriate discretion.[47] The charge of formalism is also a question about the substantive
ends of law, and it necessarily requires that a positivist deal with the moral issues thought by positivists to be outside the domain of jurisprudence proper.[48]

The exercise of discretion, if it is not to be the arbitrary exercise of judicial power disparaged by Bentham, must be informed by equitable principles
of justice, something also disparaged by Bentham.[49] By concentrating on the
first question—what is law (and whether the laws of a band of robbers ruling a territory constitutes laws)—Hart ducks the deeper issue, which is the
key to fairly dealing with the formalist charge. That is addressed in the third
question, concerning the relation of justice to law within jurisprudence.

The remainder of Hart's jurisprudence is not important for the purposes
of this study, other than to point out the degree to which he differs from—
and tempers somewhat—Austin's positivism.[50] For example, Austin's severe
limitation of law to the commands of the sovereign authority excludes features of legal systems involving what Hart calls "secondary rules." Hart believes that these secondary rules are required to identify and change the
"primary rules" of a legal system (for example, the duties imposed by the
criminal law), as well as to adjudicate when such primary rules have been
breached.[51]

Hart acknowledges that these rules implicitly carry with them some features of a moral notion of justice and are embedded within the functioning
of the legal system. However, Hart views the connection of such moral considerations (that might be considered features of natural law) to the workings of the positive law as merely contingently connected to the legal system
(and lacking the logical necessity required by natural law theory). Accordingly, Hart does not waver in defending Austin's truncation of jurisprudence
from ethics.

Lon Fuller advances a minimalist natural law position, where the moral evaluation of law is limited to procedural concerns relevant to the "art of law."[52] Fuller is not concerned with the unjust "application" of law to specific circumstances (the concern of this book), something that is best revealed from the framework of substantive ends (or justice). Rather, he evaluates law on its own, internal terms—an approach that, I will argue throughout this chapter, epitomizes the formalism of some legal injustices.

In my opinion, the subject matter of justice cannot be reduced to mere procedural concerns without losing something. But according to Fuller, there are only eight ways for a law to fail from the standpoint of procedural justice.[53] Although some features of some of my examples of injustice illustrate the failure of a few of Lon Fuller's factors, it would take some ingenuity (lacking in myself) for a reader to find ways to characterize each of my legal injustices in such a manner.

Additionally, many of my examples of legal injustices violate none of his eight factors. That is, the law was publicized and known, was not retroactive, and so on. Although some would exclude such examples from my list of injustices, it is my view that this merely indicates the inadequacy of Fuller's eight factors. Accordingly, I argue that Fuller is an illustration of a strict formalist within what is claimed to be a version of natural law doctrine. (And, to my way of thinking, he is not that far apart from Hart, much as they debate each other.)

John Finnis illustrates a contemporary version of natural law thinking that is more compatible with my view than is Fuller.[54] However, his points of emphasis are slightly different than mine, insofar as the role of epieikeia and the community, although included by him, are not dealt with in the same manner (or level of detail). Additionally, I do not know the degree to which he might differ with me on the details of my program, as much as we might overlap in some of our views.

He makes the first question somewhat subsidiary by emphasizing that, as a natural law thinker, he is merely trying to ascertain the constituents of "practical reasonableness" in order to provide a "rational basis for the activities of legislators, judges, and citizens."[55] He moves away from Hart's favored battleground in the first question by pointing out how the issue of whether unjust laws are, in fact, laws is not the primary point of natural law thinkers when their position is fully and fairly represented. He then shifts the discussion to the issues of question three, which point out how blind are the positivists who would remove the question of justice and its relation to law from the domain of jurisprudence.[56]

Finnis correctly points out that removing the question of justice from jurisprudence proper renders its descriptions of how lawyers and judges actually deliberate incomplete and impoverished.[57] He then details in which areas Hart himself has not consistently excised moral considerations from his jurisprudential writings.[58] The most significant contribution made by Finnis for my purposes, however, resides in his discussions of the relationship of the distinctive types of rational analysis appropriate to four different orders of unifying experience within the human community: the first order studied by natural sciences; the second order studied reflexively through logic, epistemology, and metaphysics; the third order studied in the arts, technology, and literary criticism; and the fourth order pertaining to action such as ethics, political philosophy, psychology, and history.[59]

Finnis points out that his jurisprudential examination of practical reasonableness is properly examined within the fourth order of unifying experience (or community), and that any degree of unity achieved in the other three orders is not dispositive of the degree of unity (or lack thereof) in the fourth order.[60] Much of positivism is an unsuccessful attempt to confine jurisprudence to the second or third orders. And when Dworkin, as I will show later, attempts to bring community into jurisprudence within the positivist framework at the level of the third order, he has not attained the desired social unity that he claims he has.

Iredell Jenkins falls completely outside the framework of debate between positivists and natural law thinkers, and the formalist criticisms as well.[61] His jurisprudence is probably closer in spirit to the framework of my own studies, and I therefore offer it as an example of a thinker (like myself) who has not devoted the bulk of his jurisprudential writings to this stale battleground.

His principal emphasis is that law, to be effective and just, must act as a "supplement" to and not a substitute for the social order upon which it relies for its very workings. As such, law must be minimal, lest it interfere with the very social underpinnings that make it effective. Accordingly, he justifies a citizens' "obedience" to the rule of law, rather than the "coercion" of the rule of law.[62] This is a very important shift in emphasis from natural law thinkers, who would view the role of the state as enacting through the positive law the duties required by the natural law.

Jenkins criticizes natural law thinkers as submerging the individual in the social order. Likewise, he traces the emergence of natural right doctrine to its natural law roots.[63] He correctly argues that although natural right is the antithesis of natural law, it shares with natural law one very important feature, in that both submerge the individual in the social order. Where natural law emphasizes the duties that individuals owe to society, natural right emphasizes the duties that society owes to its members. "One doctrine imposes duties; the other protects rights: but both submerge the individual in the social order and treat the human person as an abstraction upon which duties and rights are to be hung at the will of the state."[64]

Roberto Mangabeira Unger illustrates a contemporary leftist variant of realism, called critical legal studies.[65] He criticizes what he calls the antinomy between the supposedly apolitical and impartial, rule-based, formalist view of law (where correct legal outcomes may be deduced within the framework of law) and the subjectivity of liberal notions of the good, for which formalist adjudication is supposed to substitute.[66] Unger rejects the line demarcating legislative from adjudicatory functions and argues that this imagined separation exemplifies the "formalist fallacy."[67]

On the one hand, under the liberal framework criticized by Unger, an impartial adjudication separated from lawmaking is needed because of the subjectivity and plurality of values. On the other hand, according to Unger, such mechanical and impartial adjudication is impossible, precisely because of this subjectivity of values. According to Unger, formalist adjudication would be possible only if the good were transparent and objective.

Although I reject Unger's premise that values are subjective, I believe he is correct to point out the incoherence of this premise of liberalism and the legal formalism often coupled with it. The way in which Unger's criticism is relevant to Dworkin will become evident later in this chapter, because Dworkin is both a formalist and liberal in the very sense criticized by Unger. Insofar as Unger's prescription calls for greater governmental and legal interference in the social order, he is opposed to Jenkins (and the working hypothesis of this book). Unger reveals, however, how even the more benign versions of liberalism at some point have to resolve their self-imposed antinomy (as he puts it) through leftist activism. Of course, I would advocate getting out of the antinomy altogether by accepting the objectivity of the good (assuming one is rational) and by rejecting formalism.

As for my own position within the above framework, I agree with the positivists as far as the first question is concerned: something may constitute a law and still be immoral and unjust. However, as far as the third (and more meaningful) question is concerned on the relation of law and justice, I completely differ with the extreme positivists (such as Thrasymachus, Hobbes, Holmes, and Kelsen); and I differ to a significant degree from the more moderate positivists (such as Bentham, Austin, and Hart), insofar as I believe that confining jurisprudence proper to the descriptive project explicitly or implicitly commits one to a formalist notion of justice (in responding to question number two).

More significantly, and for reasons explained at greater length in Chapters

3 and 4, I differ from natural law thinkers (such as Kant) who establish formalistic or legalistic notions of justice. I see grave dangers in translating the moral order into a framework of moral laws analogous to the legal order. Accordingly, the key to my position is my rejection of formalism, the focus of question number two. I cannot make the case for this position in this preliminary sketch of jurisprudential history, but the underlying thread of this book is that the roots of many legal injustices reside in formalism, and that both legal positivism and (some) natural law thinkers illustrate a type of formalism. The positivists do so by overtly or effectively excluding morality from evaluations of law, and some natural lawyers do so by infecting morality and justice with legalistic notions. And to the degree that some early American realists (such as Frank) fail to recognize the moral dimensions at the root of their criticisms of formalism, or the degree to which they are amoral (such as Holmes), realism has to be seen as an inadequate and incomplete framework.

Natural law theory recognizes the need for justice to inform judicial decisions. However, to the extent that justice under natural law theory is itself a set of rules or duties, it is difficult to reconcile with the flexibility and mercy that I would associate with an equitable notion of discretion grounded in natural justice and community. For instance, does one merely say under natural law theory that one must exercise equitable discretion, or does one say something more: that one must exercise equitable discretion in a particular way in a particular circumstance, without regard to the rules' impact on the social connections that exist or ought to exist between persons?

The other problem associated with reconciling natural law theory with discretion is natural law's common association with a perfectionism that requires the enactment of positive laws whenever the natural law requires a duty. This requirement would at some point seem to close off opportunities for equitable discretion (that is, truly leave no gaps)—and not just in the case of officials, but also in areas often described as comprising private morality. (Yes, the flexibility underlying equity is not merely a matter for officials.)

On the other hand, positivism appears to be of two minds on the appropriateness of judicial discretion. Bentham apparently believed that it was possible to legislate a complete, fully transparent body of law making judicial resort to discretion (at least in the manner of the common law judges) arbitrary. Hart recognized the possibility of statutory ambiguities and gaps in the law where the exercise of judicial discretion could conceivably arrive at a variety of legitimate outcomes.

But the regulative idea of this study is that discretion is not merely a function of so-called gaps in the law. Rather, the very notion of discretion ultimately implicates moral concerns (that is, justice), and as much as the realists recognized the need for discretion, they often did not fully comprehend it as providing the critical link between law and justice. Realism recognizes the need for discretion but does not completely recognize this moral dimension that prevents this discretion from being arbitrary.

The sense of *arbitrary* presupposed by a traditional jurisprudence that accepts the legal distinctions of our legal system as it has historically developed would regard the failure of a judge to defer to legislative enactments as being arbitrary. The substantive effects of the judge's actions are not what makes his actions arbitrary, under this view. Rather, the degree to which a judge confines his actions to adjudicative functions defines the degree to which he has not exceeded his authority—his jurisdiction. This constricted viewpoint assumes that exceeding authority is the only way to be arbitrary, and that it is somehow illegitimate to embark upon a moral evaluation of the consequences of official actions that would criticize such actions when they are not deemed arbitrary under this view.

On the other hand, the sense of *arbitrary* argued for throughout my analysis of legal injustices is a broader one and does not derive its necessity from the historically contingent events that make up our legal system, with its allocations of authority and the distinctions based upon those allocations. This latter sense is not legal, but moral, and it derives its necessity not from mere accidents of history. Under this latter sense, the consequences of an official's actions are a legitimate and essential consideration that must not be excluded from an evaluation of the correctness of those actions.

The historically contingent distinctions presupposed by our legal system cannot be imported into such a moral evaluation without collapsing the two senses of *arbitrary* and rendering any external moral critique of the legal system impossible. Accordingly, an action can be legally arbitrary in the narrower sense, because an official exceeds his authority, and yet be morally correct. Conversely, an action can be morally arbitrary in the broader sense, because of the evil consequences of the official's actions, and yet that same action will not be legally arbitrary if that official has acted within his jurisdiction and authority.

Thus justice, to the extent that it carries with it some notion of the flexibility and mercy of equity (in the original sense of epieikeia), cannot be simply reduced to an egalitarian notion of justice without obliterating this very flexibility and mercy. And the flexibility inherent in the equitable (rather than egalitarian) type of justice presupposes voluntary and cooperative bonds of association not commonly associated with the rule-book approach more applicable to strangers. In other words, (1) nonarbitrary discretion requires (2) an equitable type of justice, which in turn presupposes (3) some form of friendship or community.

The problem of explaining legal injustices cannot be adequately per-formed within a rigid, formalistic framework for justice and community reduced to egalitarianism. And so, when we find Dworkin (like Bentham) ar-guing that there are not any gaps in the law that would leave room for dis-cretion, because his egalitarian notion of justice fills any gap by means of the interpretations provided by his elite "community of principle" (made up of lawyers and judges), we will find Dworkin's jurisprudence to be in-compatible with the flexibility and mercy associated with the discretion in-formed by epieikeia.[68] This is the thread underlying my description and crit-icism of Dworkin in the remainder of this chapter.

However, Dworkin does attempt to deal with the third question—the re-lation of law to justice—within the framework of the first question, What is law? Within the context of this book, I eschew that approach to avoid the inevitable dangers of reducing justice to some commonly accepted legal norm and never really getting beyond the first question—something that I believe happens in Dworkin. An analysis of law within the framework of the first question will only satisfy lawyers and jurisprudential philosophers. Such analysis will not directly confront the tension between law and justice, but only serve to hide the real problems latent in the conflict between law's co-ercion and the merciful flexibility of justice, as I understand justice.

The idea that Dworkin's jurisprudential effort somehow primarily con-fines itself to a mere description of the law and legal interpretation in so-called democratic legal systems is a pretense, because he also argues (and pre-supposes) that an interpretation of a legal rule is correct only insofar as it conforms to his interpretation. This pretense is useful to Dworkin in two ways. First, it permits him to claim that his descriptive theory is correct merely because it has the best "fit" with legal interpretations, where interpretations at variance with his theory can be discarded as anomalous "outliers." Sec-ond, it makes it appear as if he were avoiding the so-called "is-ought" prob-lem, the contemporary preoccupation that one cannot legitimately infer a prescriptive or normative proposition from a factual or descriptive proposi-tion.

But the motivating principle of my project lies in a rejection of the prac-tical usefulness of merely descriptive efforts in ethics or jurisprudence. Ap-prehending what is just in a particular situation is not necessarily something that can be best attained through reason alone. Indeed, an excess of rea-soning can often be a hindrance to appropriate moral conduct—consider

Kant's difficulties with the so-called right to lie to a murderer about the hiding place of his intended victim. Accordingly, ignoring the ontological debate concerning the status of moral reasoning is considered necessary in order to obtain a clearer view of practical legal and ethical issues, just as mathematicians do not cease using irrational numbers merely because they do not divide like whole numbers.[69]

To view the often rhetorical disagreements between "hired guns" as providing philosophical and moral insights is highly problematical for me. Accordingly, my analysis does not presuppose the necessity of the particular ways in which authority has been allocated within our system. The historical fact that in our legal system, trial courts presumably establish the factual record and appellate courts confine their review to considerations of legal error is recognized as historical fact, but not as necessary from a moral standpoint. The historical fact that our legal system is predicated upon a notion of separation of powers where there are presumably clear-cut distinctions between judicial, executive, and legislative functions is recognized as historical fact, but not as necessary from a moral standpoint.

Insofar as my examination of legal injustices is concerned with the relationship between morality and law, a consideration of traditional jurisprudential problems is not directly pertinent. Moreover, these moral principles have a necessity utterly lacking in purely jurisprudential inquiries.[70] As such, my analysis of legal injustices is a consideration of how well law fulfills its substantive ends. It is not properly a descriptive analysis of the art of law or its degree of fit or coherence.

Accordingly, the statute and the process of lawmaking do not form the starting point of my analysis, precisely because it is the consequences of particular legislative enactments that matter for my purposes. While inartful lawmaking may or may not be exemplified in many of my examples, that is not the reason that I consider these examples to be unjust. It is, instead, their particular applications that render them unjust. The legality, or source of authority, or legal artfulness of official actions, whether legislative actions, judicial actions, or enforcement actions, is simply not relevant to my analysis of legal injustices.

Rather, it is the morality of presumably legal and illegal actions that I am subjecting to criticism, a criticism that looks to the consequences of such actions. How lawful an action is, from the standpoint of traditional jurisprudential distinctions, is irrelevant to the question of legal injustices, unless one wants somehow to collapse legality and morality together or argue that the consequences of legal actions are not subject to moral review. But these are the very positions against which I am contending. The evil or good of the consequences of a legal or illegal action, from a moral standpoint, are absolutely independent of the legality or authority of that action. The criteria for assessing the morality of a legal system are external, not internal to that system, and, as such, they may (and indeed must) be established independently of any account of the legal system or its fit. At this point, let us return to Dworkin, the primary focus of this chapter.

2. Introductory Summary of Dworkin's Jurisprudence

Dworkin's notion of interpretation in chapter 2 of *Law's Empire* emphasizes what an interpreter brings to an interpretation and criticizes an "intentionalism" that would purport to limit legal interpretation to the so-called original intention of the authors of legislation.[71] He analogizes legal interpretation to artistic interpretation where, according to Dworkin, meanings never conceived by the creative artist can be legitimately added as part of the interpretation of an artistic work. Although this analogy only becomes clear after considering the entirety of *Law's Empire,* Dworkin appears to be setting the stage, by means of his notion of interpretation, for displacing legislative intention with adjudicative interpretation as the authoritative source of meaning for a legal text.

A reader might misconceive Dworkin as somehow broadening interpretation, particularly with his analogy to artistic interpretation. However, I argue (later in this book) that he really is replacing one limited view of interpretation—the original intention view—with another limited view of interpretation (Dworkin's Herculean judge).

Under either view, there is only one correct interpretation. This inflexibility, inherent to an emphasis on textual interpretation, effectively disregards the particularity and teleological character of human action. In this way, even allegedly broadened notions of interpretation are incompatible with the notion of epieikeia that I will explore in Chapter 4.

While Dworkin does not pretend to deal exhaustively with all possible alternative jurisprudential theories, he does find it instructive to articulate his theory as a pragmatist interpretation of the law, in contrast to the various forms of conventionalism of the positivists. He characterizes the economic approach to the law[72] as an alternative theory—but one that is conceivably also within the pragmatist framework, as characterized by Dworkin.

According to Dworkin, the principal difference between a pragmatist approach and conventionalism is that "consistency" with some extralegal principle or notion of justice underlies a pragmatic interpretation, whereas conventionalism requires "consistency" with (1) prior adjudications (that is, stare decisis), and (2) the past political decisions of legislatures (that is, judicial deference to legislative enactments).[73] Dworkin characterizes his own theory of legal interpretation as a refinement of the pragmatist variety, labeling his own theory as "integrity" in legal interpretation, by which he means having integrity or consistency with some extralegal principle as a "source of legal rights." In contrast, according to Dworkin, positivism (or conventionalism) rejects this integrity-based conception of consistency as a source of legal rights.[74]

Understanding how Dworkin's use of the notion of consistency provides an overall framework for his theory of interpretation will be important to understanding my criticisms of the related universalizability principle in Kant's categorical imperative (in Chapter 3 of this book) and my arguments favoring the Aristotelian notion of epieikeia (in Chapter 4).

Dworkin's principal method for concluding that the pragmatic approach to legal interpretation is superior to conventionalism consists in arguing that pragmatic interpretations have a better fit with judicial opinions.[75] Accordingly, he argues, when one examines judicial opinions over the past two hundred years in England and the United States, pragmatic interpretations offer better explanations of changes in law and legal practices than does conventionalism.[76] Moreover, Dworkin criticizes conventionalism because he believes that it results in an unfortunate skepticism that denies that there are "right" answers to so-called "hard cases."[77] According to Dworkin, such positivism argues for a judicial discretion to come to many different answers (rather than one right answer) where so-called gaps in the law exist because of legislative failure to anticipate the circumstances being adjudicated.[78]

The principal difference between Dworkin's interpretive theory from rival pragmatist theories is that his theory of integrity "takes rights seriously," whereas rival pragmatist theories are characterized as skeptical concepts of law because of their rejection of "non-strategic legal rights."[79] What Dworkin means by "taking rights seriously" may be gleaned from his criticism of the economic approach to the law in chapter 8 of *Law's Empire,* where he argues for egalitarian-based rights rather than libertarian-based rights.

The content and justification of his egalitarian-based (and Rawlsian) extralegal principles of integrity are assumed in *Law's Empire,* which is principally oriented toward articulating the overall interpretive framework of integrity and illustrating its better fit with legal practice. For example, near the conclusion of chapter 8 of *Law's Empire,* Dworkin states: "Since my main purpose is to show the connection between a conception of equality and accident law, I shall not argue but only assume that equality of resources is superior to the libertarian conception: it fits our legal and moral practices no worse and is better in abstract moral theory."[80]

Accordingly, I have reserved my principal criticism of the underlying justification of the moral "necessity" of Dworkin's notion of equality and rights for Chapter 3. There I discuss what I believe to be the strongest justification of modern liberalism's notions of "equal concern," in Kant's notion of the "kingdom of ends" in his categorical imperative. While the notion of "fit" may have an appeal to the legal community, one ultimately must look to Kant and Rawls for finding some ontological justification of the moral necessity of Dworkin's assumed extralegal principles.

Dworkin identifies three extralegal principles, which he also labels "political virtues" underlying his theory of integrity: (1) justice, (2) fairness, and (3) procedural due process.[81] It is unclear how Dworkin can characterize such nonteleological principles as virtues in the ordinary sense of *virtue*. Moreover, Dworkin does not state that these three principles are equal. Indeed, he explicitly recognizes that they may conflict and must be balanced with each other.[82] However, in his application of these three principles, it appears that justice is the most important and seemingly overrides questions of fairness (but, for reasons that I will offer later, Dworkin is not always consistent on this score, and he does not supply clear criteria in this regard, other than fit). It is unclear what status procedural due process has vis-à-vis the other two principles, although I suspect that it carries less weight, for Dworkin, than does justice.

Dworkin characterizes justice as an "institution we interpret" for which there are senses in which there is no consensus (such as disputes between egalitarians and libertarians on tax policy) and other senses in which there is a core of agreement (such as abhorrence of slavery).[83] Nonetheless, in his applications and characterizations of this principle,[84] Dworkin ultimately appears to identify justice with equality in the broadest possible sense, and he further characterizes equality (or justice) as a "political virtue."

He gives the principle of equality the greatest emphasis in his discussions of "fit" in *Law's Empire*. In other writings he makes clear that what he means by equality is a Rawlsian notion of what distribution of rights and resources any rational person would agree to in hypothetical circumstances, where that person was under a "veil of ignorance" as to what their real circumstances would be. These abstract discussions are cast as hypothetical auctions, or as decisions by persons as "reasonable insurers."[85] Accordingly, in chapter 8 of *Law's Empire*, Dworkin emphasizes that "differences in talent" are "differences in resources," and that, under his favored approach, the less talented should be compensated "beyond what the market awards them."[86]

What Dworkin means by equality or justice as a principle of legal interpretation is revealed further by his important distinction between the public and private sphere of duties. Dworkin distinguishes between the private duties and self-interested rights that a person has with respect to property that has been clearly assigned him *by law* and the public duties and weaker claims to rights that a person has with respect to property that has not been clearly assigned to him *by law*. In the latter circumstance, the claims of equality and public duty override other private interests of a person in the property.

Accordingly, defining the sphere of public and private duties is important, and ultimately this turns on the interpretation of law, since it is legal interpretation that is the source of legal right (that is, the basis of an assignment of property to a person).[87] Legal interpretation determines the line separating private from public duty and is the source of any legal rights in either sphere. Accordingly, implicit in Dworkin is the possibility of legal interpretation's adjusting the boundaries between the public and the private. Indeed, this line is fairly elastic, as far as the expansion of the public into the private is concerned, insofar as the domain of the public can intrude into the private to the extent that a plaintiff's attorney is creatively able to fashion an egalitarian-based claim of discrimination against some newly defined, protected classification. It is in the sphere of public duty that equality reigns supreme, and only in the elastic and shrinking realm of private duty that equality is allegedly less paramount.

Dworkin characterizes fairness as responsiveness of officials to public opinion.[88] As such, fairness embodies Dworkin's apparent assumption of the necessary superiority of democratic legal forms. Dworkin apparently sees no need to justify this assumption. The necessity for such an assumption is critically examined in the section on Aristotle's treatment of custom in Chapter 4.

However, there is a further refinement whereby Dworkin clarifies when such fairness may be limited by the legal interpretations of enlightened judges: namely, in his distinction between "choice-sensitive" and "choice-insensitive" issues.[89] In the latter, responsiveness to majority opinion may not be appropriate where it conflicts with the strong sense of equality of outcomes (not opportunity) advocated by Dworkin in his Rawlsian "veil of ignorance" models. However, ascertaining which issues are "choice-sensitive" and which are "choice-insensitive" is the province of the legal elite—judges and the lawyers who argue before them—which Dworkin apparently trusts more than he does the general public.

As discussed in some detail later, legal argumentation has not been consistent in dividing between "choice-sensitive" and "choice-insensitive" issues, and Dworkin, unsurprisingly, mirrors that inconsistency because of his reliance on "fit." As a result, the only minimal constraint on the legal elite is a notion not much discussed by Dworkin: that of procedural due process.

Dworkin apparently presupposes the commonly accepted notion of procedural due process that has been articulated in recent Supreme Court opinions and constitutional law treatises: he does not discuss or use this principle in *Law's Empire* or in any other writing that I have examined. It is arguable that procedural due process should not be viewed as an extralegal principle, but as a part of the adjudicative interpretations of the due process clause of the Fifth and Fourteenth Amendments to the United States Constitution. However, since Dworkin apparently incorporates this complex body of law by reference into his theory of interpretation without ever characterizing or defining it, I criticize its notions as if they were part of his theory. Because he refers to due process, it will be presumed as having some importance in his theory. However, it is arguable that it is not the most important principle in his theory, because of his failure to use it to the same degree as he does the notions of justice and fairness.

There is one final refinement to Dworkin's theory of legal interpretation as integrity—his "community of principle."[90] This notion of a "liberal community"[91] is probably the most significant additional feature to his interpretative scheme, since it is conceivably that which most distinguishes his scheme from positivism. Dworkin articulates three hypothetical models of community: (1) "community as a matter of circumstance," (2) a rule-book community, and (3) the community of principle.[92]

The first type of community is that of strangers thrown together on a desert island, compelled to associate for certain common interests and lacking any overriding principle of trust or justice. They act only out of expediency.[93] In the rule-book community, the members of the community negotiate certain rules that they obey literally, with no sense that there are common underlying principles that might further obligate them.[94] In contrast, the community of principle exists where the source of legal rights and duties arises out of legal interpretations that have integrity consistent with Dworkin's three principles of equality, fairness, and due process.[95]

Dworkin uses the fraternal bonds of community to justify the legitimacy of the coercive authority of the law.[96] Indeed, this move to community is required because, according to Dworkin, the coercive demands of the law are not justified at the merely descriptive level of establishing the "grounds of the law."[97] Rather, Dworkin argues that the "force of the law" or its legitimacy can only be established by this move to community because of the strength of its natural fraternal bonds.[98] However, Dworkin criticizes most natural communities as sometimes being unjust to their members or strangers.[99] Accordingly, he ultimately grounds legal interpretation and his principle of integrity in the community of principle as the sole source of legal rights and duties.[100]

In addition, Dworkin claims that he has "personified" the community of principle as if it were a "chain novel" created by a "single author."[101] He appeals to a hypothetical superhuman judge, Hercules, in his applications of this principle.[102] This appeal suggests that Dworkin conceives of the community of principle as largely limited to judges and lawyers.[103] Indeed, such an inference is consistent with his method of fitting his integrity theory to the practices of the legal community (and to the opinions of appellate judges).

3. Dworkin's Interpretative Method Excludes Teleology

Dworkin's notion of interpretation may be conceived as an indirect way of leaving room for justice while pretending to apply the law. However, the circumlocution involved in his broad notion of interpretation is not necessary where there is an open recognition of natural justice (as will be amplified in Chapter 4). Where the status of natural justice is legitimate (and at least equal with the law), there is no need to bring justice in through the back door in the guise of legal interpretation.

When I assert a statement, my intention as the author of that statement is not something that can be ignored without changing my statement's meaning. Indeed, if it appears that my listener is interpreting my statement in a manner contrary to my intention, I am quick to correct such misinterpretations. Otherwise, a listener could turn left and claim that his misinterpretation of my statement that he should turn to the right was somehow legitimate.

Moreover, there are important distinctions that need to be made between contemporaneous speech and historical texts as well as between speech or texts enjoining certain actions or conduct and artistic speech or texts. Historical texts may legitimately take on a life of their own as circumstances change. In addition, there is, conceivably, an even greater latitude in chang-

ing artistic texts through interpretation, something that is not available to interpretations of texts prescribing certain actions.

There is greater clarity in acknowledging that although a law may mean
one thing, natural justice requires something else, than in pretending that
the law includes justice through legal interpretation. Indeed, there is a
greater danger of reducing justice to a legalistic notion when one attempts,
as Dworkin, to bring some notion of justice in to the application of law
through the back door of legal interpretation. By making interpretation so
central, Dworkin runs the danger of making it seem as if only laws are being
interpreted. Further, he risks implying that law, properly interpreted, and
justice never conflict.

At some point, simple honesty and clarity require that one acknowledge
that interpretation, as envisioned by Dworkin, can conceivably create something new and different from that which is being interpreted. This does not
exclude the legitimacy of taking ideas expressed in historical circumstances
and using them in altogether different circumstances, or even changing the
ideas. But this manner of applying such ideas in different circumstances, as
a species of interpretation, must be distinguishable from the transmutation
of the ideas into something new.

Thus, my first concern with Dworkin's notion of interpretation is that it
confuses justice with (and reduces it to) mere legal interpretation. However,
there is an even larger, related problem. To the extent that his notion is used
to limit interpretations to one correct interpretation (that also happens to
exclude an author's original intention), he is distorting the nature of interpretation and is not much better than the intentionalists he criticizes for
limiting interpretation to an author's original intention.

The debate between Dworkin and the intentionalists is really about
whether the authoritative source of meaning for legal texts resides in legislative enactments or in judicial interpretations. In effect, the intentionalists give authoritative weight exclusively to legislative bodies to which, under
this view, judges must defer. On the other hand, Dworkin gives authoritative
weight primarily to Herculean judges—who may change laws in the guise of
interpretation, so long as this interpretation has integrity with his egalitarian notion of justice.

When seen in this light, the very framework at the root of Dworkin's debate with the intentionalists is beside the point, if one wishes—as I do—to
introduce overt moral considerations of the just that can potentially conflict
with and override legal authority. It is important to leave room for inconsistency if one wants to leave room for justice coming into conflict with the
legal realm. Moreover, neither judges nor legislators—even Herculean ones

in a universe exclusively populated with Dworkins—ought to be viewed as having some infallible reservoir of wisdom giving meaning to legal texts in a just manner in all circumstances.

In one circumstance, the "just" application of the law might require one *action,* whereas in a quite different circumstance, the "just" application of the law might require a completely different *action.* I use the word *action* rather than *interpretation* in order to stress that while Dworkin's project involves determining what the law is, my endeavor is concerned with the appropriate application of the law and the ways in which preoccupation with what the law is seems often to preclude any consideration of the just or unjust application of law.

In either case, the application of law involves more than mere legal interpretation, and one single interpretation is not possible without at least obscuring the very real differences that are better explained by a more overt appeal to justice. In this important sense, Dworkin's notion of interpretation is less accommodating to the notion of epieikeia that I will interpret in Chapter 4. With due apologies to the pretensions of Dworkin's Hercules, I maintain that there cannot be one correct, Herculean interpretation that somehow embraces all the disparate circumstances involving the application of a legal rule.

This is not to imply that in any given circumstance there are many different right or just outcomes (or actions), but only that the right or just action in one circumstance may be different from the right or just action in another circumstance. Further, legal interpretation alone cannot suffice to accommodate these very real differences that are better revealed through a more overt recognition of the potential conflict (and inconsistency) between law and justice.

A rule or abstract principle in its generality can not adequately accommodate the inherent particularity of practical action through mere interpretation of the rule or principle. One must attend to the action and its purpose, something that interpretation of the legal rule does not accommodate where it is merely a question of assessing the consistency of one's interpretation with those of other judges, in the light of Dworkin's egalitarian notion of justice. Egalitarianism is simply not a flexible enough surrogate for the absence of teleology.

Thus the question of whether there is one or many correct legal interpretations in a given circumstance is different from the question of whether there is one correct or just action or outcome in a given circumstance. Nor is it practically possible to find a single rule that completely specifies one action that will be just in one circumstance and a different action that will be just in another circumstance—unless one reduces justice to a universalizable principle. But the essence of justice is having a sensitivity to particularity, that is, the particular ends or purposes desirable for an individual on his or her own terms.

Where just *actions* and particularized ends are the concern, the question of legal interpretation is beside the point. Using a theory of legal interpretation to pretend that law and justice—through mere interpretation—will never conflict ultimately diminishes the importance of justice, unless one reduces justice to an impoverished, inflexible, egalitarian notion of justice. But recognizing the need for preserving the potential for inconsistency between law and justice ultimately forces one to displace the legal text (the exclusive focus of jurisprudential legalism, from intentionalists to Dworkin) with the realm of human action (and justice) in all its particularity, as the primary subject matter of jurisprudence.

In each example of formalism in Chapter 1, interpretation of a legal rule consistent with some legal or extralegal principle was emphasized, rather than the consequences or resulting outcome of the adjudication. In *Corcoran,* a law drafted with the intention of protecting the pension interests of employees was interpreted in a manner that injured the interests of employees who were covered by employee health-benefit plans. In *Zabolotny,* the IRS tried to financially destroy the beneficiaries of an Employee Stock Ownership Plan (ESOP) because the ESOP acquired land owned by the beneficiaries, a technical violation of a statutory conflict-of-interest provision intended to protect the interests of beneficiaries. In *Harmelin,* a first-time nonviolent drug offender was sentenced to life imprisonment without possibility of parole, and this was sustained by the Supreme Court as not constituting cruel and unusual punishment, based on the types of punishments that were in effect at the time the Constitution was adopted. Prosecutors have successfully prosecuted and imprisoned persons for violating the environmental wetlands regulations, based on elastic definitions of what constitutes a wetland. In the *McCummings* case, the New York courts interpreted the burden of proof and legal presumption rules in a manner that permitted a mugger to sue police for injuries sustained when the police prevented him from robbing. Persons defending themselves from violent criminals have been prosecuted for violations of gun-control laws, in some cases with greater vigor than the prosecutions of the violent criminals. None of these obvious examples of breakdowns in the legal system can be adequately diagnosed as legal injustices by a purely descriptive jurisprudential theory confined to the level of legal interpretation. Indeed, in each of these examples, the emphasis on interpretation of a legal rule or principle, independently of its conse-

quences on a particular person, is the common thread. While such an emphasis on interpretation is not unique to Dworkin, he developed the theory
that best fits the reasoning underlying these examples.

Dworkin argues at length at the beginning of *Law's Empire* that all he is
doing is describing what law is (what he characterizes as the "grounds of
law"), and that those who raise concerns about the moral legitimacy of law
in democratic legal systems (what he calls the "force of law") are committing a logical error, which he terms the "semantic sting."[104] According to
Dworkin, disagreements between lawyers about what the law is do not require an underlying semantic theory of common rules (or a tacit shared criteria) when one properly understands the nature of legal interpretation as
a descriptive effort. Dworkin characterizes those who argue for such underlying shared semantic criteria as guilty of the semantic sting.[105]

By analogizing interpretation with artistic creation and aesthetic interpretation, Dworkin argues that he is able to accommodate in his descriptive
theory the fact that lawyers disagree about what the law is, while at the same
time yielding correct answers through his interpretive principle of integrity,
or consistency with egalitarianism and responsiveness to the majority in a
democracy. According to Dworkin, there are no gaps in the law (areas where
it would conceivably be appropriate to argue about what *ought* to be the law)
in adjudicating a dispute, but the nature of interpretation is exclusively concerned with correctly determining what *is* the law. Dworkin argues that his
interpretive framework permits one to view law as complete (without any
gaps) because his interpretive principles, when used by judges and lawyers—
even when they disagree about details—fill in any gaps left by lawmaking
bodies, and, overall, has a fairly good fit with accepted legal modes of argumentation.

Insofar as one is merely descriptive at the interpretive level, it is misleading, according to Dworkin, to argue against the "correctness" of a "proposition" of law arrived at through interpretation by appealing to noninterpre-
tive concerns external to the legal system (concerns dealing with the "force
of law" or its moral legitimacy). In effect, the so-called semantic sting as characterized by Dworkin involves treating the legal system as if it were not self-
contained and self-sufficient, but required an appeal to some extralegal
source of authority for its legitimacy. Thus my own approach is guilty of
Dworkin's semantic sting, but only provided Dworkin has fully exhausted
the alternatives to his theory. In a sense, Dworkin does not conceive of any
jurisprudential criticism outside the question of what the law is. Accordingly,
he assumes that an external critique of the legal system, such as mine, argues for the need for an underlying semantic theory of common rules for

determining what the law is. But I do not care about the "what is law" question. The question of explaining the possibility of meaningful disagreement about "what is the law" is not something I have to explain in order to mount my external critique. It may be remembered that we began with the point that the "what is law" question, or the equivalent question of legal "interpretation," is ultimately beside the point and irrelevant in real legal disputes that are really about justice, that is, what the law ought to be in the particular circumstances being adjudicated.

Lawyers often pretend to be arguing about what the law is on the point in question, when, in fact, they are really arguing about what the law ought to be. And when lawyers argue about that, they often argue about whether a principle may be derived from a legislative or a judicial source, or from an extralegal economic or an egalitarian principle. The fact that this is the way lawyers argue, and the fact that Dworkin (consistent with much of contemporary jurisprudence) fits his jurisprudential theory to this legal manner of interpretation, does not foreclose the legitimacy of criticisms of the legal system. Rather, such criticisms as advanced by my present examination into the origins of legal injustices are not intended to have a close fit with legal interpretation, as it has historically evolved in our culture.

Although Dworkin and most contemporary jurisprudential thinkers may disagree, it is appropriate to attempt an external, moral critique of the legal system without establishing an account of the sources of legal authority. The justice of an adjudication has nothing to do with the legal interpretation that produced a given result, but has only to do with whether that result is just. In other words, the acquittal of an innocent person and the conviction of a guilty person are correct adjudications because of the result achieved, and not because of the legal interpretations of procedural due process that were rendered during the course of the trial.

Conversely, the claim that the system works when a guilty person is acquitted, because the procedures mandated by that legal system were followed and produced a result (even an erroneous one) illustrates the type of thinking that permeates current jurisprudential thought. This outlook emphasizes the interpretation of legal rules and principles, as if these were the results of the system when properly working.

If medicine were evaluated in the same way (and it once was, five hundred years ago), we would similarly argue that a medical procedure worked even if the patient died, so long as the medical doctor followed the procedure as prescribed in the authoritative textbook. On its face, such an argument appears ridiculous. Yet it is repeatedly made and presupposed in much contemporary discussion of the legal system. Indeed, it underlies even the most subtle of reflections, such as those of Dworkin.

Namely, a legal result is deemed just by Dworkin if it conforms to his interpretive principles. He does not care about particular factual applications, except as they illustrate the workings of his principle. In other words, he would probably not change his arguments favoring affirmative action in the face of examples of its use to promote the fortunes of middle-class minorities over those of poor persons who happen to not fall within any privileged category of minorities. This is because the principle of affirmative action is so important to Dworkin that any such deviation from it would be viewed as a threat to that principle. It is the effect of an adjudication on the fashioning of rules and principles that is so important when legal interpretation is emphasized (as in Dworkin), not the effect of an adjudication on a particular person.

This recognition is, indeed, arguably at the root of John Finnis's insightful criticism[106] of the inadequacy of Dworkin's notion of interpretation—as analogized to artistic interpretation: "Interpretation resists being taken for the whole of practical reasoning; or, perhaps more clearly, practical reasoning—e.g., political *praxis*—resists being rendered as 'interpretation of a practice.' Adjudication and juristic interpretation resist being taken for the constitutive and legislative moments in the life of the law; those moments resist being understood through and through, as interpretive."[107]

According to Finnis, then, the "practical reasoning" underlying legislative and adjudicative actions involves more than the making, or *poesis* (*factio*) descriptive of artistic creation, but also embraces doing, or praxis (*actio*). For Dworkin to confine the practical reasoning of legislation and adjudication to a notion of interpretation analogized to artistic interpretation is to reduce legal practical reason to making.[108] And to take this notion further than Finnis, I will argue in Chapter 4 that only at the level of doing can the relevance and merit of Solomon's decision make any sense—whereas confining one's analysis to interpretation renders him incomprehensible. Where the particularity and teleological character of human actions, and not a legal text, becomes the subject matter of jurisprudence, the very notion of interpretation becomes somehow inappropriate altogether, or at least misleading.

Thus, while interpretation has a role, its role ought to be secondary to that of mediating between the excessive generality and rigidity of a legal rule and the particularity and intentionality of human action. Interpreting a legal rule so that it is consistent with other legal rules and the interpretive framework shared by lawyers is a very different enterprise than determining what is a just outcome in an adjudication. The very subject matter of human action is particular and not subject to abstract simplifications, without doing violence to justice itself—something that making interpretation so central to jurisprudence does. Indeed, where particular human actions displace the centrality of the text (that is, the law), as I will show in Chapter 4, the central role of interpretation in Dworkin, with its amenability to obfuscation, is likewise displaced.

4. "Fairness" as Responsiveness to Public Opinion

In *Law's Empire*, Dworkin calls "fairness" one of the so-called political virtues from which the truth of a legal proposition is derived.[109] Under his notion of integrity, an interpretation of the law is "better" (that is, more true and not morally right) if "it reflects convictions that are dominant or at least popular in the community as a whole than if it expresses convictions unpopular or rejected there."[110]

Indeed, herein lies his second major reason for favoring the woman's "right to choose" an abortion over the fetus's right to live. The fact that there is such "deep disagreement within our culture" on this issue makes it wrong for the government legally to coerce women not to have abortions, according to Dworkin.[111] Dworkin distinguishes the illegitimate legal coercion against having an abortion from legitimate legal compulsion of citizens to pay taxes (even if used to fight a war considered immoral by some of those citizens), on the ground that the justification for coercion to pay taxes involves an appeal to the rights and interests of other people, rather than an appeal to a religious or moral belief (as in the case of abortion).[112] The interest of the fetus in living is reduced and replaced by Dworkin with the religious belief in the "intrinsic value" of life, an abstraction for Dworkin that only has meaning within certain religious contexts. Dworkin's liberalism recognizes the inseparability of a tradition and notion of the good associated with the pro-life position while, at the same time, failing to recognize that his liberalism lies within a tradition with its own notions of the good. The result of this is a failure to confront opposing traditions on their own terms, and a corresponding failure to truly justify his own presuppositions of the good. This failure is exemplified in those women who proclaim that they would never get an abortion themselves but would also never presume to bar others from that choice—however unrestricted and absolute the choice might be.

The problem with Dworkin's position is that there were deep divisions involving the issue of slavery in the America of the early nineteenth century, yet Dworkin views the sanctioning of slavery by a legal system as illegitimate and outside of the "normal circumstances" of democratic legal systems. One hundred years later it is easy for Dworkin to dismiss this problem by saying it is not included in his legal system. Using his criteria of fairness in a contemporaneous setting in the 1840s would make it much more difficult for him to dismiss slavery's legitimacy under his very principle of integrity. Indeed, Chief Justice Roger Taney used Dworkin's fairness argument to support his atrocious holding in *Dred Scott*:

> They [African Americans] had for more than a century before been regarded as beings of an inferior order; and altogether unfit to associate with the white race, either in social or political relations; and so far inferior, that they had no rights which the white man was bound to respect; and that the negro might justly and lawfully be reduced to slavery for his benefit. He was bought and sold, and treated as an ordinary article of merchandise and traffic, whenever a profit could be made by it. *This opinion was at that time fixed and universal in the civilized portion of the white race. It was regarded as an axiom in morals as well as in politics, which no one thought of disputing, or supposed to be open to dispute; and men in every grade and position in society daily and habitually acted upon it in their private pursuits, as well as in matters of public concern, without doubting for a moment the correctness of this opinion* [emphasis added].[113]

Indeed, most abolitionists were viewed as religious fanatics, just as most pro-lifers are viewed today. Moreover, the fact that opposition to slavery in the 1840s was motivated by a religious view of the intrinsic value of human life—when the legal system and U.S. Constitution at the time did not view African Americans as "persons"—would have been a further reason for supporting it if Dworkin's fairness principle had been applied to slavery consistent with his use of it in the abortion context.

This, in turn, reveals the ultimate intellectual bankruptcy involved in determining issues of morality and justice purely in legalistic terms—otherwise known as Dworkin's principle of integrity in judicial interpretation. In each case—that of slavery and that of abortion—the Supreme Court did not adequately deal with the morality of slavery or the importance of the fetus's right to life. Rather, it avoided the real moral issues by dealing with them purely on jurisdictional grounds. It addressed only the questions of whether Dred Scott was a "person" for legal purposes, and whether a fetus is a "constitutional person" for purposes of the Fourteenth Amendment.[114]

Something quite similar occurred in the Michigan Supreme Court's jurisdictional evasion of the real issue of the adopted child's interest in the *Claussen* case. One hundred years ago, there was not a consensus about slavery. Today there is not a consensus about fetuses or young children. In both cases, courts have avoided the issue by arguing in strictly legalistic terms. It is my contention that grave injustices were done and that Dworkin's notion of fairness and integrity in interpretation provides no basis for distinguishing the results in the pro-abortion cases (favored by Dworkin) from the result in the slavery case (condemned by Dworkin).[115]

"Fairness," characterized and used by Dworkin as the responsiveness of officials to the electorate or public opinion, cannot be a constraint that tempers the potential injustice of a legal decision and may even operate as one of the motivating forces behind an unjust legal decision. While public opinion may give a regime political legitimacy, it certainly cannot be seriously argued that it gives it any moral legitimacy. The times when public opinion has been wrong and has served as a force for scapegoating unpopular individuals or groups are well known from historical and contemporary examples.

However, Dworkin conceivably limits the notion of fairness with the sole trump in his system, his notion of equality. In a separate essay on "political equality," which he defines as concerned with the "distribution of political power" within an "egalitarian community," he asks which is the best "approach" to democracy: a "dependent interpretation of democracy" or a "detached interpretation of democracy."[116] He defines a dependent approach as one that "supposes that the best form of democracy is whatever form is most likely to produce the substantive decisions and results that treat all members of the community with equal concern."[117] He contrasts this to the "detached" approach, which he characterizes as insisting that "we judge the fairness or democratic character of a political process by looking to features of that process alone, asking only whether it distributes political power in an equal way, not what results it promises to produce."[118]

He concludes that the "dependent" approach is the best, particularly with respect to "choice-insensitive issues," because it produces equal outcomes.[119] He introduces the distinction between "choice-sensitive" and "choice-insensitive issues" to distinguish between issues that should not be sensitive to preferences in a community (such as opposition to the death penalty, according to Dworkin) and those for which input from the community is appropriate.[120] The distinction between choice-sensitive and choice-insensitive issues conceivably parallels his distinction between the public and private.

At any rate, I suspect that issues implicating Dworkin's rigid egalitarianism would be the most choice-insensitive, issues such as his advocacy of affirmative action, unrestricted abortions, rationing health care through a government-mandated system, and minimizing the role of religion as much as possible in the so-called public realm. Dworkin argues that an appropriate way to design a "dependent conception of democracy" so as to "improve the accuracy" of decisions concerning "distinctly substantive goals of an egalitarian political process" would rely heavily on this distinction between choice-sensitive and choice-insensitive issues.[121]

Dworkin concludes that the constitutional practice of judicial review, although elitist from a detached democratic view, best fulfills the "dependent" democratic approach with respect to choice-insensitive issues. Accordingly, for Dworkin, fairness is for the most part an allegedly subsidiary value to that of justice, understood in an egalitarian sense. But in issues like that of abortion, where there are arguably competing egalitarian considerations— that of the unborn fetus and that of the mother, it is not an egalitarian notion of justice, but so-called fairness that ultimately determines for Dworkin which egalitarian concern should carry greater weight. This elasticity, in effect, reduces egalitarianism to fairness, or, at the least, it renders egalitarianism into an effective limit on fairness only when the judicial elite so opines.

One would hope that even the least attentive reader would readily discern the difficulty here: namely, that Dworkin is able to avoid confronting the moral incompatibility between his espousal of egalitarianism for some classes of persons (runaway slaves and so-called "defectives"), and rejection of it for others (an unborn fetus), when these cases are viewed exclusively at the level of legal interpretation. That is, has Carrie Buck been afforded due process, or does Dred Scott or an unborn fetus have standing as a legal "person" under the Constitution?

And this moral confusion at the root of Dworkin's inordinate emphasis on legal interpretation in part reveals how it happens that his notion of integrity in interpretation has such a good fit with judicial opinions. When out of historical accident the majority believes that slavery of African Americans is right, judicial opinion in deference to majority opinion sustains slavery against egalitarian arguments. But when the majority believes slavery of African Americans to be wrong, judicial opinion interprets African Americans to be entitled to equality before the law. When the majority believes that unborn fetuses do not have equal rights, judicial opinion sustains the limitations on state regulation of abortions. Dworkin argues that his notion of integrity in judicial interpretation is "true" because of its fit with both strands of American judicial interpretation. Yet he supplies no basis for reconciling these conflicting interpretive strands, other than the historical accident that his interpretation has a perfect fit with contemporary judicial interpretation. But if judicial interpretation is revealed to be incoherent, then a jurisprudential theory that is based on its fit with judicial interpretation must also be somewhat incoherent.

5. Toward a "Liberal" Redefinition of Justice Reduced to Simple Equality

Because Dworkin reduces the notion of justice to a rigid egalitarianism, it cannot operate as a constraint on unjust coercion in democratic legal systems. One does not have to be a libertarian to recognize the historical violence often associated with egalitarian movements. Equality does not exist naturally and, therefore, it must be imposed artificially, necessitating coercion or violence.

Yet equality is ultimately a chimerical goal that can never exist or be imposed without coercion, whether through the legal system or through violence. The act of leveling one group necessarily requires empowering another group that, in turn, has no reason to limit its newly found power based on the principle of equality. It is the supreme paradox of theoretical egalitarianism that in practice—at the level of action—it is elitist, insofar as it requires an elite priesthood (lawyers) to interpret and implement its abstract principles. Whether or not one finds egalitarianism attractive, it requires coercion and, consequently, cannot operate as much of a constraint or limitation on the coercion of the law.[122]

This is a very practical problem inherent to redistributive schemes. The rigid pursuit of equality often requires coercion that is in one way or another at odds with equality—and this is ignored by Dworkin. Instead, he views the problem in a completely theoretical manner. He stipulates that the only appropriate liberty is the liberty that does not conflict with equality, where there is an equality of resources: "How can a plausible conception of liberty require that anyone have more power than he would have if freedom of choice was unlimited and resources fairly distributed?"[123]

Dworkin constructs an artificial model based on an "imaginary auction" on a desert island where, after specifying certain liberties as essential to equality, the resources are auctioned off in a series of transactions from an initially equal stock of resources, with the auction not ending until everyone is content (that is, his "envy test" is met).[124] The idea is to provide a redistributive model on the "insurance decisions members of the community would make under certain appropriate circumstances," so that these redistributive legal institutions would "make the resources available to any one person depend so far as possible on the opportunity costs of those resources to others, in the way the imaginary auction and post-auction transactions make them so depend."[125]

The basic problem with this model is the fact that it is a model, that is, an artificial, mechanical model of human society—as if societies were a machine or a set of isolated billiard balls with no connection with one other. It ignores the fact that no group of humans would ever agree to an artificial auction of the sort hypothesized, that none has ever occurred nor ever will. If such a scheme were ever implemented, it would be through fraud or force, and ultimately it would break down, like the Soviet system, through its own corruption and inefficiency. If societies arose naturally in the manner of Dworkin's "imaginary auction," he would not be advocating restructuring society based on this scheme. Natural societies, from this viewpoint, are raw materials for an economist, mechanic, engineer, or sculptor playing the role of a lawyer/judge/legislator able to fashion and manipulate through the coercion of the legal system alone.

But even if Dworkin's scheme were enacted into law (and many of its features already exist, in our tax system), it would not function in the manner intended, because it would be implemented in a society of people who already had natural ways of interacting with one other outside of and independent of this artificial legal scheme—just as in our tax system. (Efforts to "soak the rich" more often than not affect small businessmen and farmers, with the real rich avoiding taxes through loopholes.) Ultimately, it would provide just another means for one group of persons to coerce the rest of society in the name of the noble goal of equality.[126]

Another good illustration of my point is supplied by a historical example dealt with at length in *Law's Empire*. It is agreed that racial segregation by law of so-called separate but equal schools under *Plessey v. Ferguson* was wrong. Dworkin uses the *Brown v. Board of Education of Topeka* and *Bakke* affirmative-action decisions to illustrate in an idealized manner the proper application of his principle of integrity in judicial interpretation.[127] He assumes an "ideal judge" with omniscient knowledge (called Hercules) who, in a nutshell, would have decided *Brown* to order desegregation of schools, and who would also have decided *Bakke* to establish a more aggressive version of affirmative action. The irony of all this is the fact that just forty years after *Brown,* ample evidence exists that despite the ordered desegregation of the public schools in Topeka, its schools remain as segregated as ever, because of "white flight" to the suburbs.[128]

The coerciveness inherent in egalitarianism fosters tensions, in part because of the inherent injustice of compulsion. If justice is more appropriately defined and grounded in terms of social connections (as I argue in Chapter 4), rather than in abstract notions of a theoretical egalitarianism, the social connections underlying justice cannot be artificially compelled without undermining those very social connections (and, therefore, justice itself). Accordingly, *Brown* illustrates the inadequacy of using the legal system alone to tackle a larger social problem. Coercive legal remedies are similar to an overeager surgeon: sometimes one needs surgery, but more often than not, it is best to let nature take its course.

In addition, Dworkin couples with this notion of equality, from which the idea of integrity in interpretation of the legal system is derived, another erroneous distinction: the distinction between public duties of government and private duties of individuals.[129] This very distinction illustrates the absence of any real recognition by Dworkin of the importance of natural communities in constituting just or unjust societies, notwithstanding his alleged appeal to community (which I will address later in this chapter): "Government has a general, pervasive duty that private citizens, as individuals, do not. Government must constantly survey and alter its rules of property, radically if necessary, to bring them closer to the ideal of treating people as equals under the best conception."[130]

One might justly ask Dworkin how individuals manage to interact with each other at all, in a cooperative or social manner, without the coercive guidance of government. Nor does this leave any role for natural communities that have a notion of the good life, a telos or summum bonum, a morality, or a religion. Society is viewed almost as an empty vessel to be filled with laws, or a computer that needs software and a programmer. Society has been replaced by the government and its laws.

The other troubling implication of Dworkin's public/private distinction is that there are no moral or social obligations owed by individuals to other individuals, apart from duties imposed upon them by the legal system or the government. One logical extension of this is for people to give less to charity because they view that as the exclusive role of government; they do their civic duty when they pay their taxes.[131] Such a society is alienated, crime-ridden, and ultimately unworkable.

One only has to look to the community of the Amish as a counterexample of the artificial character of Dworkin's egalitarian program.[132] In this distinctive religious community, the public and private realms have not been separated. The Amish spurn connections with the national government and pay their taxes, but do not accept any government benefits in return, such as Medicaid or farm subsidies. Family members and the community care for their aged members, rather than relegating them to institutions. The social connections between the young and the old are maintained in a more humane manner in this arrangement. The community voluntarily insures itself for its own health care. Benefits are provided according to need, and contributions are voluntarily paid according to ability to pay—all without elaborate legal enforcement mechanisms. If a member of the community suffers financial reverses, the rest of the community assists that member. The community is filled with prospering small businesses, even though the Amish spurn much modern technology. Serious crime is virtually nonexistent. The care and protection of members of the community is provided voluntarily, without legal compulsion by other community members.

But the coerciveness and artificiality inherent in egalitarianism are only partial dimensions of the problem. To the extent that one's notions of justice are concretely realized in the practical world, rather than in that of abstractions, egalitarianism will often appear rigid, blind, and inflexible. Equality, by its own terms, looks elsewhere than to the facts before it. Ultimately it appeals to some type of abstract standard of measure for filtering those facts and sifting out or accommodating with verbal locutions and distinctions those uncomfortable facts that just do not fit neatly within its rigid formula.

For example, Dworkin argues for the justness of a racial classification operating as a preference for African American law-school applicants over a Jewish law-school applicant with higher academic credentials in *DeFunis v. Odegaard.*[133] Dworkin purports to reconcile his argument favoring racial preference in *DeFunis* with his condemnation of a racial classification operating to exclude an African American law-school applicant from admission to law school in *Sweatt v. Painter.*[134] Dworkin argues that the exclusion of the Jewish student from law school, based on a racial classification in *DeFunis,* was just, but that the exclusion of the African American student from law school in *Sweatt* was unjust.[135] His interpretation distinguishes between the right of "treatment as an equal," which he calls more fundamental than the derivative right of "equal treatment." Dworkin's interpretation uses a combination of a "preference utilitarianism," where "external preferences" are discounted in favor of "personal preferences," and an "ideal" notion of justice favoring greater equality as his means of justifying the unjust treatment of DeFunis in the particular circumstances based on the overall welfare to the community. This exemplifies the legalist fallacy, where justice in particular circumstances is sacrificed to a general principle—in this case, equality of outcomes and greater utility to the community as a whole.

Justice and injustice are so particularized that a consistent application of a rule that would be just in one circumstance may be unjust in another circumstance. The aim of Chapters 3 and 4 is to establish the particularity of justice and the injustice of rigidly pursuing consistency. In a way, the coherence or consistency inherent in the notion of integrity parallels Dworkin's proclivity to reduce justice to a rigid egalitarianism. The petty complaint of the modern bureaucrat, "If I made an exception for you, then I would have to make an exception for someone else," perfectly epitomizes the egalitarian element of consistency. As Dworkin says: "Law as integrity, then, requires a judge to test his interpretation of any part of the great network of political structures and decisions of his community by asking whether it could form part of a coherent theory justifying the network as a whole."[136]

To determine the ultimate justice of a particular application of a law based on its consistency with the legal system as a whole is to construe a body of rules and principles, namely the law, as overriding any particular person or circumstance. This epitomizes the legalist fallacy discussed at the beginning of my examination of legal injustices.

Another recent example involves the use of statistics that argue against capital punishment for murder based on an alleged lack of equality between the percentage of criminals executed for murdering whites as compared with black victims. The notion that equality is more important than obtaining the most retribution that is ever possible for murder (execution) is a perversion of traditional notions of justice. While one might legitimately disagree about the appropriateness of capital punishment because of a lack of confidence in the judicial system's actually convicting the right person, introducing equality as a competing consideration to justice is a dangerous notion that confuses the real issue—particularly if there is little doubt that the person convicted of the crime did, in fact, commit the crime. The real issue is whether a particular person committed the murder, not whether persons belonging to a certain group were unjustly executed in circumstances not being adjudicated.

The problem inherent in a theory of the law where consistency in the body of rules, or their overall fit as a legal system, is the overriding principle of interpretation, rather than the manner in which the application of the law fits the facts, lies in the absence of any telos for the law other than

the legal system itself. But this, in turn, is the source of the rigid inflexibility of such an approach. Egalitarianism and coherence as principles of legal
interpretation are opposed to a flexible application of the law, one that treats
people as ends in themselves.

Egalitarianism expands "law's empire" in a limitless manner, whereas
epieikeia (as developed in Chapter 4) limits and directs the application of
the law in recognition of the telos of the person to whom it is being applied
and his or her place in the social order. This treatment of the person as an
end is not the same as Dworkin's notion of equal concern.[137] Treating a person the *same as something else* is emphatically not equivalent to treating that
person on his or her own terms.

The *Harmelin v. Michigan* case, identified as a breakdown (or injustice) in
our legal system in Chapter 1, is a good illustration of this point. Dworkin
would probably argue that life imprisonment without parole was cruel and
unusual punishment for a nonviolent crime. The rationale of the Supreme
Court minority objecting to this punishment has a better fit with Dworkin's
principle of equality than does the opinion of the majority, which tracks
more with the conventionalist approach.

But the greater fit of the majority opinion with conventionalism does not
make it a better opinion from the standpoint of my examination of legal injustices, insofar as Dworkin's method of fit has already been emphatically
rejected. As discussed in Chapter 1, the majority in *Harmelin* focused on the
history of punishments during colonial times when the Eighth Amendment
was first enacted. The majority happened to be conservative justices favored
by Republicans, and the minority consisted of the court's liberals, generally
favored by Democrats.

This reveals the historical contingency of the method of fit shared between
Dworkin and positivists. Further, it shows that fit is insufficient to supply a
philosophically rigorous or necessary justification for one theory over another. As more Republican judges are appointed, the pragmatist economic
approach to the law and conventionalism will have better fits to opinions,
while as more Democratic judges are appointed, Dworkin's theory will have
a greater fit. Such accidents of history do not supply adequate philosophical justification.

Although the Supreme Court majority was wrong from the standpoint of
my framework for exploring legal injustices, the reasons for this conclusion
are problematic if one confines one's rationale to Dworkin's egalitarian principle and the court's dissenters. The dissent was based on the notion of proportionality or equality. If all fifty states imposed the same punishment of
life imprisonment for this particular nonviolent offense, the punishment

would be justified, according to the same principle of equality that the dissenters made the basis for opposing such an unjust sentence. But the real reason that such a punishment would be cruel and unjust, even if not unusual, would be the disproportionate nature of the punishment relative to the *particular* crime (taking into account the unique circumstances of the person convicted of that crime). And this would be cruel and unjust whether or not that punishment was inflicted with equality.

The fact that the punishment was also disproportionate on the grounds of equality is a significant consideration, but that should not be the only consideration. Justice is always particularized and cannot be reduced to mere equality without forfeiting the sense of flexible proportionality that is unique to justice. Dworkin's notion of integrity as justice reduced to equality misses that subtle distinction: that there is a difference between treating persons as ends valued in themselves and treating them with so-called equal concern. Treating persons with so-called equal concern is a limitation (and not an expansion) on treating them as ends valuable in their own right.

But recognizing this distinction would require setting aside Dworkin's moral neutrality about the good life. This commitment to some sort of view of the good life is something that is lived out in a practical sense in day-to-day living by everyone, but it is conveniently forgotten when engaging in philosophical speculation. Any choice of an action has some end or good in view for the sake of which the action is done.

There is every reason to think that a legal system grounded in moral neutrality about the good life must ultimately place the legal system itself on a higher plane than any particular human. As applied to this person, if I applied the law to him as if he were my son, I would interpret the rule with flexibility and, I would say, with justice—with an eye toward the best end in view for that person. But if I applied the law with a view to its consistency with the principle of equality—as an abstract principle—it is conceivable that I would treat this person as an object that ultimately must be sacrificed to the need to universalize the rule.

A jurisprudence that studies rules rather than the facts to which these rules are applied misses the point of the legal system, because the facts arise out of a context that gives meaning to the rules, and that context is within a particular community and within a given teleological framework of the good for man, albeit a tacit one. Equality as conceived by Dworkin reduces justice to just another mechanical rule to be added to the other rules that compose the body of law and its principles of interpretation.

Indeed, Congress largely eliminated judicial discretion in imposing criminal sentences for federal crimes because of egalitarian concerns. A complex set of rules involving cross-references to various factors affecting the ultimate sentence for a criminal, with mandatory minimums, has replaced the discretion of judges. After a decade under the new rules, most legal practitioners agree that harsher sentences have resulted and that poor minority criminals have fared worse under the complex rules.[138] Many federal judges have resigned in disgust at the severity of the penalties and draconian limitations on their discretion.

The complexity of the rules make having an experienced and expensive attorney the determining factor in the likely outcome. Prosecutors and police can "game" the rules and stack the deck against certain defendants based purely on how they charge the defendant. The complexity of the rules makes them so subject to manipulation that their seeming objectivity and exactitude are largely viewed as a sham. Ironically, much of the focus on reforming the sentencing guidelines does not appear to question their underlying egalitarian premise. Accordingly, the penalties for drug crimes, for which minorities are more likely to be charged, are being scrutinized for possible reduction, rather than focusing on repealing the guidelines altogether, to return discretion in sentencing to federal judges.

The exclusive focus is on assuring uniformity in the sentencing rules, rather than giving judges the discretion to flexibly tailor a sentence based on the particular characteristics of the defendant. Thus the focus is on the purity of the sentencing rules from an egalitarian framework (that is, language), and not on justice in the particular circumstances (that is, action). This shows very starkly how equality and legal interpretation go hand in hand with the obliteration of epieikeia, or equity from the moral vocabulary of reform. This example ought to lay bare the potential harshness and inflexibility at the root of Dworkin's egalitarian interpretive principle of integrity, which fits so well contemporary legal thinking.

6. The Relationship Between Dworkin's Moral Neutrality and His Rigid Egalitarianism

There are a number of confusions latent in Dworkin's notion of moral neutrality and his related egalitarianism.[139] For example, Dworkin's private/public duty distinction can conceivably be extended by some to hold that no moral obligations exist apart from those imposed by the legal system constituted by the government (which is not the same as the community). This confusion is further abetted by Dworkin's misleading characterization of his three principles of integrity (fairness, equality, and due process) as so-called political virtues. Such a characterization is misleading, in part because the notion of a virtue more properly implies perfection toward some end or purpose by a person having intentionality, rather than a thing.[140]

This is not to deny that a political community—as an *aggregation of individual choices*—can be more or less virtuous. But it is an impoverished and misleading notion of a "political virtue" to call a community virtuous based solely on its principles of legal interpretation, its legal constitution, or its legal system. Rather, it is the customs of a political or a legal community—as exemplified in the aggregation of *individual* actions of its citizens—that may improve upon, ameliorate, or pervert the noblest-sounding or harshest-sounding framework of legal interpretation. In a very practical sense, ignored by Dworkin, a political community cannot be virtuous apart from the virtue or lack thereof of its individual citizens, and this further means that virtue cannot be compartmentalized into a narrower species of political virtues that can exist in the absence of other virtues.

Thus, "fairness" defined as responsiveness to public opinion can hardly be viewed as what is traditionally accepted as moral virtue, and certainly it has nothing to do with the virtue of any individual. In addition, it is difficult to see how liberty or equality can be properly deemed virtues in such an avowedly morally neutral system. By what criteria or necessity does Dworkin select certain virtues as meriting favor by a political community, to the exclusion of other virtues? In sum, Dworkin purports to define his notion of justice as a political virtue—a real potential improvement upon contemporary jurisprudential thought. But this potential advance is severely undercut by his impoverished notion of virtue. Indeed, his so-called political virtue of justice or equality is, paradoxically, a morally neutral virtue that is also a reduction of political virtue to a species of legal interpretation. But the essence of equality as a so-called virtue is self-contradictory, because one cannot treat everything with equality or tolerance without giving preference to something and expressing intolerance for something else.

The purported tolerance of alternative moral conceptions is required, according to Dworkin, because giving preference to any particular conception of the good life would result in the legal system not treating persons holding different conceptions of the good life as equals with those holding the preferred conception.[141] Laws involving prohibitions of homosexuality and restrictions on abortion are prime examples, for Dworkin, of legal conceptions incompatible with his notion of equality. Dworkin also advocates public funding of art without consideration of its content, giving priority to diversity and innovation over excellence.[142]

The extent of this toleration has resulted, however, in the preferred treatment of many alternative lifestyles over the moral and religious views of the majority—something that, at some point, conflicts with Dworkin's notion of fairness. Thus, prayer is banned in the public schools and yet homosexuals, for a time, were allowed to proselytize their views to elementary children in a borough of New York City. A so-called performance by an AIDS activist cutting another actor with a knife was funded by the National Endowment for the Arts, while public funding of parochial schools remains illegal.[143] In other examples, homosexual activists are allowed to disrupt religious services while Congress enacts a law making it a crime to demonstrate in front of abortion clinics. Landlords have been fined by state human-rights czars for refusing to rent their properties to cohabiting couples and homosexuals. Homosexual activists have used the legal system to disrupt St. Patrick's Day celebrations within the Irish community.[144]

The problem with Dworkin's egalitarianism is that its purported morally neutral view of the law cannot really be morally neutral with respect to those having moral views that are opposed to such neutrality: that is, practice that passes for moral neutrality is not morally neutral. Indeed, any enforcement of this principle necessitates coercion against the group deemed to have an advantage over others, with the so-called victimized group receiving preferential treatment to compensate for this inequality. Dworkin's unjustified premise that it is somehow possible for officials to be morally neutral is a dangerous pretense that, in effect, denies that there is a notion of the good life underlying the pluralistic liberal position. This pretense is dangerous because it fails to face up to its use of coercion through the law when it imposes this so-called moral neutrality on communities that are avowedly committed to some moral point of view.

Indeed, the pretense of moral neutrality is particularly insidious because it masks the coerciveness inherent in the law and the implications of this coercion for that supposed moral neutrality. The legal system is not some abstraction with no practical consequence. The legal system always and necessarily involves the use of force, either to induce or to constrain the actions of individuals. Action is the realm of morality, and anything that induces or constrains action cannot be viewed as morally neutral. Constraining others to be morally neutral is not a morally neutral action.[145]

What Dworkin, in essence, is doing when he grounds the legitimacy of the law's violence in his theory of integrity is tacitly assuming that might makes right in these circumstances. But might can never make right, even in the few areas where I would agree with Dworkin that the law has some legitimacy. For example, there is a certain legitimacy to a law that punishes a person for committing murder. Complete justice would restore the murder victim to life, an impossibility. Therefore, it may be argued that the next best approximation to justice involves taking the life of the murderer or imprisoning the murderer. But it must be recognized that this can never be mistaken for real justice itself.

The coercion of law and egalitarianism can be exposed by examining one instance in which Dworkin acknowledged some problems with too rigid a notion of equality. In this circumstance Dworkin himself abandoned equality, because he considered strict equality to be too unjust and coercive. This exception to equality cannot be easily reconciled with his general theory of equality. Dworkin rejected the clearly extreme notions of Professor Catharine MacKinnon that freedom of speech and thought must be restricted by the principle of equality, because certain speech (particularly pornography, broadly defined to encompass criticisms of her position favoring censorship) contributes to unequal opportunities for women.[146] In the context of Professor MacKinnon's application, Dworkin found it to be a "frightening principle that considerations of equality require that some people not be free to express their tastes or convictions anywhere."[147]

But Professor MacKinnon's use of the notion of equality is a logical extension of Dworkin's own general theory of equality as a limit on permissible liberties. That his is a theory according to which tolerance of diversity can actually be used to subvert toleration reveals Dworkin's failure to face this dilemma or at least to recognize the inconsistency of his position. As repulsive as Professor MacKinnon's views are, she at least is consistent with Dworkin's theory of equality. He has yet to articulate a basis for his failure consistently to apply his notions of equality in the circumstances that she singles out. The only rationale that he articulates against Professor MacKinnon, that liberty must constrain equality in the circumstances involving free speech, is a major exception to his general theory's notion that it is equality that limits liberty and determines what liberties are permissible, and not the reverse.

7. Due Process: An Inadequate Constraint on Law's Coercion

At this point, the fundamental incoherence of Dworkin's reliance on fairness and equality as supposed constraints on abuses of power in the legal system should be apparent. If anything, these two notions are often the very sources of abuses of power and breakdowns in the legal system. This leaves due process as the only remaining constraint apparently recognized by Dworkin on the coercive use of the law. To some degree due process is, in fact, a constraint. Interestingly, he never develops the way it acts as a constraint, nor does he explain or develop its relative importance vis-à-vis equality and fairness. While the omission of extended treatment of due process by itself does not definitively establish its relative unimportance, this omission is certainly an arguable indication that due process is less important, for Dworkin, than are justice or fairness.

Constraining the coercion of the legal system does not appear to be Dworkin's principal concern, since he more often states the problem as finding justification for such coercion. It is a justification that he, indeed, claims to find in his three principles of equality, fairness, and due process. While equality and fairness are conceivable justifications for legal coercion, due process is more of a constraint and limitation on the law than it is a justification of legal coercion.

However, due process by itself is hardly a sufficient constraint on the coercion of the legal system; one merely has to review some of the paradigmatic cases that I examined in Chapter 1. In *Buck v. Bell,* a person was forcibly sterilized with due process. Developers have been sent to prison under the wetlands regulations, with due process. Innocent persons accused of sex abuse have been sent to prison, with due process. The government has unjustly confiscated private property under the forfeiture laws, with due process.[148] Due process involves purely procedural considerations that hardly encompass the full range of moral theories that might constrain the exercise of state power through the law.

Certain procedures, for example, are thought to carry with them greater risks of convicting an innocent person. Other procedures are thought to carry with them greater risks of letting a guilty person go free. Weighing these risks and assessing the appropriateness of certain procedures based on what is deemed an appropriate mix of risks is a due process analysis. While due process may be the only effective constraint on the abuse of power in a legal system, it is hardly the only legitimate moral constraint.

Indeed, one could conceive of a legal system, such as ours, with procedures theoretically weighted against convicting an innocent person, that nonetheless frequently convicted innocent persons and let guilty persons go free—the worst possible outcome. Procedures by themselves assure nothing. The moral character of officials following those procedures is much more important than a particular mix of procedures that assign weight to the risks one way or the other.[149]

Any constraint on the unjust application of the law ultimately comes from the community within which the law is applied. A community or an individual with a clear sense of right and wrong can bring about great good or evil. There can be no rule book or system of laws that programs a person to have the requisite moral sensibility that prompts moral actions. The individuals and communities who defied legal authority to save Jews and other persecuted enemies of the state from the Holocaust acted not in conformity with the law, but contrary to it.

One might counter these reflections with the argument that some of the persons erroneously convicted of sex abuse based on fabricated testimony of programmed child witnesses have been released from prison (in some cases after serving five years), after their convictions were overturned on appeal for some violation of procedural due process. However, it was legalistic interpretations of due process rules that got them into prison in the first place, and the initial impetus for gaining their release came through exposure by the press, most notably the *Wall Street Journal*'s editorial page. What prompted exposure by the press was the basic teleological consideration that innocent persons were in prison—a consideration not requiring elaborate intellectual analysis and legal interpretation.

8. Toward a "Liberal" Redefinition of Community

If the morality of a community, rather than its legal system, is the only reliable constraint on the abuse of power in that legal system, it is appropriate to unpack the role of community and Dworkin's so-called community of principle. Indeed, the role of the community, in particular a community of principle, is explicitly introduced by Dworkin as the basis for grounding the legitimacy of a democratic legal system within the interpretative scheme of integrity. After earlier claiming that his notion of integrity would be at the level of the grounds of law only, he makes the following assertion midway through *Law's Empire:* "We now turn to the direct connection between integrity and the moral authority of the law, and this bends our study back toward the main argument of the book . . . [which]—connects law with the justification of official coercion."[150]

After rejecting the traditional Enlightenment social contract models of political legitimacy as artificial models that fail to explain political legitimacy adequately, he turns to natural communities—families, friends, neighbors, and similar associations.[151] He recognizes that the obligations of such natural communities arise indiscernibly, rather than in the deliberative contractual manner presupposed by the social contract models.

He acknowledges that philosophers, in general, have ignored his approach of grounding political legitimacy in such natural communities, justifying such neglect on the basis of the small size and parochialism (or even racism) of such communities. He correctly notes that "communal obligations" depend on "emotional bonds that presuppose that each member of the group has personal acquaintance of all others."[152]

Dworkin is correct in recognizing that moral obligations are less abstract and more important to most people at this associative level. He even implicitly acknowledges that there is no public duty in competition with a private duty at such a level of communal obligation, but rather that responsibilities between the members of the group are "personal" and "run directly from each member to each other member, not just to the group as a whole in some collective sense."[153] He further correctly distinguishes these natural associations from the social contract models on the basis that communitarian obligations, unlike contractual ones, need not be voluntary in the deliberative sense.[154]

However, Dworkin departs from such a conception of association, perhaps best exemplified by Aristotle's conception of friendship, when he affirms that such associations are inherently egalitarian.[155] While this claim may be easily disputed by merely observing families and communities in a sociological sense, it is not, at this point, as useful to dispute Dworkin's egalitarianism as it is to discern the potential of his focus on the notion of community. His analysis of community begins rather auspiciously: "We are at last able to consider our hypothesis directly: that the best defense of political legitimacy—the right of a political community to treat its members as having obligations in virtue of collective community decisions—is to be found not in the hard terrain of contracts or duties of justice or obligations of fair play that might hold among strangers, where philosophers have hoped to find it, but in the more fertile ground of fraternity, community, and their attendant obligations."[156]

These remarks are followed, however, by a reintroduction of the artificial counterfactual models so beloved by post-Enlightenment thinkers. He examines three artificial models of "community."[157] The first is a desert island community of strangers, more akin to the Hobbesian state of nature.[158] The second, the "rulebook" model of community, as well as the third, the community of principle advocated by Dworkin, are indiscernible from the artificial social contract models.[159]

The advantage of the community of principle over the rule-book model of community, according to Dworkin, is that it more closely approximates the moral obligations that are felt in the natural communities briefly discussed earlier—and it paradoxically does this in a "morally pluralistic society."[160] According to Dworkin, these moral obligations that are felt in natural communities are egalitarian, and, accordingly, the members of a community of principle agree that his three extralegal principles fill in any gaps in the letter of the law. Such a society is permissive of diverse moral ends, so long as the core egalitarian morality is accepted. In contrast, the rule-book community confines the law's prescriptions to the letter of any explicit political agreements arrived at in constituting and maintaining a community.

It should be apparent, at this critical point in the argument, that Dworkin is no longer talking about natural communities—communities that, as a liberal, he would obviously want to avoid because of their prejudices and insularity—but about an ideal community. According to Dworkin, this ideal community, as an abstraction that is no longer a real community, can thereby serve to ground the legitimacy of the full coercive force of the legal system and the modern nation state.[161]

While Dworkin initially considers the phenomenon that—at the level of small local and parochial associations—people naturally cement bonds that are felt by them to impose greater moral and communal obligations toward each other, he ultimately shies away from exploiting this insight wherever it might lead, for two reasons that I explore in the next two subsections.

8.1 Dworkin's Discontent with Natural Communities Rooted in Moral Neutrality

First, Dworkin finds it more important to ground an assessment of the ultimate moral legitimacy of the law in a morally pluralistic community than to retain the features of a genuine community. Genuine communities more ordinarily attain a cohesion through a moral consensus and telos: that whatever is good for one member is good for the other members of the associative group.[162] This cohesion is, indeed, recognized by Dworkin in his discussion of natural communities. There is an unrecognized contradiction (discussed earlier) between adopting Dworkin's egalitarian political virtues and tolerating the moral expressions of more traditional moralities, which are inherently nonegalitarian because of their stipulation that some behaviors are more perfect than others.

Dworkin also fails to recognize that the cohesion of traditional communities that he claims to capture in the community of principle is a result of the sense of responsibility and purpose that results from such traditional, nonegalitarian moralities. These traditional moralities are explicitly not neutral with respect to certain ends or purposes, and this intentionality with respect to certain ends as being more desirable than others does not recognize a private/public demarcation of duties as presupposed by Dworkin.

There is, accordingly, a broader notion of what is involved in living in a community, in the traditional sense, which presupposes a rejection of moral pluralism. It is difficult to raise children in a society where the public authorities emphatically spurn and reject the expression of the morality accepted by the parents in a public forum, while this public authority, at the same time, in the name of an egalitarian-based tolerance for diversity, promotes in a public forum the so-called alternative lifestyles rejected by the parents. Any sense of responsibility and fraternity with the community comes from the parents, family, and friends, and it cannot be imposed by some public institution. To the extent that a public institution makes the morality of the parents, family, and friends less legitimate than the egalitarian morality of promoting diversity, both the traditional community and morality are undercut.

Accordingly, there is a fundamental incoherence, indeed, a mixed message, in limiting the grounding of the legitimacy of the legal system in Dworkin's so-called political virtues, or the principles of fairness, equality, and due process, while at the same time claiming to start from a morally pluralistic premise.[163] At some point, equality and tolerance for diversity have to undermine standards as understood within traditional moral frameworks. As a result, a pale reflection of community, as personified in Dworkin's community of principle, becomes the source of supposed feelings of fraternity between persons who otherwise share no common sense of purpose other than that permitted by the egalitarian principles.[164] But then the issue turns on a more complete examination of whether the principles of Dworkin's community of principle may be located in real, bona fide communities.

8.2 Identity of the "Community of Principle" and Lawyers

Second, what Dworkin calls the political community and the community of principle within it are not coextensive with any natural communities that might actually exist.[165] In an essay published after *Law's Empire,* he defines the political community as the nation state.[166] Therefore, it is not surprising that he is able to define such a so-called community purely in terms of the formal acts of its legal institutions (executive, legislative, and judicial arms of government), as if it were a "collective agency" for its citizens.

He analogizes this so-called community, as embodied in the institutions of

the democratic nation state, with an orchestra, to show that the citizens of
this so-called political community are "integrated" for the purposes of the actions of these institutions, without requiring any further "integration" as to
the pursuit of a summum bonum.[167] Thus, a split between the pluralism (that
is, the absence of a single notion of the good life for its citizens or the absence
of integration at this level) and the collective agency of the political community does not result in a lack of integration at the level of the political
community.[168]

This so-called integration at the level of the political community is
achieved, according to Dworkin, through voting, speaking, lobbying, and
demonstrating. The low levels of participation in these activities by most of
the public, and general alienation or disaffection with the political process,
are ignored by Dworkin. In effect, Dworkin essentially replaces the natural
communities with a rather elite political community and a still more elite
community of principle within the political community. The unstated assumption would appear to involve a displacement of the smaller and local
natural communities by the larger political community. Further, the tacit assumption is that integration at the level of the political community somehow suffices for the lack of integration, or even a breakdown of community,
at the level of the natural communities. Indeed, Dworkin's aim appears to
be to displace the natural communities with the nation state while purporting to retain the associative and integrative bonds of the natural community, by merely renaming the nation state a political community.

Symptomatic of Dworkin's thinking in this regard is his account of the orchestra. His characterization of an orchestra as having a collective identity
only for the purposes of making music ignores the natural sociability of persons as an attribute apart from the purpose of whatever common enterprise
they are engaged in. To the extent that an orchestra is also a real orchestra,
its members will, indeed, become involved in each other's lives beyond their
cooperation in making music, and this involvement may affect their per-
formances for better or ill, as much as do the formal institutional structures
of the orchestra. As in any activity that involves another person, the social relationship becomes a factor, in addition to the activity itself.

There are other features of Dworkin's analogy of the political community
to an orchestra that I find rather jarring and incongruous. Most members
of a political community are born into their community, and in a practical
sense, they have little real choice, as far as joining other political communities is concerned. Moreover, the talents and fortunes of each member of
most political communities will be less equal than those of more specialized
associations, such as orchestras. Indeed, orchestras will not include as their

members nonmusicians or musicians who play instruments that are not commonly included in their orchestra. Further, they will include musicians of roughly comparable abilities. On the other hand, selection for membership in an orchestra is voluntary and is not egalitarian, since only persons with very specialized skills are included as members—otherwise the orchestra could not produce music.

There are other incongruities with the orchestra metaphor as well. For example, the conductor is analogous to Dworkin's appellate judges, the musicians to lawyers, the passive audience (never referred to in his analogy) to the citizenry, and the music to liberal and egalitarian principles (that is, judicial opinions consistent with the principles underlying Dworkin's community of principle). But this image seems far more sterile, structured, elite, and regimented than that created by Dworkin's professed neutrality toward competing and pluralistic notions of the good, supposedly accommodated by his "democratic" approach.

However, Dworkin might argue that I read too much into his orchestra metaphor, and that these differences between an orchestra and a political community are beside the point and not important for the purposes of his analogy, insofar as he was merely making the point that associations do not have to consider broad notions of the good or well-being of their members in order for the association to be integrated for its special purposes. But this conceivable objection leads to my next point.

Even special-purpose associations, such as orchestras or businesses, ignore the unique needs of each of their component parts (musicians or employees) at the peril of fulfilling the special purpose of the association. To foster meaningful participation in any association, its members have to get something beneficial for themselves, as individuals, out of the association. Each individual member will not actively participate at his or her best level merely to serve the association's ends. To the degree that they feel the association's ends do not accommodate fully their particular needs, they will feel alienated from that association and not perform at their best.

Good conductors and good managers will recognize each musician or employee not just as a musician but also as a person. Musicians and employees have full lives apart from making music or producing profits for a business. As common as this view has become in our contemporary American society, members in a healthy association ought not be viewed as mere tools for that association's special purposes.

But the question remains: Why would Dworkin so transparently displace the natural community with the nation state (called the political community), and, more particularly, with the officials and lawyers interpreting and applying the legal system of the nation state (called the community of principle)? Why indeed, especially after his brief consideration of the unique type of integration, sense of obligation, and associative bonds that arise naturally at the level of local, natural communities (in his case, families and neighborhoods)? While it is clear that he has some discomfort with these localized natural communities because of their potential parochialism, at one point in *Law's Empire* he also acknowledges, very briefly, the strength of the sense of communal obligations at this level.[169]

It is possible that he ultimately has to ignore the nature and genesis of natural communal obligations, because there is really not an antiseptic way to find a moral sanction for the law in natural communities, given the existence of the nation state—that modern empire containing a myriad of communities. He is so intent on proving that the legal system has a moral sanction for its coercion that he is not open to the possibility that the very nature of natural communal obligation is incompatible with such a sense of obligation being imposed through legal coercion without destroying the very sense of natural communal obligation in the first place. Dworkin is really, in a sense, arguing that the artificial is natural, that the coercion of the state is somehow as voluntary as the social bonds that exist at the level of friendship (or smaller natural communities).

But the social bond compelled by law can never adequately or completely substitute for the natural bonds of friendship. Accordingly, Dworkin's aim of justifying legal coercion blinds him to the possibility that there might not, in fact, be an airtight moral sanction for the legal system at all—that perhaps the legal system is the result of force and violence, with a mere pretension of morality to cloak its actions. This consideration introduces my most basic objection to Dworkin's legal philosophy and the fundamental core of this critique: his slippery conception of a so-called community of principle.

Dworkin calls it an interpretative community. In a very tangible and practical sense, his community of principle can be nothing more than the community of lawyers and governmental officials charged with interpreting and applying the law. Much of his discussion of the integrity of interpretations that arise out of this community of principle might lead some to restrict it to the level of appellate court judges.[170] But appellate court judges probably constitute too narrow a group, since the entire legal community is involved in framing the arguments that channel judges to render their interpretations.

If the practices and opinions of the legal profession make up what he means by the community of principle, then, after unraveling the philosophical trappings of his argument, his theory is ultimately reducible to a grounding of the legitimacy of the law in the legal profession. While this might give lawyers and the legal system their power and privilege in a particular political system, I submit that this is not a credible justification of the moral basis for the coercive use of the law.

8.3 Dworkin's Fallacious Use of *Personification*

Dworkin uses *personification* to describe his community of principle, in order to argue that just as individuals can be committed to particular principles of justice, so too can a political community.[171] Dworkin gives an ontological weight to this personification of the legal community: he emphasizes that his personification, exemplified by the community of principle, enables him to give more weight to its principles of integrity, as adjudicated or legislated by its officials, than may be accorded to the beliefs of its individual members.

This essentially serves to emphasize in another way his public/private and choice-sensitive versus choice-insensitive framework that really is quite elitist. This also indicates the abstract nature of his shift from the natural community, with which he started, to the community of principle. That is, he seems to assume that it is primarily principles or ideas, and only secondarily people, that constitute this strange notion of a community. It is difficult to see how such an abstract notion of community retains the natural bonds that Dworkin acknowledges, to a greater degree, in more natural communities. The sense of legitimacy arising out of the bonds of natural communities was his original impetus for declaring that the move to community was to be his route for linking his descriptive project to the more difficult project of establishing legitimacy for the coercion of the democratic legal system.

Accordingly, it is fallacious to personify, or even to analogize, collective groupings of individuals (or individual wills) as if these groups together reflected one will, whether as the general will, the Volk, or the community of principle. The act of not revolting against the sovereign power or of voting for one's rulers or lawmakers are somehow deemed as manifestations of the ways in which individual wills indicate the presence of one general will. But the very notion is ultimately self-contradictory. If there is one general will, there cannot be the multitude of individual wills. If there are many individual wills, there cannot be one general will.

It is more accurate to say that the so-called collective will is the will of the officials empowered to make laws and to enforce or adjudicate them in particular circumstances. Whatever label one gives to the will at the collective level (the label does not matter, whether one calls it divine right or the community of principle), the object of this fallacious argument is to purport to justify the power of whoever is deemed to be the ruler or ruling class. The arguments for sovereign authority throughout the history of jurisprudence have been essentially the same, with the only difference lying in who was deemed to be the official (or ruling class) with whom the philosopher was attempting to curry favor. At first it was kings, but now it is lawyers. But the contention of this study is that such an endeavor is constructed on a deception.

I have only to look to my own experience with raising young children to find a classic illustration of this fallacy. Suppose a three-year-old named Bobby hits another child, Tommy, with a toy soldier. The parent tells Bobby not to hit Tommy. Bobby responds that he did not hit Tommy, but that it was the toy soldier that hit Tommy. A reader may chuckle at the example, but it is not that different when transferred to the level of personifications of sovereignty. The notion that when an official acts, he is somehow acting in the name of every citizen, rather than merely acting as himself, is not really distinguishable from the example of the child.

The terminus of all personifications of sovereignty, whether democratic or totalitarian, is a policeman with a gun saying: "In the name of the will of the people [or lawful authority], I hereby execute, imprison, or otherwise punish Tom." Paradoxically, it is Tom's will that Tom be punished, because Tom is one of the individual wills constituting the general will on whose behalf the policeman with a gun is punishing Tom. How absurd.

The effect of turning the analysis into one of locating the source of legal authority or sovereignty in some collective will is to obliterate all particular, individual wills from view. But the world is only made up of individual wills, so that the real consequence of arguing for a collective will is to argue for the individual will of the official claiming to act for the collective wills. Once one buys into this fallacious equation of each individual will to the aggregation of individual wills, one buys into the basic building unit for legal authority in jurisprudence—sovereignty (or, more honestly, Leviathan).

While the goodness of the will at the individual level is certainly relevant at the level of individual morality, the supposed morality of the notion of a collective will is a confusion, since it ultimately can only be analyzed by collapsing law and morality together. The moral legitimacy of actions at the collective level is thus reduced to consideration of their lawfulness. The real dividing line in jurisprudence would appear to be between those who see no need to establish the moral legitimacy of sovereignty and those who attempt to either assume it or justify it.

I opt for neither approach, because I hold that there is not a sufficient moral justification for sovereignty—unless sovereignty is limited to a substantial degree. The community of principle and the divine right of kings are essentially rooted in the same metaphor of an unlimited sovereign power greater than the sum of its parts. It is a legal Leviathan, where considerations of the legitimacy of lawful authority (or integrity) are the exclusive preoccupations. And this limitation cannot be effectively imposed internally through the legal system alone: sovereignty cannot truly limit itself. That is, law cannot be much of a limit on law. The limitation, if any, must come externally from the moral realm, properly understood. Changes in sovereignty, whether by means of the illusions and machinations of voting or by means of the violence of the revolutionary, merely displace one set of elites with another set of elites, each with their own, unique brand of evils.

Thus Dworkin's effort fails, because there can be no credible justification for the coercive use of the law on moral grounds, except in a jurisprudence that imposes limitations on the scope and force of the law. Dworkin's system of integrity and community of principle are ill suited to impose such limitations. Indeed, his community of principle is more a motive force for the expansion of the law. The very title of his tome, *Law's Empire*, connotes this very well. There are no limits of the law in Dworkin's view, and, consequently, there can be no justifiable moral sanction for a legal system grounded in his theory.

This absence of any effective limits exists because Dworkin's notion of integrity is his only limit on his notion of sovereignty, or the so-called community of principle. That is, consistency with some historically contingent principles that accord with Dworkin's egalitarian principle is his only limit. The problem with this is that egalitarianism is often as morally empty of content as is the notion of consistency.

It is easy to argue for the absence of consistency in Anglo-American law, whether one confines one's review to a one-year slice in time or takes in the full history of the law. Law can only be deemed internally consistent by choosing to ignore legal principles deemed inconsistent with the legal principle that one wants to select as the grounds for consistency. Dworkin does this with his choice-sensitive versus choice-insensitive distinction and with his selection of equality as his bedrock principle. But egalitarian considerations are inadequate, because, in a sense, egalitarianism is a species of consistency: How different in principle is treating everyone the same from a notion of consistency? It really begs the question. Some notion of the good for man is needed in order to establish which principles are to have priority over others in order for Dworkin's notion of consistency or integrity to work.

8.4 Natural Communities Are Not Egalitarian

However, if natural communities are egalitarian and devoid of teleological moralities, and if the artificial community of principle effectively reflects such egalitarianism, then Dworkin may be able to argue credibly, to some degree, that the force of communal obligations arises out of this egalitarianism. The problem with this assumption of a natural egalitarianism is threefold:

1. The force of communal obligations and bonds of friendship arises out of partiality, not impartiality. As such, communal obligations and friendship inherently run counter to egalitarianism in their exclusivity and favoritism. But this very partiality is the source of their strength. Human beings are more prone to be flexible and generous with persons they encounter on a personal level than with persons that are more remote. Indeed, a further irony of Dworkin's position is that as the range of the law expands, the bonds of communities are frayed into distrust and dissension. His very notion of a community of principle as a basis for grounding law's empire is inimical to real natural communities.

   Not incidentally, the distinction between public duties and private duties within Dworkin's notion of integrity and the community of principle is diametrically opposed to his earlier description of the kinds of bonds that exist in natural communities. There is, as a result, considerable irony to his assumption that the community of principle better approximates these bonds than the desert-island community or rule-book community, as if the only alternatives that existed were these artificial counterfactual communities. If his community of principle has the kind of communal bonds of natural communities, he needs to explain why the public-duty versus private-duty distinction obtains in the realm of law's empire ruled by his community of principle, given that earlier, he correctly points out that one of the essential features of natural communities is essentially the absence of such a distinction.

2. Natural communities are not inherently egalitarian. One merely has to look to the natural communities that one encounters in everyday life to see this. To the extent that there is a moral consensus binding a natural community together, egalitarianism is particularly absent, at least as far as Dworkin's moral pluralism is concerned. Indeed, I submit that social tinkering with the distinctive moral bonds of particular communities through the legal system can ultimately destroy the community itself.

Inasmuch as this claim implies that a certain moral cohesion is inherent in strong communities, the notion of an inherent egalitarianism just does not fit in the way Dworkin uses it when he discusses natural communities and their peculiar attributes. Of course, just a few pages later he contradicts the notion of an inherent egalitarianism in such natural communities, when he acknowledges that natural communities can be unjust to their members and particularly to those outside the group, which is ultimately the reason that he probably shies away from grounding the law's legitimacy in any real form of community.

3. The artificial community of principle is not egalitarian. While the legal community may express liberal and egalitarian views, the way it operates in society and the nature of its privileges make it a distinctly elitist rather than an egalitarian institution. Dworkin appears to take the view that if its results are egalitarian, it is the best form of democracy—a so-called dependent democracy. Legal coercion in the guise of egalitarianism ultimately subverts true egalitarianism and only furthers the interests of the legal elite.[172]

Conclusions

Moral neutrality about the good life, a definition of justice purely in terms of equality, and legal interpretation as integrity or a rigid consistency determined by equality—these tenets epitomize the legalistic morality at the root of the breakdowns in the legal system identified in Chapter 1. Under such a scheme, "law's empire" has been ever expanding while not performing its basic function of protecting communities from the violence of criminals. Not only is such a system oppressive in its expanded roles, but it compounds this oppressiveness by being ineffective in performing what should be its principal function. Such a system lacks moral legitimacy. Accordingly, the unpersuasiveness of Dworkin's defense of such a system is unsurprising.

Interpretation of legal texts and a descriptive fit with the beliefs and practices of the legal elite are inadequate for the purposes of diagnosing and remedying the legal injustices outlined in Chapter 1. Textual interpretation, where action is required, might be highly creative and subtle, but it is also ultimately blind to the more important teleological considerations involving natural justice. Moreover, an interpretive theory that displaces natural justice with the empty political virtues of egalitarianism and responsiveness to public opinion fuels, rather than retards, the coercive power of the law and its potential for inflicting legal injustices.

As stated earlier, it is the supreme paradox of egalitarianism that it requires a legal elite to enforce it and that such enforcement is ultimately destructive of the natural bonds of association that make living together bearable. At bottom, it must be recognized that there is a fundamental difference between legally compelling cooperation between people, an artificial act, and any voluntary cooperation that arises naturally. For Dworkin to slip from such nonegalitarian natural communities to his elitist community of principle is tantamount to equating compelled action with voluntary action. Dworkin's egalitarian notion of justice and his elitist interpretive community of principle are incompatible with the flexibility inherent in epieikeia, a part of natural justice that we will attempt to recover in Chapter 4.

Notes

1. Alexis de Tocqueville, *Democracy in America,* vol. 2, trans. Henry Reeve (New York: Alfred A. Knopf, 1980), 290, 295, 302.

2. The split in Dworkin's theory between his influential description of the legal system as highly regarded by lawyers (an "internal" account of law's legitimacy from the perspective of lawyers) and his larger project of providing an "external" account of law's legitimacy from the perspective of ordinary citizens is aptly depicted and criticized by Paul Kahn in "Community in Contemporary Constitutional Theory," *Yale Law Journal* 99 (1989): 77, 80.

3. Ronald Dworkin, *Law's Empire* (Cambridge: Harvard University Press, 1986), 410.

4. Ibid., 120, 130, 154, 411.

5. Aquinas conceivably articulates this more nuanced position as a qualification of a quotation he makes from Augustine, that an "unjust law" is not a law at all. The Augustinian formulation is the version commonly used as a straw man for attacks by positivists. Saint Thomas Aquinas, *Summa Theologica,* trans. Fathers of the English Dominican Province (New York: Benzinger Brothers, 1947), I-II, qu. 95, art. 2.

6. Ibid., I-II, qu. 94, art. 4.

7. Ibid.

8. Ibid., I-II, qu. 96, art. 6; qu. 97, art. 4.

9. Ibid.

10. Ibid., I-II, qu. 95, art. 1.

11. Thomas Hobbes, *Leviathan* (London: Penguin, 1968), chap. 26.

12. Ibid., chap. 14.

13. Ibid.

14. Ibid., ch. 26. However, in defining what makes a good judge, Hobbes leaves room for a notion of equity, which has some superficial similarity to the Aristotelian notion of epieikeia explored in Chapter 4, viz., it "depend[s] not on the reading of other mens Writings, but the goodnesse of mans own natural Reason." Hobbes, *Leviathan,* chap. 26.

15. Hobbes, *Leviathan,* chap. 26.

16. Ibid.

17. Jeremy Bentham, *Of Laws in General,* ed. H. L. A. Hart (London: Athlone Press, 1970), section 1.2; Bentham, *A Fragment on Government,* ed. F. C. Montague (Oxford: Oxford University Press, 1891); Bentham, *An Introduction to the Principles of Morals and Legislation,* eds. J. H. Burns and H. L. A. Hart (London: Oxford University Press, 1970). See also Gerald J. Postema, *Bentham and the Common Law Tradition* (Oxford: Oxford University Press, 1986).

18. See Jeremy Bentham, "A Comment on the Commentaries," in *A Comment on the Commentaries and a Fragment on Government,* eds. J. H. Burns and H. L. A. Hart (London, 1977), 204–5; 223, app. F.

19. For an excellent criticism of Bentham's consequentialism, with citations to other contemporary criticisms, see John Finnis, *Natural Law and Natural Rights* (Oxford: Oxford University Press, 1980), 111–18.

20. Finnis, *Natural Law and Natural Rights,* 131, summarizing the work of Neil MacCormick, *Legal Reasoning and Legal Theory* (Oxford: Oxford University Press, 1978), 105–6.

21. The modern law of evidence is more commonly recognized as specifically being favored by Bentham. Its highly technical and intricate rules are oriented toward determining what evidence may be presented to a jury.

22. John Austin, *The Province of Jurisprudence Determined,* ed. H. L. A. Hart (New York: Humanities Press, 1965), 184–85.

23. Immanuel Kant, *Metaphysik der Sitten,* vol. 6 (Berlin, 1914), 232 (trans. John Ladd, *Metaphysics of Morals: The Metaphysical Elements of Justice* [Indianapolis: Bobbs-Merrill Co., 1965], 37).

24. Ibid., 39–40.

25. See Immanuel Kant, *On a Supposed Right to Lie Because of Philanthropic Concerns,* trans. James W. Ellington (Indianapolis: Hackett, 1993), 427.

26. Kant, *Grundlegung zur Metaphysik der Sitten,* vol. 4 (Berlin: Konigliche Preussiche Akademie der Wissenschaften, 1913). (Trans. James W. Ellington, *Grounding for the Metaphysics of Morals* [Indianapolis: Hackett, 1984]). *Kritik der praktischen Vernunft* (Berlin: Konigliche Preussiche Akademie der Wissenschaften, 1913). (Trans. L. W. Beck *Critique of Practical Reason* [Indianapolis: Bobbs-Merrill, 1956]).

27. Kant is a major reason why I am offering my moral-based criticisms of positivists and Dworkin outside of a natural law framework.

28. Oliver Wendell Holmes Jr., "The Path of the Law," *Harvard Law Review* 10 (1896): 457–78; letter to Sir Frederick Pollock of 1 Feb. 1920, in *Holmes-Pollock Letters* 36, ed. Mark DeWolfe Howe, 1961; *Gitlow v. New York,* 268 U.S. 652, 673 (1925).

29. See Robert Axelrod, *The Evolution of Cooperation* (New York: Basic Books, 1981), where game theory is used to explain why most people cooperate, and why Hobbes's notion of man as asocial really does not work. In noniterative zero-sum games, the egoist wins and takes advantage of other players, but in iterative games, the egoist is ultimately ganged up on by the other players, who cooperate with each other to keep the game going.

30. Roscoe Pound, *An Introduction to the Philosophy of Law* (New Haven: Yale University Press, 1922), 102–43.

31. Ibid.

32. Ibid., 111.

33. Jerome Frank, *Law and the Modern Mind* (New York: Brentano's, 1930), 253.

34. Ibid., 3–47.

35. Ibid., 32–41.

36. Ibid., 39.

37. Ibid., 42–7.

38. Ibid., 170–85.

39. Hans Kelsen, *Pure Theory of Law,* trans. Max Knight (Berkeley and Los Angeles: University of California Press, 1978), 47–50.

40. Ibid., 279–319.

41. Ibid., 49.

42. Ibid., 67–69.

43. Ibid., 348–56.

44. H. L. A. Hart, "Positivism and the Separation of Law and Morals," in *Essays in Jurisprudence and Philosophy* (Oxford: Oxford University Press, 1983), 49–87.

45. Ibid., 62–66.

46. Ibid.

47. Roberto Mangabeira Unger, *Knowledge and Politics* (New York: Free Press, 1975), 88–100.

48. Ibid.

49. For a comparison of Hart and Dworkin on discretion, see Section 3.2 of Chapter 4 and the last two sections of this chapter. See Ronald Dworkin, *Taking Rights Seriously* (London: Duckworth, 1977), 1–130.

50. H. L. A. Hart, *The Concept of Law* (Oxford: Oxford University Press, 1961).

51. Accordingly, Hart rejects the "rule skepticism" inherent in Austin's position (and, arguably, in that of some of the legal realists, such as Frank) without rejecting realist criticisms of certain features of formalism (which Hart unfairly ascribes to natural law thinkers alone).

52. Lon L. Fuller, *The Morality of Law* (New Haven: Yale University Press, 1964).

53. These are: (1) failure to achieve rules at all, (2) failure to publicize the rules, (3) abuse of retroactive legislation, (4) failure to make rules understandable, (5) enactment of contradictory rules, (6) rules requiring conduct beyond powers of affected party, (7) frequent changes in the rules, and (8) failure of congruence between rules as announced and their actual administration.

54. Finnis, *Natural Law and Natural Rights*.

55. Ibid., 290.

56. Ibid., 351–66.

57. Ibid., 357–59.

58. Ibid., 359.

59. Ibid., 135–39.

60. Ibid., 138.

61. Iredell Jenkins, *Social Order and the Limits of Law*.

62. Ibid., 192–213.

63. Ibid., 312–23.

64. Ibid., 322.

65. Unger, *Knowledge and Politics*; Roberto Mangabeira Unger, *The Critical Legal Studies Movement* (Cambridge: Harvard University Press, 1986).

66. Unger, *Knowledge and Politics*, 88–100.

67. Ibid.

68. Dworkin, *Taking Rights Seriously*, 1–130; Dworkin, *Law's Empire*.

69. These traditional ontological questions concerning ethics are meaningless to the extent that the aim of jurisprudence as a branch of applied ethics is practical. Thus, in the spirit of Aristotle's ethics, the aim of this study is action, not knowledge. Whatever its flaws, Aristotle's ethics attempts to avoid applying the inappropriate methods of the more rigorous sciences to this very practical area. Aristotle, *Nichomachean Ethics* (*EN*) 1095a5–6 ("our aim is not knowledge but action"); Aristotle, *Physics*, 193a5–7 ("to try to prove what is evident through what is not evident is a mark of a man who cannot judge what is known through itself from what is not known through itself"); Aristotle, *Metaphysics*, 993b20–23 ("the aim of theoretical knowledge is truth; of practical, deeds").

70. I recognize that Kantian or deontological thinkers would reject the significance of the necessity claimed for the moral principles justified throughout my examination of legal injustices, insofar as such principles are teleological and based upon human nature. But of late, certain contemporary philosophers have devised arguments to refortify the basis of a teleological ethic. See, for example Henry B. Veatch, "Modern Ethics, Teleology, and Love of Self," *Monist* 75 (January 1992): 52–70, and Mary Hayden, "Rediscovering Eudaimonistic Teleology," *Monist* 75 (January 1992): 71–83. Moreover, Hadley Arkes in *First Things* (Princeton: Princeton University Press, 1986) links categorically necessary "first principles" with certain substantive ends derived from human nature and uses these first principles as a basis for grounding his ju-

risprudence. While my inquiry sets to the side the issue concerning the type of necessity underlying "natural justice," some sort of necessity is tacitly assumed throughout the arguments.

71. Dworkin, *Law's Empire*, 45–86.

72. The Chicago school is really a modern form of utilitarianism that defines justice as efficiency, obtaining the result with the lowest transaction costs, or avoiding waste. Richard A. Posner, *The Economic Analysis of Law*, 2d ed. (Boston, 1977).

73. Dworkin, *Law's Empire*, 136, 151.

74. Ibid., 160, 224.

75. Ibid., 151–60.

76. Ibid., 157.

77. Ibid., 120–36.

78. Ibid.

79. Ibid., 160.

80. Ibid., 301.

81. Ibid., 164, 224.

82. For an example, see Dworkin, *Law's Empire*, 374.

83. Dworkin, *Law's Empire*, 73–76.

84. Ibid., 164–65.

85. Ronald Dworkin, "What Is Equality? Part 3: The Place of Liberty," *Iowa Law Review* 73 (1987): 1–60.

86. Dworkin, *Law's Empire*, 298.

87. Ibid., 300.

88. Ibid., 164, 374.

89. Ronald Dworkin, "What Is Equality? Part 4: Political Equality," *University of San Francisco Law Review* 22 (1987): 1–40.

90. Dworkin, *Law's Empire*, 213–15.

91. Ronald Dworkin, "Liberal Community," *California Law Review* 77 (1989): 479–504.

92. Dworkin, *Law's Empire*, 206–15.

93. Ibid.

94. Ibid. Dworkin likens the rule-book community's outlook to the conventionalism of positivism.

95. Dworkin, *Law's Empire*, 206–15.

96. Ibid.

97. Ibid., 190–215.

98. Ibid.

99. Ibid., 202–5.

100. Ibid., 213–15.

101. Ibid., 225–32.

102. Ibid., 245–66.

103. Ibid., 245.

104. Ibid., 108.

105. Ibid., 45–86.

106. I am not sure that Finnis would go as far as my argument for epieikeia, which is why I say it is arguably at the root of his criticism of Dworkin.

107. John Finnis, "On Reason and Authority in *Law's Empire*," *Law and Philosophy* 6 (1987): 363.

108. Ibid., 360–61.

109. Dworkin, *Law's Empire*, 164, 224.

110. Ibid., 374.

111. Ronald Dworkin, "Unenumerated Rights: Whether and How *Roe* Should Be Overruled," *University of Chicago Law Review* 59 (1992): 381, 411–12.

112. Ibid., 412. Alasdair MacIntyre, "The Privatization of Good," *Review of Politics* (1990), 353–54.

113. *Dred Scott v. Sandford*, 60 U.S. (19 How.) 393 (1856).

114. Ronald Dworkin, *Life's Dominion: An Argument About Abortion, Euthanasia, and Individual Freedom* (New York: Alfred A. Knopf, 1993), 111–12.

115. Dworkin, *Law's Empire*, 374.

116. Dworkin, "What Is Equality? Part 4: Political Equality," 1, 8.

117. Ibid., 3.

118. Ibid., 3–4.

119. Ibid., 23–30.

120. Ibid., 23–24.

121. Ibid., 25–28.

122. Only due process and fairness may conceivably constrain legal coercion. Equality is only a source of legal coercion.

123. Dworkin, "What Is Equality? Part 3: The Place of Liberty," 1, 48. Dworkin calls equality a "shadow over liberty," such that "any genuine contest between liberty and equality is a contest liberty must lose" (p. 7). Dworkin argues that there is no general right to liberty, which may be construed, in a limited way, by *equality*. Dworkin, *Taking Rights Seriously*, 266–78.

124. Dworkin, "What Is Equality? Part 3: The Place of Liberty," 17–18.

125. Ibid., 18.

126. See my discussion of the role of custom in rendering democratic constitutions oligarchical and vice versa, in Chapter 4.

127. Dworkin, *Law's Empire*, 387–97.

128. See, for example, Paul Ciotti, *Money and School Performance: Lessons from the Kansas City Desegregation Experiment* (Washington, D.C.: Cato, 1998).

129. Ibid., 295–301.

130. Ibid., 310.

131. The public/private distinction is probably also at the root of the ethical rule for lawyers (discussed in Chapter 1) that views lying in a business relationship as more egregious (subjecting one to bar discipline) than lying to one's spouse (not sanctionable).

132. Ingersoll, "Old Order: GOP's Plans to Curtail Government Benefits Bring No Pain to Amish."

133. *DeFunis v. Odegaard*, 94 S.Ct. 1704 (1974).

134. *Sweatt v. Painter*, 339 U.S. 629 (1945).

135. Dworkin, *Taking Rights Seriously*, 223–39.

136. Ibid., 245.

137. Michael Sandel effectively argues that Dworkin's argument in favor of affirmative action conflicts with treating persons as ends in themselves, in "Liberalism and the Claims of Community: The Case of Affirmative Action," *Ronald Dworkin and Contemporary Jurisprudence*, ed. Marshall Cohen (Totowa, N.J.: Rowman and Allanheld, 1984), 231:

> On Dworkin's argument for affirmative action, this perplexity takes the following form: Once admission or exclusion cannot plausibly be seen to depend on a notion of 'merit' in the abstract or on an antecedent individual claim, the alternative is to assume that the collective ends of the society as a whole should automatically prevail. But the bounds of the relevant society are never established, its status as the appropriate subject of possession never confirmed. Once the self, *qua* individual self, is dispossessed, the claims of the individual fade to betray an underlying utilitarianism which is never justified. And as Rawls implies early on, utilitarianism is in a sense the ethic of the unbounded subject, the ethic that fails to take seriously the distinction between persons. For Dworkin, however, utilitarian considerations are precisely the ones that distinguish the legitimate discrimination involved in affirmative action from the unjustifiable sort based on prej-

udice and contempt. If it cannot be said that some are inherently more *worthy* than others, it can at least be said that some are more *valuable* than others with respect to the social purposes at hand, and discrimination on this basis is justifiable. So long as a policy of preferential treatment *uses* people for the sake of worthy ends rather than *judges* people as more or less worthy in themselves, it is permissible.

138. Flaherty and Biskupic, "Rules Often Impose Toughest Penalties on Poor, Minorities." See 28 United States Code Section 991 et. seq. See also commentary by the Commission in preface to Title 18, Federal Sentencing Guidelines (1995), 6–10.

139. Larry Alexander cogently argues that Dworkin's notion of equality is morally empty, and, for that reason, is subject to potential misuse. See Alexander, "Striking Back at the Empire: A Brief Survey of Problems in Dworkin's Theory of Law," *Law and Philosophy* 6 (1987): 426–31.

140. Dworkin, *Law's Empire*, 164–65.

141. Ronald Dworkin, *A Matter of Principle* (Cambridge: Harvard University Press, 1985), 191. But this so-called moral neutrality at the level of the nation state, which is where Dworkin locates his community of principle, marginalizes natural communities precisely because this purported moral neutrality cannot really be morally neutral.

That some of these marginalized communities are ethnic minorities is aptly noted by Adeno Addis in "Individualism, Communitarianism, and the Rights of Ethnic Minorities," *Notre Dame Law Review* 67 (1991): 647. In particular, Addis notes that so-called communitarians of the Dworkin variety who view the nation state as a community "attempt to 'cure' the society of multiple (and at times contradictory) traditions by assuming a coherent tradition."

142. Dworkin, *A Matter of Principle*, 221–33.

143. Jacqueline Trescolt, "Honeymoon's Over: Legislators Threaten Arts Agency Again," *Washington Post*, 22 June 1994, D1, D8.

144. In fact, it took the Supreme Court to overturn the Massachusetts courts holdings that required St. Patrick's Day parade organizers to include gays, lesbians, and bisexuals as distinctive groups in their parade. See *Hurley v. Irish-American Gay, Lesbian, and Bisexual Group of Boston*, 132 L.Ed.2d 487 (1995).

145. The tendency of Dworkin's theory to obscure the problematical nature of the "violence" of the law has been pointed out by some thinkers who are, commendably, not averse to recognizing the corrupting nature of the coercion inherent in the law. See Austin Sarat and Thomas R. Kearns, "Making Peace with Violence: Robert Cover on Law and Legal Theory," in *Law's Violence*, ed. Austin Sarat and Thomas R. Kearns (Ann Arbor: University of Michigan Press, 1992), 213–14.

146. Ronald Dworkin, "Women and Pornography," *New York Review of Books*, 12 October 1993, 37–42; Ronald Dworkin, "Reply to Catherine MacKinnon," *New York Review of Books*, 3 March 1994, 48.

147. Dworkin, "Reply to Catherine MacKinnon," 40.

148. See, for example, *Bennis v. Michigan*, 134 L.Ed.2d 68 (1996). For examples of occasions where government agents have abused the forfeiture laws, see Henry Hyde, *Forfeiting Our Property Rights* (Washington, D.C.: Cato, 1995); and Bovard, *Lost Rights*.

149. See the discussion of custom and epieikeia in Chapter 4.

150. Dworkin, *Law's Empire*, 190.

151. Ibid., 191–208.

152. Ibid., 196.

153. Ibid., 199.

154. Ibid., 199–201.

155. Ibid., 200.

156. Ibid., 206.

157. Ibid., 208–315.

158. Ibid., 208–9.

159. Ibid., 210–12.

160. Ibid., 213.

161. Ibid., 196–99.

162. John Finnis makes a similar criticism of Dworkin's spurious connection of the fraternal bonds of natural communities with his artificial community, particularly in light of his alleged moral neutrality, in "On Reason and Authority in *Law's Empire*," 377–78.

163. Williams further notes that Dworkin's description of the benefits of being "integrated" in a community just as strongly supports rival, more conservative conceptions, and that he fails to provide convincing criteria for his dismissal of the conservative position as meritless. Bernard Williams, "Dworkin on Community and Critical Interests," *California Law Review* 77 (1989): 515, 519. It should be noted that Williams wrote his criticisms as a liberal who was in agreement with many of Dworkin's goals, if not with his theory justifying them.

164. This is one of Philip Selznick's principal criticisms of Dworkin's notion of community, in "Dworkin's Unfinished Task," *California Law Review* 77 (1989), 508–10.

165. This is the basic criticism of sociologist Philip Selznick in "Dworkin's Unfinished Task," 506. "Dworkin slips easily from 'community' to 'political community.' Community includes politics, but much more as well, including much that is collectively experienced though not necessarily coordinated."

166. Dworkin, "Liberal Community," 479.

167. Ibid., 495–504. Selznick criticizes the inadequacy of the orchestra analogy to a political community in "Dworkin's Unfinished Task," 505–6.

168. Dworkin, "Liberal Community," 495–504.

169. Dworkin, *Law's Empire*, 196–202.

170. See, for example, Dworkin, *Law's Empire*, 225.

171. Dworkin, *Law's Empire*, 167.

172. For a view conceivably contrary to my questioning of a "natural egalitarianism" in "natural communities," see Richard Wilkinson's interesting argument that draws a relationship between public health and the distribution of wealth in a society from anecdotal and statistical analysis in *Unhealthy Societies: The Afflictions of Inequality* (New York: Routledge, 1997). As interesting and suggestive as Wilkinson's study is, I am not sure that "egalitarianism" is the real, underlying variable that best explains the phenomena pointed to in his study (e.g., lower mortality rates in Japan, Sweden, Greece, Italy, and 1970s Eastern Europe as compared to less egalitarian societies such as Britain and the United States), and even it it were, I am not sure that "economic equality" would be an adequate surrogate for broader notions of political, social, and gender equality. Although Wilkinson rejects income distribution as a mere "proxy" for "social cohesion," he acknowledges the importance of the connection between social cohesion, income distribution, and public health in a society, as evidenced in a number of studies surveyed by him. Wilkinson's method of comparing mortality rates to income distribution does not seem to fit feminist notions of equality very well, given the longer life spans of women, in general, and the well-known absence of equality for women in some of the countries deemed to be more egalitarian by him (e.g., Japan). It would appear that Wilkinson's measure of economic equality is with regard to individuals in family units, and therefore does not consider the inegalitarian nature of the family unit itself, a unit he acknowledges as important for the social cohesion underlying his statistical finding of a relationship between health and relative equality in income distribution. These distinctions are important to assessing the viability of Dworkin's "community of principle" because mere manipulation of greater economic equality through the coercive power of the law would foster social cohesion and improvements in public health if Wilkinson is right, but such manipulations could be counterproductive to the social cohesion requisite to improvements in public health if Wilkinson's emphasis is misplaced, or if such manipulations are extended to broader notions of equality not embraced by his theory.

3

Kant's Moral Foundations and Legalism

While by no means a new problem, the disconnection of theoretical ethics from lived experience is one that is and must be grappled with by anyone who seeks to think about ethics and to have his or her thoughts taken seriously, as more than an exercise in logical argumentation. . . . We now know—certainly we ought to know—that the level of violence and destruction coming out of Germany during the 30s and 40s would not have been possible were there not a set of great moral ideas at work here and a rationally, bureaucratically organized mechanism for turning these ideas into action. After Kristallnacht, the brown-shirted gangs of the SA—whose random, disorganized acts of violence characterized the early form of Nazi violence—were replaced by the SS, a highly organized, disciplined, and lawful body. The subsequent history of Nazi violence is a history of increasing discipline, increasing rationality, increasing order, increasing lawfulness, and increasing violence. The death camps in particular, precisely in order to have achieved the high degree of success that they did, had to have been highly efficient, well-organized, rationally structured factories that received the sanction of the public. The kind of thought required for all this is, as rational, calculative, scientific thought, of course, "antithetical to the wild passions of barbarism." This is precisely what is prized by Western culture: a way of thinking that is uncorrupted by passion, that cannot be moved by self-interest, and that acts on the basis of law. Yet this kind of thinking, we now know, is not at all antithetical to dispassionate destruction, slaughter, and torture.[1]

Before establishing the Aristotelian alternative to jurisprudential legalism, I will briefly digress to discuss Kant's moral philosophy. There are a number of important reasons for this digression, among which the most significant is my view that certain features of Kant's moral philosophy—in particular his categorical imperative and his emphasis on the importance of practical reason in moral action—are the most substantial obstacles to a reconsideration of epieikeia. This exploration is useful, because the categorical imperative and epieikeia are so opposed to each another, as illustrated by the following:

1. Kant's moral philosophy emphasizes universalizable rules and argues that this emphasis amounts to treating a person as an "end" rather than as a "means" in a "kingdom of ends."
2. Aristotle's notion of epieikeia emphasizes exceptions to rules, based on treating a person with flexibility and mercy in accordance with the ends of natural justice.

Of course, epieikeia is discussed in a political-legal-ethical context, whereas the universalizability of the moral law is developed in Kant's exploration of the metaphysical foundations of morals.

But the difference between Aristotle and Kant in problems considered on this score is immaterial to recognizing the fundamental incompatibility between the two notions. And the fact that Kant's notions of impartiality, universalizability, and the moral law (as developed in his foundational works on morals) do not reflect the completed features of his jurisprudential philosophy is, again, immaterial to an exploration of the fundamental incompatibility between these notions developed in his foundational works and epieikeia. The point of this digression is not Kantian exegesis, but to illuminate the differences between the categorical imperative and epieikeia, and in so doing, to reveal what is gained and what is lost by moving from a Kantian framework to an Aristotelian ethic.[2] The principal point of this digression is not to illuminate directly any particular legal injustices, but rather to clear the way for epieikeia, a notion more directly pertinent to understanding the legal injustices that are the direct topic of this study. However, as a secondary matter, conceivable applications or misapplications of the categorical imperative to moral issues in a legal setting will be described for the purposes of showing that there is, indeed, a difference between Kant's inflexible notion of a kingdom of ends and Aristotle's flexible notion of an epieikeia that treats a person with mercy and compassion.[3]

Kant's grounding of moral philosophy in the categorical imperative subordinates the happiness and well-being of particular persons to acting in a way so that one's actions could be legislated by a rational will as a universal law: "Act only according to that maxim whereby you can at the same time will that it should become a universal law."[4]

In the remainder of this chapter, this formulation is referred to as the universalizability formulation. One effect of this formulation has been to subordinate the well-being of individual persons to a legalistic morality, interpreting and applying moral rules in a way that emphasizes their universality without any exception being made that would otherwise accommodate individual human happiness. Kant's emphasis on moral rules, his characterization of them as moral laws, and his description of the self-legislation of the will indicate a legalistic frame of mind applying legal metaphors in what is supposed to be an examination of the metaphysical foundations of morals. The universalizability formulation of the categorical imperative would appear to have little to do with teleology.

But Kant's kingdom of ends is an apparent attempt to camouflage the universalizability of the moral law in some sort of teleology. As such, Kant's kingdom of ends formulation of the categorical imperative presents the greatest challenge to the arguments in the next chapter because of Kant's attempted linkage of his formalism (in the notion of universalizability) to his appealing and, apparently, Christian-based kingdom of ends notion—where humanity is viewed as an end in itself, valued in its own right, that must never be subordinated as a means: "Act in such a way that you treat humanity, whether in your own person or in the person of another, always at the same time as an end and never simply as a means."[5]

On its face, the kingdom of ends prevents Kant's categorical imperative from being applied in the inhumane manner described above, and, therefore, ultimately it can be seen as the strongest defense of formalism. Attacking versions of formalism that overtly ignore the so-called kingdom of ends notion is easy, but attacking a formalism that has a supposed basis in the kingdom of ends would appear to be much more difficult and, therefore, a worthy undertaking. Indeed, appropriately considering Kant's kingdom of ends is particularly important for our purposes, when it is recognized that this notion is also at the root of contemporary notions of equality that, I contend, are, likewise, ultimately formalistic and morally empty.[6]

Accordingly, the central question of this chapter is not only what Kant says (or can be taken to mean) regarding his kingdom of ends, but also, more importantly, what Kant should have said or meant in regard to it.[7] How can a so-called kingdom of ends retain its alleged teleological cover if it is reducible to universalizability, as Kant claims? Moreover, even if a suitable definition and elaboration of the kingdom of ends were forthcoming, what would this more meaningful notion of kingdom of ends do to the necessity of the universalizability notion underlying the categorical imperative?

The working hypothesis of this chapter is that a meaningful notion of kingdom of ends cannot exclude the possibility that what is entailed by the principle of the kingdom of ends, suitably understood, sometimes conflicts with what is entailed by the principle of universalizability. If universalizability and kingdom of ends formulations necessarily never conflict, because they are the same thing, then the central point of the next chapter cannot be made. In the next chapter, the argument is made that justice is grounded in Aristotle's notion of epieikeia and friendship as its necessary (but not sufficient) conditions.

In the present chapter, it is argued that the Kantian notion of a kingdom of ends is, in the last analysis, morally vacuous, and so, too, are Kant's formulations of the categorical imperative in terms of universalizability. Kant's equation of the kingdom of ends with the categorical imperative serves to emphasize the moral emptiness of Kant's concept of the kingdom of ends in the first place, since it ultimately lends itself to a reduction to universalizability.[8] In effect, the equation of the concept of the kingdom of ends with that of universalizability does not so much define universalizability as it does kingdom of ends and so reduce it to universalizability.

By asserting that Kant's equation of kingdom of ends with the notion of universalizability underlying the categorical imperative is a reduction to universalizability, I am not interpreting this equation in the sense of identity. Rather, a reduction in the sense described here can arise even if the two notions are distinctive but amount to the same thing. My problem with Kant's equation is its clear suggestion of the moral necessity of universalizability. The possibility of conflict between universalizability and what I (not Kant) would define as a meaningful kingdom of ends must be left open. For me, a kingdom of ends must view both the promotion of happiness of others and friendship as necessary conditions for justice, rather than merely desirable virtues. The emphasis in Kant is, in short, misplaced. Moral necessity should be grounded in a different, broader, and more flexible notion of the kingdom of ends, thereby making universalizability less central.

As such, I am less concerned than Kant with the type of necessity underlying moral judgments; for me, what is paramount is the content of the moral system arising out of a particular form of necessity. When Kant argues that morality can only be grounded on categorical imperatives not derived from the special characteristics of human nature,[9] but from an unconditioned necessity of action holding for all rational beings, it is because he explicitly presupposes that any morality based on human nature and the ends suited to human nature can only yield subjective principles lacking any universal application. Merely by extending his universe beyond human beings to so-called rational beings, Kant avoids the problems inherent in the empirical character of concepts of human nature. Avoiding these problems is consistent with Kant's requirement for the a priori unconditioned demands of morality.

Some contemporary thinkers have also viewed Kant's approach as a way of avoiding the Humean and twentieth-century concern over the so-called is-ought problem.[10] Most important, Kant's emphasis on universalizability is a direct result of his emphasis on the importance of freedom, exemplified in his notion of the "autonomy of the will as the supreme principle of morality."[11] For Kant, all other morality—and, by obvious implication, Aristotle's grounding of his ethics in human nature and man's social nature—fails on this score, because the act of willing for such "spurious" moralities, as far as Kant is concerned, is not completely autonomous and unconditioned. That is, its necessity is merely "hypothetical" rather than "categorical," and its will is heteronomous rather than autonomous.

But this emphasis on metaphysical rigor ultimately leads to an impoverished notion of justice in legalistic terms.[12] For me, a socially grounded notion of justice (and not a reduction of justice to legalistic terms or coercive right), achievable by real human beings, is more important than attaining a theoretical perfection in the act of willing by supposed rational beings. I will argue in this chapter and in Chapter 4 that emphasizing our social connection with one other based on a notion of justice that recognizes that connection is more important than the theoretical moral perfection obtainable by the completely unconditioned freedom of theoretical rational beings.

Confining justice to legal justice—as a coercive right or claim against another, rather than as an Aristotelian social virtue—carries with it some significant problems, not only in morality (which then becomes legalistic), but also in the realm of the positive law itself.[13] Whatever the theoretical merits of Kant's original motive in emphasizing freedom and the importance of the type of necessity underlying morality, the point of my examination of legal injustices is that such an emphasis can obscure more important and practical concerns about the content of morality. Indeed, I will argue in Chapter 4 for a more humane and flexible morality, which results from a weaker type of moral necessity requiring a less unconditioned notion of freedom. Modest aims in metaphysical foundations may achieve greater results in practical morals. My basic point is that the content of a moral system can be adversely affected by too great an emphasis on the foundational questions of morals, which can be overly parsimonious or overly inclusive.

1. What Is the Nature of a True Kingdom of Ends?

Kant's notion of the kingdom of ends in the *Grundlegung*—or, what is the same, his notion of treating a person as an end rather than as a means—is morally vacuous for three significant reasons.

First, Kant denies anything more than a contingent relation between morality and happiness.[14] To treat persons as ends rather than as means signifies for Kant that one treats oneself and others in a way consistent with retaining the autonomy of the moral agency (or freedom) of each, something that is distinct from their happiness.[15]

Second, treating a person as an end, for Kant, is not treating that person as having value as a particular individual, but, rather, it is treating that person qua humanity in general, so that one preserves, by the universalizability of one's action, the autonomy of that other person's rational will.[16]

Third, in the *Kritik* and *Grundlegung,* Kant recognizes only one kind of partiality—that of self-love, with the result that treating a person with partiality is treating that person as a means rather than as an end.[17] The only way, according to the arguments in the *Kritik* and *Grundlegung,* that one can treat another person as an end is to do so with impartiality—without regard for the material consequences of one's action. This argument ultimately excludes the possibility of grounding the moral necessity of just behavior in human sociability and friendship. Each of these problems is briefly treated in turn.

1.1 Morality and Happiness Are Connected.

Treating a particular person as an end rather than as a means seems to be a fairly empty notion, unless it specifically includes the effect of an action on that person's happiness or well-being. However, Kant emphatically rejected anything but, at best, a contingent relation between morality and human happiness on the grounds that: happiness is not (strictly speaking) our natural end, there is no necessary connection between reason and happiness, and there is no correspondence between virtue and happiness in our world.[18]

It may, perhaps, be assumed that moral actions are often not rewarded by rendering the actor happy, or that often immoral acts do not render the malefactor unhappy. However, this fact does not warrant any assumption that one could define treating a person as an end rather than as a means without any regard for the happiness of the person being affected by the action.[19] The consequences of an action do matter, and the consequences of an action on human happiness in particular are significant, if one is to define a kingdom of ends in the ordinary manner of understanding.[20]

For Kant, our well-being has nothing to do with the moral grounds of our actions, but merely pertains to the pleasantness of our circumstances. Conversely, the good or evil of our actions is exclusively related to the autonomous exercise of our will as rational beings in conformity with the universalizable moral law. "'Well-being' or 'woe' indicates only a relation to our condition of pleasantness or unpleasantness, or enjoyment or pain; if for that reason we desire or avoid an object, we do so only in so far as it is related to our sensibility and to the feeling of pleasure or displeasure which it produces. But *good* or *evil* always indicates a relation to the will so far as it is determined by the law of reason."[21]

"But even if a rational being himself strictly obeys such a maxim [the categorical imperative], he cannot for that reason count on everyone else's being true to it, nor can he expect the kingdom of nature and its purposive order to be in harmony within him as a fitting member of a kingdom of ends made possible by himself, i.e., he cannot expect the kingdom of nature to favor his expectation of happiness."[22]

The two distinct notions, that of well-being and that of autonomous moral actions in accordance with the categorical imperative, are not equated by Kant.[23]

Promoting the happiness and connection of a person with his or her society cannot be limited to merely promoting their independent agency as a potential actor, as might be gathered from Kant's overemphasis on autonomy in his foundational works. Rather, promoting such happiness must consider the unambiguous promotion of appropriate ends consistent with that person's ultimate happiness and connection with society. For Kant and his followers, the primary significance of the notion of treating a person as an end lies in a consideration of the effect of one's actions on the autonomy of the other person's rational will (that is, of his or her free agency as a potential actor).[24] And the effect that Kant would look to is even more limited and attenuated, as it involves an abstract consideration of the effect of the universalizability of one's action on the autonomy of that other person's agency as a rational being.

For example, it is recognized by most persons (both experts and ordinary persons)—from the standpoint of human experience (not the metaphysics of rational beings)—that young children should not be treated as things or as means to some end, merely because they have not yet developed the ability to deliberate about the universalizability of their actions as potential future rational beings. However, this does not foreclose restrictions being imposed on the autonomy of children. (For example, a parent will hold a toddler rather than let the child run in front of a car.) Indeed, such restrictions are consistent with the well-being of the child and would be considered as treating that child as an end by most persons. Accordingly, children are restricted to the extent that it is thought best that they be cared for by a parent or guardian.

The post-Enlightenment, in keeping with the Kantian emphasis on freedom and autonomy as the ultimate and exclusive ends of morality, provides a putative justification for an unfortunate practice in our society of treating insane persons as if they were rational agents.[25] Such persons, like children, lack the ability to care for themselves. However, some persons actively resist efforts to have certain insane persons who are homeless on the streets from being cared for in institutions—out of theoretical concerns for preserving the autonomy of the insane persons as potential rational agents. (Apparently, the insane are better off homeless on the streets than cared for in institutions.) In my present sane state, I would hope that I would be forcibly cared for in an institution, in the event of my insanity, rather than left wandering the streets—notwithstanding protestations of civil-liberties advocates on my behalf.[26]

This issue exemplifies the conflict between treating a person as an end from the standpoint of their well-being (however limited their capabilities may be) and treating that person as an end from the theoretical standpoint of their potential, albeit not presently extant, autonomy as a rational being. Thus, the family of an insane person, trying to keep that person off the streets—by force and institutionalizing them, if necessary—is more concerned with treating the insane family member as an end than as a means. Conversely, the legal advocate trying to preserve the insane person's theoretical rational agency at the expense of being thrown on the streets is less concerned with treating the insane person as an end than as a means.[27]

Some might argue that it is impossible for Kant's notion of well-being to be interpreted in this way; indeed, it might be argued that for the insane person to irrationally decide to remain homeless violates the categorical imperative. But others would argue that for the legal advocate to attempt to keep the insane person homeless rather than institutionalized out of a regard for the insane person's potentially autonomous rational agency is somehow acting in a way that violates the categorical imperative.

I am not so sure that an application of the categorical imperative necessarily excludes either of the above interpretations. I am not so certain that the categorical imperative would require a legal advocate to attempt to keep the insane person homeless rather than institutionalized (or vice versa). If I were to act as a legal advocate in these circumstances, I would institutionalize the insane person, because that is how I would want myself or other loved ones in similar circumstances to be treated—for me, the universalizable maxim would mandate institutionalization. But if another person with a different view of the matter were to act as a legal advocate in these same circumstances, it is very conceivable that that person might view the universalizable maxim as mandating against institutionalization—even if that meant the insane person remained homeless.

The categorical imperative by itself does not, by its very terms, determine just what would fulfill the well-being of a rational being, even a minimally rational being (such as an insane person), other than to stipulate that any such well-being must be in accord with the categorical imperative.

1.2 The Justice of an Action Is Relative to Its Effect on a Particular Person in Concrete Circumstances.

Differences in kind or differences in circumstances are most often seen, in moral contexts, from the standpoint of the consequences of an action. An action can be universalized solely because Kant excludes the consequences from the moral calculus. There is an enormous difference between the universality and necessity of an imperative to simply do X in a given set of circumstances and the universality and necessity of the categorical imperative to do X *without exception* and *without regard to the consequences.*

The difference between the two types of universality illustrated here is essentially the difference between a universal imperative that can be consistent with a true kingdom of ends, since consequences are considered, and a universal imperative that can only be consistent with an impoverished notion of the kingdom of ends, since consequences are not considered. Because Kant's foundational notions of morality that exclude the consequences of an action from an assessment of its morality cannot accommodate differences in circumstances as exceptions to universalizability, Kant ultimately cannot equate the kingdom of ends with universalizability without perverting the very notion of a kingdom of ends.[28]

There really is a difference between lying to a murderer about the location of his intended victim and lying to another person in most other commercial or family relations. That Kant failed to recognize this fact in his example is not a defect in the example, as claimed by his recent defenders,[29] but a defect in the categorical imperative. Where the immediate consequences do not matter, but only the action and the universalizability of its rule, the Schindlers and Wallenbergs who lied to the Nazis to save lives violated the categorical imperative—and Kant would have said so based on his own illustration.

There is, or should be, a broader universe than the murderer and oneself in deliberating about the morality of lying to the murderer about the hiding place of his intended victim. The intended victim as an end valuable in his own right should also enter into one's deliberations and, indeed, should be the paramount consideration. Kant's interpretation of the categorical imperative as requiring the preservation of the metaphysical autonomy of a potential rational will of another who is at any moment about to perform an action that is not autonomous or rational (such as murder) indicates that Kant conceived of the kingdom of ends too narrowly in two ways.

First, Kant should not have limited the kingdom of ends to the universe of oneself and the murderer, to the exclusion of the intended victim of the murderer, when deliberating about the morality of lying to the murderer to save the victim's life. Second, the importance of a reified abstraction—such as the autonomy of the will of a rational being who is about to act in disregard of the autonomy of his will, as a potentially rational being—should not take priority over what is actually happening in the circumstances. That is, moral deliberation cannot and should not be divorced from actual experience.

There is a danger that one can confuse or deliberately obfuscate what is the obviously right thing to do in a given set of circumstances, if one confines oneself to metaphysical bubbles divorced from concrete experience. Even if Kant erred in his example of the categorical imperative in his consideration of the right to lie, at the very least his alleged error illustrates the ambiguity underlying the application of the universalizability and kingdom of ends notions in ordinary circumstances, where the morally correct action is not so paradoxical to most persons.

The dangers of a consequentialist position are not entailed by the argument advanced here. The notion of hypothetical moral imperatives chosen by rational beings is not being rejected. Rather, the notion of a categorical imperative as being a sufficient condition for a moral act is being rejected. Something more than acting in accordance with a universalizable moral law is required, and that additional something comes into play by broadening the so-called kingdom of ends based on notions of friendship and human sociability (as developed more fully in Chapter 4). Arguing that consequences also must be considered, or that the categorical imperative by itself is an inadequate and incomplete grounding of moral action, cannot be fairly construed as somehow entailing consequentialism. The issue is not that of either buying into the categorical imperative or somehow lapsing into consequentialism.

1.3 Morality and Human Sociability (Love and Friendship) Are Connected.

To elaborate further, there is more than one way for a person to be treated as a means rather than as an end, and conversely, there is more than one way of treating another person as an end rather than as a means.[30] Kant appears to assume, in his foundational works, that the only way one can treat another person as a means is to use that person for one's own advantage—hence his narrow notion of partiality as a partiality limited to self-love.[31] He does not appear to consider the prospect that more often than not, men treat other men as means to ends that are wholly unconnected with any personal advantage to the actor. Nor does he consider the possibility that men sometimes treat other men as ends (in the broad sense envisioned here, rather than the narrow Kantian sense) out of a partiality toward the person affected by the action, a partiality arising out of love or friendship toward the affected person.[32]

Indeed, sacrificing another person to an idea that itself is of no advantage to the actor is an all too common form of treating another person as a means (rather than as an end). The Robespierres, Hitlers, Mao Tse-tungs, and Pol Pots of history are among some of the more extreme, but obvious, examples of this. Indeed, in Eichmann's trial in Jerusalem, he apparently defended his atrocities by emphasizing that he was merely following Kant's categorical imperative and Kant's rigid notion of duty. As Hannah Arendt explains this:[33] "Much of the horribly painstaking thoroughness in the execution of the Final Solution—a thoroughness that usually strikes the observer as typically German, or else as characteristic of the perfect bureaucrat—can be traced to the odd notion, indeed very common in Germany, that to be law-abiding means not merely to obey the laws but to act as though one were the legislator of the laws that one obeys. Hence the conviction that nothing less than going beyond the call of duty will do."

Further, Arendt elaborates:

> Whatever Kant's role in the formation of the "little man's" mentality in Germany may have been, there is not the slightest doubt that in one respect Eichmann did indeed follow Kant's precepts: a law was a law, there could be no exceptions. In Jerusalem, he admitted only two such exceptions during the time when "eighty million Germans" had each had "his decent Jew": he had helped a half-Jewish cousin, and a Jewish couple in Vienna for whom his uncle had intervened. This inconsistency still made him feel somewhat uncomfortable, and when he was questioned about it during cross-examination, he became openly apologetic: he had "confessed his sins" to his superiors. This uncompromising attitude toward the performance of his murderous duties damned him in the eyes of the judges more than anything else, which was comprehensible, but in his own eyes it was precisely what justified him, as it had once silenced whatever conscience he might have had left. No exceptions—this was the proof that he had always acted against his "inclinations," whether they were sentimental or inspired by interest, that he had always done his "duty."[34]

Eichmann had two conceivable maxims to be tested as universal laws here—
and they are completely incompatible:

1. Murdering persons is not an action that arises from a maxim that could
   become a universal law. Eichmann could not hold such murder to be a
   universal law that he would want to apply equally to himself (permitting
   his own murder) as well as to his Jewish victims. Alternatively:
2. Disregarding the law of the state (even when the law says to murder) is
   not an action that arises from a maxim that could become a universal law,
   because disobedience to the positive law just because it is wrong would justify disobedience to other laws, if this disobedience to an unsuitable law
   were universalized.

Clearly, the first interpretation of the categorical imperative has to be the
only correct one. But what distinguishes the second interpretation from the
first? Is it that the first exhibits the exercise of practical reason and the latter does not? I am not so sure. Indeed, the latter is an all too common illustration of the defective use of practical reason (Eichmann is only one of
the worst examples), but it is not solely within the realm of practical reason
(in the deliberative sense involving the application and knowledge of mere
rules) that one apprehends the defect.[35]

Man's rational nature by itself is insufficient, that is, utterly inadequate, as
the all-encompassing grounding of moral action. Moral action is not merely
a matter of the proper deliberation to the correct action through the possession of mere knowledge of the appropriate maxims or rules of conduct
that ought to govern one's actions. There is a moral sensibility exhibited by
wisdom (not knowledge) that apprehends the differences between the correct and incorrect maxim in the two conceivable interpretations of the categorical imperative. And that wisdom (or moral sensibility) arises through
habitual living and sharing one's life with other people in friendship.

In a defense of Aristotle against a self-styled Kantian-based critique of Aristotle's ethical and political philosophy by Arthur W. H. Adkins, Roger J. Sullivan noted some critical distinctions between the various workings of practical reason as a ground for moral action in Aristotle as contrasted with Kant.
Among these distinctions are the following:

1. For Aristotle, education and habituation in the virtues are the ways in
   which a man fulfills his natural potential to act morally, rather than
   through the categorical necessity of a so-called rational being.[36]
2. For Aristotle, this education and habituation occur within a social frame-

work where the political is not separated from the ethical—where justice is grounded in friendship and a natural sociability, without any concern that this somehow might implicate the infamous is-ought inference of Hume.[37]

3. For Aristotle, there is a concern about the potential injustice arising from generalizing from a practical rule as a universal, "because moral rules do not include in themselves a standard for *when* and *how* they apply." (This concern with the particularity of justice is the topic of Chapter 4.)[38]

These distinctions between Aristotle and Kant may be more strikingly seen in a recent sympathetic discussion of Kant by Daniel N. Robinson and Rom Harre.[39] Robinson and Harre emphasize the metaphysical nature of Kant's so-called kingdom of ends as a way of avoiding the is-ought problem.[40] They emphasize that the kingdom of ends involves a rational being, and not the empirical concept of a "social being."[41] They take this notion of a nonsocial rational being so far that they argue that the demography of the kingdom of ends can consist of a single rational being.[42]

A Kantian, of course, will argue that Eichmann's application of the categorical imperative can be seen to be a misapplication completely within the nonsocial framework of a theoretical rational being (an angel, I suppose, or something of the sort). My contention is that Eichmann's obvious misapplication can only be seen as such when one broadens the framework outside of the narrowly metaphysical realm of Kant's strict notions of practical reason into something like an Aristotelian ethic—at the risk of offending philosophical purists, as far as the is-ought inference is concerned.

Those who would reject the aptness of the Eichmann example, as far as the potential misapplication of the categorical imperative is concerned, are making two debatable assumptions. First, they are assuming that the moral content of the categorical imperative is completely transparent and obvious. This transparency is belied, however, by the fact that Kant's own contemporary defenders treat the "right to lie" to a murderer very differently from the way Kant does. If the moral content of the categorical imperative is so obvious, why the difference in treatment of this so-called right to lie between Kant and his contemporary defenders?

Second, those who dispute my example have to assume the sufficiency of practical reason and freedom of the will as the basis for grounding moral action without regard to human sociability and friendship. The fact that Kant does this in the theoretical realm of asocial rational beings (such as angels) rather than real human beings living together does not preclude this assumption from being tacitly made when the categorical imperative is ap-

plied in the practical realm of human action. Unfortunately, our rationality—and the autonomy of our will to the extent of our rationality—is only a
necessary, but not a sufficient, condition of moral action.[43] We also need a
notion that sounds like the kingdom of ends—but not as defined by Kant.

The converse of the Eichmann example obtains, of course, as well. Just as
there are ways of treating a person as a means rather than as an end, ways
that are impartial from the Kantian standpoint and yet incompatible with a
meaningful notion of the kingdom of ends, there are also ways of treating a
person as an end rather than as a means that are not impartial from the
Kantian standpoint but involve partiality toward another (rather than the
self), and that are incompatible with the notion of universalizability.

Of course, it would be far better, I suppose, that an individual helped another not because they liked that particular person, but because they liked
humanity in general, whatever that means. But I have never known a person who liked humanity in general who did not like particular human beings.
In fact, based on human experience, I doubt that one could find one without the other. One of the consequences of Kant's excessive concern for
grounding morality with the necessity of an a priori notion of universalizability is his posing of a false dichotomy between the partiality that views
one's self as an end and an impartiality that regards other persons as ends
in themselves.[44]

But this totally excludes from consideration the possibility of establishing
the necessary foundations of an ethic on the partiality that a friend has toward another friend, whether it is a purely utilitarian or a contractual friendship, a friendship based on status (such as family or community ties) or one
of the higher forms of friendship recognized in Aristotle—where one loves
one's friend for the friend's own sake. While an ethic grounded in human
sociability may be more modest than a universalist ethic contemplated by a
Kantian, it is certainly a bit excessive and unwarranted for Kant to exclude
the possibility of such an ethic. Kant is simply ignoring the most relevant
data of moral experience when he does this.

Historical and personal experience confirm that human beings are more
likely to behave justly toward those humans to whom they are connected by
some social bond, than toward those humans to whom they have weaker or
no social connection. This is not to say that members of communities and
even friends never behave unjustly toward one another. Rather, when such
injustices occur, it is due to a weakening of the bonds of association or in
spite of this association. Indeed, more injustices occur where the bond of
association is weak than where it is strong. At least as early as Christ and

Boethius it was recognized that the love of others presupposed a love of one-self, and that a hatred of others ultimately arose from self-hatred.

There is no metaphysical proof of this, but it is merely a fact of experience that just behavior toward another person seems to be associated more with partiality than with so-called impartiality toward another person. Stated in another way, seeing another person as an end valuable in his or her own right seems often to require a partiality toward that person, a partiality that has to do with some level of friendship or association. On the other hand, seeing another person as a mere means is, more often than not, associated with an impartiality, a notion better described as an indifference to the value of that person as an end in his or her own right. This is why impartiality, more often than not, can rationalize the sacrificing of a particular person with his or her own ends to some abstract universal notion.

The realm of the most perfect friendship is where people act "for the sake of the end" of their friend. The appropriate problem of a true morality is to extend that action for the sake of another, in this case a friend, and to extend the feeling (or motivation) associated with this action, as well, to others who are not friends. It is not appropriate to take the approach of Kant, so as to deny any intrinsic moral worth to concrete actions that are done for another, for the sake of their own end, just because these actions are not impartial and indifferent to the end of the other person.[45] The true kingdom of ends at least encompasses the altruistic actions motivated by true friendship—and this is the case whether or not one friend acting for the sake of the end of another friend rationally considers the universalizability of his or her actions.

If an empirical study were undertaken asking people who have performed clearly altruistic actions whether they contemplated the universalizability of their actions under the categorical imperative at the time, I suspect that few, if any, would state this motive as the basis for their actions. Rather, concern for a friend for his or her own sake, or even better, concern for another who is not a friend for his or her own sake, likely have seldom involved conscious considerations of the universalizability of actions. Such altruistic actions must not be robbed of their true nature by the efforts of those purporting to defend Kant.

Indeed, if any so-called friend acted on one's behalf based on the categorical imperative, they would hardly be a "friend" that one could trust. If one's very life were at stake, or the lives of one's children, one would probably rely on a friend who did not quibble over whether acting for one's sake or one's children's would be treating a potential murderer as a means, or whether lying to this murderer would result in a universalizable maxim. Or, if one were a judge in a custody battle over children, one would choose the parent who expressed love for the child over a parent who expressed complete indifference but insisted that actions would be motivated impartially by duty to act toward the child in accordance with a universalizable maxim. Indeed, such a recognition is at the core of Solomon's judgment favoring the real mother over the mother expressing indifference when confronted with the prospect of an "equal division" of the child.

Society and friendships would never exist or be maintained, were the categorical imperative ever instituted as the true grounding of moral action. Such an imperative presupposes the grounding of morality independently of any social bonds—indeed, it rejects the morality of any action grounded in these social bonds. At best, the categorical imperative is unworkable. At worst, it is a source of confusion that can even serve as a subterfuge for ostensibly moral action that actually is quite immoral and unjust.

2. The Problems of Universalizability

Paul Grueninger, as police chief of St. Gallen, Switzerland, had the duty to enforce Swiss immigration laws in 1941. Grueninger bent the rules by lying and falsifying records to save hundreds, perhaps thousands, of Jews fleeing from the Nazis. When the authorities learned of his actions, Grueninger was fired, stripped of his pension, and convicted as a criminal in court. In 1994, the Swiss still refused to rehabilitate Grueninger. The St. Gallen council stated that although Grueninger "deserves recognition and respect," he did not deserve a pardon or full legal rehabilitation because this could set a precedent that would justify any breach of rules with the mere allegation that the law was contrary to morality.[46]

This example illustrates the relationship between a Kantian notion of duty and a legalistic morality. Recognition of the morality of an action in particular circumstances is sacrificed to the larger principle of universal legal rules (that is, morality is confused with and reduced to legality) precisely because a strict application of the categorical imperative can, in practice, be used to justify compliance with all positive laws without exception.

In the face of Kant's unequivocal and wrongheaded discussion of the right to lie, it is inconceivable for me to see how one could argue that this example does not illustrate an application of Kant's notion of universalizability underlying the categorical imperative, notwithstanding Kant's distinction between the moral and positive law. The way Grueninger broke the law was by lying and falsifying records. Kant had a documented concern with lying—even to save the life of a person from a murderer. At the very least, there is enough ambiguity in Kant's notion of universalizability that an appeal to Kant's distinction between the positive and moral law is beside the point here, precisely because it is unclear where universalizability sanctions breaking the law—particularly where breaking the law involves lying.

Moreover, I fail to see any essential difference between Kant's arguing that it is wrong to lie to a murderer because lying is not universalizable and arguing that it is wrong to break the positive law because breaking the positive law cannot be universalizable—even in the face of Kant's distinction between the positive and moral law.[47] At any rate, the Grueninger example is a classic example of Kant's right to lie to a murderer, with the only distinction being that Grueninger happened to be breaking the positive law as well as the moral law by his lying.

The problem with the Kantian emphasis, and, ultimately, with the Kantian reduction of morality to the universalizability of an action or duty, is that universalizability is empty of content—unless the so-called kingdom of ends formulation of the categorical imperative fills universalizability with meaningful moral content. This was recognized by one of Kant's great defenders, Lewis White Beck, who acknowledged that the universalizability of a maxim is but a "negative test of its validity," since "many maxims can in fact be universalized which do not have the status of [moral] law."[48] According to Beck, this is because Kant also grounds morality in the regulative principle of a teleological order—a realm of ends or a community of rational beings under a universal (moral) law.[49] In other words, formulations of the categorical imperative given the most emphasis by Kant, those pertaining to the universalizability of a maxim, require something else to give them a positive moral content: the notion of a kingdom of ends.

But the problem is that those formulations cannot be truly given this positive moral content when the kingdom of ends is redefined and equated with a mere notion of universalizability. To add something of positive moral content to the universalizability notion, the kingdom of ends would have truly to supplement and, therefore, ultimately limit and compete with the universalizability principle. By equating the two principles of universalizability and the kingdom of ends, Kant manages to avoid the problem of balancing and reconciling these conflicting notions in his foundational works.

Hadley Arkes reasons that the categorical imperative cannot be properly interpreted, so that certain immoral ends result.[50] According to Arkes, Kant must have been mistaken to quibble over the so-called right to lie to a murderer (that is, the categorical imperative was not so morally empty as to support genocide or slavery). I find it instructive, however, that Arkes reaches this conclusion by managing, in effect, to limit the scope of the categorical imperative's universalizability, for example, through his notion that "it is wrong to speak other than the truth *without justification.*" For Arkes, the "justification" for not lying, or, in effect, for lying, depends on the factual circumstances—for example, is one lying to Nazis to save Jews from genocide?

I would add that the apprehension of this justification and its moral (if not categorical) necessity ought to be grasped without requiring erudite and elaborate reasoning from universalizable first principles. I would also argue that the real significance underlying Arkes's notion of a justification that sometimes limits a categorical imperative is that a categorical principle can still be categorically necessary, even if its universalizable scope is limited by a "justification." While I concur with Arkes that this justification has a moral necessity to it, I am not sure that a categorical imperative limited by such a justification may properly be viewed as universalizable. (Universalizability is not always identical with the universal; that is, holding that any given person in the same circumstances ought to do the same thing is different from constructing a rule from that circumstance that is universalizable in other circumstances.)

For the purposes of this inquiry, it is the moral necessity of the action that is important (even if that action is not self-legislated from a universalizable rule), not the first principle from which that action might be conceivably deduced. This is because there always are conceivably limiting factual circumstances that might justifiably limit the universalizable scope of a proposition, however noble it might seem in the abstract.

It is very important to recognize that Kant's ultimate concern in formulating the categorical imperative is freedom. It is the autonomy of the will that is his concern, for having a completely unconditioned will is the only way to assure categorical necessity, for him. The moral law, to be such, is universalizable without exception (that is, without any limiting justification on that universalizability) in order to assure this completely unconditioned, autonomous state for the will. That is why "without exception," for Kant, means without exception. Arkes, on the other hand, is more concerned with duty and combating moral relativism, something that he does not need a completely autonomous will to do. Indeed, Arkes's notion of the categorical imperative, unlike Kant's, I would argue, is not conceived principally in a theoretical realm of rational beings, but among humans.

For example, if one were a mother caring for an infant child in Nazi Germany, would the universalizable moral law compel one to lie to a Nazi to save a potential victim of that regime if the lie were highly likely in the circumstances to be found out and as a result place one's child at risk, or foreclose the prospects of future rescues of a greater number of potential victims? (This is a question about a moral action that is almost suicidal—an action that is derivable from pristine moral principles, yet that is likely to result in even greater harm than no action, in the circumstances.) At what point are there limits to the justifications that might limit a so-called universalizable principle?

I submit that the limits are not to be found at the level of hypothetical abstractions (universalizable first principles), but in concrete circumstances—which, by their very nature, are particular and not universalizable. It is not the deliberative process through which an action is undertaken (that is, the process that results in an unconditioned will—Kant's emphasis), however important that process is, that ultimately determines the morality or justification of that action. Rather, it is the substantive end, or the result in the circumstances that determines the morality of the action (this is what Arkes, in effect, appears to really emphasize).

I would jettison the notion of universalizability of first principles outright—while holding that there is one morally correct action in any given circumstance (and this is not a moral relativist position), whereas Arkes appears to come to the same place by a seemingly different route, through his notion of "justification." The grounding of moral action is not exclusively in the theoretical realm of freedom. The concern in such circumstances ought to be with consequences—that is, the well-being of the hidden Jew, rather than with the categorical necessity of not lying. When Arkes brings in his limiting notion of justification, that makes all the difference in the world.

In other words, in my hypothetical example involving the morality of a mother lying to a Nazi inquisitor, I have changed the categorical imperative along the lines suggested by Hadley Arkes's limitation of it (that is, Arkes limits it with his notion of justification). Accordingly, I have reversed Kant's formulation of the moral law by requiring the mother to lie to the Nazi when justified (rather than Kant's formulation of telling the truth to a murderer).

However, I have complicated the circumstances by confronting the mother with the dilemma of either (1) placing her child at risk by lying to a Nazi about the location of hidden Jewish persons in circumstances where she knows it is a virtual certainty that her lie is futile and will be discovered, or (2) saying nothing. Here, the correct course would appear to be to say nothing, given the risks to one's child.

But there is a further complication: saying nothing can itself amount to saying something in certain circumstances. If a Nazi inquisitor asked a person

if someone was hiding in her home and the person said nothing, such silence, in the real world, might potentially be construed as a yes. In such circumstances, there would appear to be a universalizable moral law without any
exceptions, notwithstanding the consequences, and that would be to lie to
the Nazi, even if this raised the risks to one's child or was 99 percent likely
to be futile. In other words, there can come a point where there is a bedrock
principle or duty for which there can be no compromise—no matter what
the result. When such circumstances occur, there are no more "justifications"
available that would conceivably limit the "universalizability" of the "principle" that describes the correct action, but such circumstances would appear
to be rare.

The problem is that the categorical imperative by itself does not provide
a sufficient framework for winnowing conceivable universalizable maxims
down to just these core, bedrock duties, but it includes other universalizable
maxims that are potentially immoral, such as Kant's notion that it is always
wrong to lie, even to a murderer. This is not a problem in the case of Arkes's
reconstructed version of the categorical imperative, because his notion of
justification has to take a great deal of its content from the particular factual circumstances; such justification cannot be arrived at if one limits oneself to deliberation about the universalizability of a principle without regard
to the particular factual circumstances.

Accordingly, discerning the rare circumstance when just such a core,
bedrock principle has been reached from one to which an exception must
be made through Arkes's notion of justification cannot be exclusively based
(if at all) on the autonomy of one's will (that is, the unconditioned manner
in which one deliberates). There is something else at work here (moving beyond Arkes's notion of justification), and I think a partial and better answer
as to what is at work is found in Aristotle's notion of a natural justice that is
grounded in human sociability, which we will explore in the next chapter.

3. The Reducibility of the Kingdom of Ends to the Categorical Imperative

Kant's equation of the kingdom of ends formulation of the categorical imperative with its primary formulations based on the principle of universalizability can be interpreted in two ways. Under one interpretation, the kingdom of ends is viewed as a broadening of the categorical imperative, so that
it is not just a rigid formalistic rule of universalizability. But if this were the

proper interpretation, the kingdom of ends would be an additional principle that might potentially come into conflict with the universalizability principle of the other formulations of the categorical imperative. The universalizability principle's necessity would be undermined, or so it seems. This
dilemma suggests the viability of a second interpretation, namely, that Kant's
equation of the kingdom of ends with the principle of universalizability ultimately involves a redefinition of the kingdom of ends in terms of universalizability.

This line of argument is not undercut by Kant's recognition in other ethical works of the positive role of friendship or the virtue of promoting the
happiness of others. Indeed, Kant rejected the *necessity* of promoting the
happiness of others, while establishing happiness as an external virtue, precisely on the basis that the promotion of the happiness of others was not universalizable,[51] just as he recognized that the nature of the idea of friendship
was such that true friendship was more likely limited to a narrow range of
persons.[52] Accordingly, Kant's favorable notions of friendship and his doctrine of virtue cannot be viewed as components of his kingdom of ends, precisely because they are not universalizable—which is the central problem I
have with his notion of universalizability and his equation of the kingdom of
ends with universalizability. The problem is that his doctrine of virtue and
friendship ought to be a central part of a kingdom of ends, but virtue and
friendship cannot have the necessity that exists in his conception of the kingdom of ends, because only universalizability purportedly has this necessity.

To argue that the categorical imperative is only a necessary (but not sufficient) grounding of moral choice (action) does not remove the pressing
concerns regarding what the kingdom of ends ought to encompass and what
potential it has to conflict with the notion of universalizability underlying
the categorical imperative. Altruism, and particularly an epieikeia grounded
in that altruism, must be recognized to be in conflict with universalizability,
if for no other reason than the nature of epieikeia itself, which is an exception rectifying the injustice of the excessive universality of a rule. A morality grounded in epieikeia cannot accommodate a morality that grounds itself in the categorical imperative as a necessary condition of morality.

4. The Diminished Status of Justice and Equity in Kant

Although the full range of Kant's jurisprudential works is far beyond the
scope of what is needed to address the very narrow problems of this inquiry

into legal injustices, there are two features of his jurisprudential works that merit some emphasis: namely, his notion of justice and his notion of equity.

Kant's notion of justice (as treated in his jurisprudential work) distinguishes him from earlier thinkers as different from each other as Aristotle and even Hume.[53] Most significantly, Kant does not even deem justice to be a virtue. For Kant, justice is merely a "right" or "authorization to use coercion."[54] Indeed, Kant's description of justice's operation is very consistent with the preceding discussion of the categorical imperative: "In applying the concept of justice we take into consideration only the form of the relationship between the wills insofar as they are regarded as free, and whether the action of one of them can be conjoined with the freedom of the other in accordance with a universal law."[55]

Accordingly, justice only applies to another person's will and not to another person's desires or needs—the latter of which are merely the objects of altruistic or charitable acts, for Kant.[56] The application of the categorical imperative to Kant's jurisprudential notion of justice exacts rather radical surgery on the social underpinnings of notions of justice as a virtue based on human sociability or friendship. Whether one agrees with Kant's or with Aristotle's notions of justice, or with the foundations of morality in the categorical imperative, one at the very least has to acknowledge, in the face of this rather radical surgery, that honest attempts to reconcile the ethical thinking of the two must ultimately flounder.

Kant's criticism of equity in strictly legalistic terms is consistent with this result.[57] Kant calls the exercise of equity by a court a self-contradiction and argues that equitable concerns are solely matters of conscience and not properly entertained by courts of law.[58] It is instructive that his examples of how equitable principles cannot be appropriately applied in a contractual law dispute before a court are, in fact, contradicted by the historical development of Anglo-American law since the mid-nineteenth century. Kant argues, using an example from contract law, that only the letter of the contract should govern the contractual relationship when unforseen events occur that would render the original contract unjust.[59]

> Again, a domestic servant whose wages through the end of the year have been paid in a currency that has in the intervening period become depreciated, with the result that he can no longer buy what he could have bought with the same money at the time of concluding the contract, cannot appeal to a right to be compensated for the loss caused by the fact that the same amount of money no longer has the same value. He can only appeal to equity (a silent goddess who cannot be heard), because nothing was stipulated about this in the con-

tract, and a judge cannot pronounce in accordance with unstipu-
lated conditions.[60]

While Kant's example might be in accord with the contract law of his time
and, indeed, with the general principles of traditional contract law,[61] at least
in the Anglo-American tradition, this harsh view has been subject to four equitable remedies, "legal fictions" or notions of justice, that have been carved
out over the past two centuries and that have significantly limited this traditional notion in certain, albeit distinct, analogous circumstances:

Frustration of Purpose:

In the seminal "frustration of purpose" case of *Krell v. Henry*, Henry saw an
advertisement of windows to be rented for viewing the coronation of King
Edward II. Henry contracted with Krell to take the rooms for the period of
26 and 27 June 1902 for seventy-five pounds, with a twenty-five-pound advance deposit. However, the coronation was postponed when the king was
operated on for appendicitis. When Henry declined to pay the remaining
fifty pounds, Krell sued for breach of contract. Krell lost, and the contract
was not enforceable based on the court's finding that "the coronation procession was the foundation of this contract, and . . . the object of the contract
was frustrated by the non-happening of the coronation and its procession on
the days proclaimed."[62]

Impracticability:

In *Taylor v. Caldwell*, Taylor, a musician, had contracted for the rental of Caldwell's auditorium for the purpose of public performance, in exchange for
one hundred pounds to be paid at the end of each performance day. However, when the auditorium was destroyed by fire in the week prior to the first
performance, Taylor sued Caldwell for breach of contract. Taylor lost, and
Caldwell was excused from the contract because the court found that "the
parties contracted on the basis of the continued existence of the Music Hall
at the time when the concerts were to be given."[63]

This doctrine has most often been applied to excuse contractors from re-
pairing destroyed buildings,[64] or to excuse farmers from delivering a given
amount of a crop because of crop failure.[65] Under the common law, courts
typically used the legal fiction of an "implied term" to the contract to give
them the basis for departing from the letter of the contract while purporting to enforce its terms.[66]

However, under the more overt, policy-based Uniform Commercial Code
governing the sale of goods, there is no pretense remaining of following the
terms of the contract: "Except so far as a seller may have assumed a greater

obligation . . . delay in delivery or non-delivery in whole or in part . . . is not a breach of his duty under a contract of sale if performance as agreed has been made impracticable by the occurrence of a contingency the non-occurrence of which was a basic assumption on which the contract was made."[67]

Mistake:

In *Aluminum Co. of America v. Essex Group,* the court found that "justice" demanded a finding that the contract was unenforceable because of a "mistake of fact" made at the time the contract was first made.[68] This mistake would have resulted in a loss of $60 million to ALCOA and a corresponding gain of that amount to Essex, if the plain wording of the contract had been strictly enforced.

The contract was entered into in 1967 for a sixteen-year term, during which ALCOA agreed to convert alumina supplied by Essex into molten aluminum. The pricing terms in the contract were based on a complex escalation formula, based in part on the Wholesale Price Index, Industrial Commodities (WPI). Twelve years into the contract, in 1979, the WPI was not keeping up with substantial increases in energy costs. ALCOA sued for relief from the contract and won.

Unconscionability:

Until the advent of the Uniform Commercial Code, courts were more reluctant to invoke the equitable notion of unconscionability except in contractual relationships involving heightened duties of trust, such as fiduciary-beneficiary or attorney-client relations.[69] However, a dictum from a case as early as 1750 specified that a court of equity would not enforce a contract "such as no man in his senses and not under delusion would make on the one hand, and as no honest and fair man would accept on the other."[70]

In *Campbell Soup v. Wentz,* the Wentz brothers agreed to sell all Chantenay carrots grown on their farm to Campbell at a price of thirty dollars a ton, to be delivered in January. The price of Chantenay carrots rose to ninety dollars a ton when bad weather decreased the supply of this type of carrot. When this occurred, the Wentz brothers sold their carrots to other buyers. Campbell sued to enforce its rights under the contract, to prevent the sales to other buyers. The court refused to enforce the contract on equitable grounds, holding that the contract terms drove "too hard a bargain for a court of conscience to assist."[71] The contract term that the court found particularly bothersome and unconscionable was one that allowed Campbell to refuse to buy carrots under certain circumstances while at the same time barring the Wentzes from selling the carrots to others without Campbell's permission.

The Uniform Commercial Code has promulgated a rule based, in part, on this case.[72] The unconscionability rule has been described by commentators as "one of the most innovative sections of the Uniform Commercial Code," in particular since there is, uncharacteristically, no precise legal definition of unconscionability provided in the code or in its commentary.[73]

Thus, Kant's jurisprudential treatment of equity happens to be harsher, more rigid and legalistic than is the actual development of contract law within the Anglo-American tradition—even for rather aged cases in this tradition.[74] While this historical fact ought to raise questions, at the very least about the sufficiency of Kant's jurisprudence at the descriptive level, it also serves to reenforce, for me, the harshness of his moral framework—in this case, as applied to his jurisprudence. The fact that his notion of the positive law and its appropriate functionings is harsher than the actual development of law (at least in Anglo-American culture) has to, arguably, infect his underlying moral foundations as well, particularly since he brings to bear upon his analysis of the metaphysical groundings of morals legal metaphors and analogies to the functioning of legal systems.

Most significantly, for the purposes of this book, this legalistic notion of morality has to make Kant incompatible with the Aristotelian notions of epieikeia developed in Chapter 4. Contemporary thinkers who wish to meld together an Aristotelian notion of natural justice with a Kantian notion of the moral law are bound to ignore this essential incompatibility between the two thinkers. While practical reason is important in Aristotle (to use a Kantian terminology), Aristotle supplements reason with justice as a social virtue and emphasizes justice's individuality through the exercise of epieikeia.[75] Kant's notion of justice as a legal right (not as a social virtue) and universalizability are incompatible with this Aristotelian social framework.

Notes

1. James D. Chansky, "Reflections on *After Virtue* After Auschwitz," *Philosophy Today* (Fall 1993): 256.

2. The historical Kant is not the issue here. Rather, my concern is with the notions of universalizability and impartiality. I question the notion that the universalizability and autonomy of the will (or freedom) notions at the core of Kant's categorical imperative are sufficient grounds for morality. I am not making the stronger claim that the free exercise of the will through the exercise of practical reason is not a necessary condition of moral action. I am merely asserting that practical reason and freedom are not sufficient grounds for moral action.

Of course, such a claim may carry with it a different understanding of the conditions required for a truly autonomous exercise of the will: that is, I am not of necessity compelled by such an admission to buy into the Kantian notion of universalizability of a maxim that can be self-legislated as a moral law without exception. (There is a difference between holding that there is one correct course of conduct in a particular set of circumstances and holding that a universalizable maxim can reflect that correct course of conduct without risking injustices in other circumstances.)

3. Some have been sympathetic to a project of reconciling the best of Aristotle and Kant. See, for example, Nancy Sherman's *The Fabric of Character: Aristotle's Theory of Virtue* (Oxford: Oxford University Press, 1989), in which she emphasizes the role of practical reason in Aristotle's ethics, a role she believes has not been properly emphasized in Aristotelian interpretation. Nonetheless, she also recognizes the ultimate incompatibility of Kant's exclusive emphasis on practical reason as a grounding of morals and Aristotle's emphasis on the role of friendship (or natural human sociability).

Roderick T. Long recently criticized Fred D. Miller Jr.'s natural right reconstruction of Aristotle's ethical-political philosophy for not going far enough in converting Aristotle into a Kantian type of thinker. Long stressed the affinities between Aristotle's concern with "rational potentialities . . . [that] enable us to choose the bad as well as the good," and Kant's emphasis on "autonomous rational agents . . . [who] transcend the motivational force of sensible appearances." See Roderick T. Long, "Aristotle's Conception of Freedom," *Review of Metaphysics* 49 (1996): 801–2.

Again, it is a bit much to claim that Aristotle emphasizes freedom or practical reason as the sufficient and all-encompassing grounding of moral action. Moreover, it is difficult to reconcile Miller's correct interpretation of Aristotle's emphasis on the individual or particular (as contrasted to Plato's emphasis on the universal) with Kant's emphasis on universalizability in the categorical imperative. For a more complete description of Miller's work, see section 3.2 in the next chapter.

4. Kant, *Grundlegung*, 421 (30). Page number in parentheses refers to the English translation, cited in the bibliography.

5. Kant, *Grundlegung*, 429 (36).

6. Although there are significant differences, John Rawls's egalitarian notion of justice has distinctive links to Kant's categorical imperative. The constraints on the conception of the good in Rawls's liberalism are at least identified by Rawls (and properly so, in my view) with Kant's notion of autonomy. And Rawls properly (in my view) links to Kant's categorical imperative Rawls's notion that justice involves the rational choice under a "veil of ignorance" of certain egalitarian outcomes.

My earlier criticisms of Dworkin's egalitarian notion of justice (for example, his "prudent insurer" test) presuppose that the egalitarian formalism of Rawls is as morally empty and subject to manipulation as is Kant's categorical imperative (Dworkin essentially appropriates Rawls's theory of justice into his jurisprudential scheme). See John Rawls, *A Theory of Justice* (Cambridge: Harvard University Press, 1971).

7. Onora O'Neill, a contemporary Kantian, at least recognizes and grants the importance of the issue of the status of the kingdom of ends to the rest of Kant's moral foundations, in "Universal Laws and Ends-in-Themselves," *Monist* 72 (July 1989): 342.

8. Kant, *Grundlegung*, 436 (41).

9. Kant, *Grundlegung*, 425 (33).

10. Daniel N. Robinson and Rom Harre, "The Demography of the Kingdom of Ends," *Philosophy* 69 (1994): 5–19.

11. Kant, *Grundlegung*, 440–41 (44–45).

12. Kant, *Metaphysik der Sitten*, 232 (37).

13. Modern liberals such as Rawls (and Dworkin, to the extent that he follows Rawls's lead), often interpret Kant's kingdom of ends in an egalitarian sense and then use this egalitarian notion of kingdom of ends as a basis for limiting their notions of freedom. That is, one is only free, in the moral sense of freedom, when one treats others with equality.

But they fail to recognize how harsh and lacking in compassion equality can often be, a topic that I explore in Chapter 4. As long as their theoretical notions of equality are satisfied, Rawls and Dworkin do not appear to be concerned with specific applications that might appear unjust to ordinary sensibilities. While I am not necessarily characterizing such thinkers as Kantians, their approach is inconceivable without Kant.

14. Kant, *Grundlegung*, 398–402 (11–14).

15. Kant, *Grundlegung*, 437–39 (42–43).

16. Kant, *Grundlegung*, 401 (13); Kant, *Kritik*, 79–85, 110.

17. Kant, *Grundlegung*, 401 (13); *Kritik*, 75–85, 110.

18. Kant, *Grundlegung*, 395–96 (8–9).

19. Of course, my argument presupposes an understanding of happiness (argued for in Chapter 4) that is not necessarily the same as any Kantian notion of happiness.

20. Rae Langton has written an interesting account that considers Kant's manner of dealing with a desperate young lady who was corresponding with him for advice, and the inadequate way in which he handled her feelings of emptiness and depression. Rae Langton, "Duty and Desolation," *Philosophy* 67 (1992): 481–505.

21. Kant, *Kritik*, 60 (62); see also Kant, *Grundlegung*, 393 (7).

22. Kant, *Grundlegung*, 439 (43).

23. The contrast between Aristotle's notion of well-being and Kant's is very aptly stated in Roger J. Sullivan's article, "Kant's Anthropology," *Review of Metaphysics* 49 (September 1995): 81.

> Aristotle's term for the good life, *eudaimonia*, is commonly translated as 'happiness,' but *eudaimonia* is not equivalent to Kant's notion of happiness as 'well-being and contentment with one's state.' For Aristotle, the notion of the eudaimonic life surely does include a psychological feeling of contentment with what one has and has done, but for him that life is essentially *moral* in nature, for it is filled with intrinsically and unconditionally good practical activities. By contrast, for Kant, the notion of happiness is an imaginative notion of a completely *nonmoral* condition in which all our desires for pleasure and all our needs are met as a whole.

24. Kant, *Grundlegung*, 433–37 (39–42); Onora O'Neill, "Universal Laws and Ends-in-Themselves," 353.

25. I am not arguing that Kant has caused this phenomenon, nor that he would approve of it, but merely using this contemporary example to illustrate the problem with emphasizing the preservation of the freedom of another person's agency over his or her happiness.

The point is that there is a significant difference between focusing on the preservation of the autonomy of the will of other persons and focusing on what would best promote their overall well-being and happiness, even at the expense of their theoretical, yet nonexistent freedom of choice.

26. Indeed, the families of some homeless persons at the age of legal adulthood have had to engage in protracted litigation with social-welfare agencies and civil-liberties advocates protecting the theoretical autonomy of irrational homeless persons, as if they were rational agents. The families would, arguably, have a greater concern and social connection to the homeless person, as a family member, than would these other institutions and advocates.

27. My use of Kant's means-ends terminology here indicates my acceptance of his terminology, when suitably understood as emphasizing the priority of kingdom of ends over universalizability.

28. Compare with Kant, *On a Supposed Right to Lie*, 425–30.

29. O'Neill, "Universal Laws and Ends-in-Themselves," 342.

30. See, in general, Lawrence Blum, *Friendship, Altruism, and Morality* (New York: Routledge and Kegan Paul, 1980).

31. Kant, *Kritik*, 79, 114 (81, 118).

32. Roger J. Sullivan states in "The Kantian Critique of Aristotle's Moral Philosophy: An Appraisal," *Review of Metaphysics* 28 (1974): 39: "But there is no logical necessity in the claim that if an action is not done from duty, it must be aimed at pleasure and so be amoral or immoral."

33. Although Arendt is not explicitly using the term *categorical imperative* in the following passage, it seems fairly obvious to me that her references to Kant's notion of duty and Eichmann's guilt at making some exceptions to his rigid implementation of the Holocaust are references to the universalizability notion of the categorical imperative.

34. Hannah Arendt, *Eichmann in Jerusalem: A Report on the Banality of Evil* (New York: Viking Press, 1963), 135–37. In fairness to Kant, he recognized the type of behavior exhibited by Eichmann very aptly, as an illustration of self-love and as not comporting with the categorical imperative, in "On Self Love," *Lectures on Ethics,* trans. Louis Infield (Indianapolis: Hackett, 1963), 137:

> In man's moral court of justice there exists a type of sophistication to which self-love gives rise. Our inner advocate becomes a pettifogger, expounding the law sophistically to our advantage. . . . Our pettifogger engages in all manner of legal quibbles; he makes use of the letter of the law for his own purposes . . . This theory of moral probability is a means of self-deception whereby a man persuades himself that he has been acting on principle and rightly. There is nothing worse, nothing more abominable than the artifice that invents a false law to enable us, under the shelter of the true law, to do evil.

The problem is that the emptiness and ambiguity of the categorical imperative makes it difficult to discern the difference between Kant's example of its application in his consideration of the right to lie to a murderer and Eichmann's misuse of it.

35. Although a consideration of Kant's jurisprudential writings is not the primary focus of this criticism, it bears mentioning that Kant repeatedly emphasizes obedience to the positive law, the priority of the state over the welfare of its citizens, and the notion that the laws of the state cannot injure unjustly a citizen in a manner compatible with my conventional reading of the categorical imperative and use of the Eichmann example: "Because all right and justice is supposed to proceed from [the legislative authority], it can do absolutely no injustice to anyone." Kant, *Metaphysik der Sitten,* 313 (78).

"But the well-being of the state must not be confused with the welfare or happiness of the citizens of the state." Kant, *Metaphysik der Sitten,* 318 (83).

"The origin of the supreme authority is, from the practical point of view, not open to scrutiny by the people who are subject to it." Kant, *Metaphysik der Sitten,* 318 (84).

"There can therefore be no legitimate resistance of the people to the legislative chief of state. . . . It is the people's duty to endure even the most intolerable abuse of supreme authority." Kant, *Metaphysik der Sitten,* 320 (86).

"An alteration in a [defective] constitution of a state, which may sometimes be required, can be undertaken only by the sovereign himself through reform, and not by the people through revolution." Kant, *Metaphysik der Sitten,* 321–22 (88).

36. Roger J. Sullivan, "The Kantian Critique of Aristotle's Moral Philosophy," 36.

37. Ibid., 46–47.

38. Ibid., 45–46.

39. Robinson and Harre, "The Demography of the Kingdom of Ends," 5–19.

40. Ibid., 10.

41. Ibid., 7.

42. Ibid., 8–9.

43. In this regard, I refer the reader back to the James D. Chansky passage quoted at the beginning of this chapter.

44. Kant states in his *Kritik,* 110 (114): "For this, happiness is also required, and indeed not merely in the partial eyes of a person who makes himself his end but even in the judgment of an impartial reason, which impartially regards persons in the world as ends-in-themselves."

45. I recognize that Kant bases the necessity of this impartiality on the need for an unconditioned will and a host of reasons not germane to the argument being made here. But I have

already stated that having the kind of moral necessity that Kant seeks is less important for the purposes of this study than the practical results of a moral theory. Accordingly, Kant is being assessed not within his own framework, but within the framework of this study.

46. Gimbel, "A Swiss Who Bent Rules to Save Jews Is Refused a Pardon."

47. In *On a Supposed Right to Lie Because of Philanthropic Concerns* (427), Kant uses an argument from analogy between the way the positive law in his day dealt with lying to the appropriate way in which the moral law against lying would be applied within the framework of the categorical imperative (apparently, the state's laws of his time dealt with lying harshly, even where the injurious consequences had not been intended, were accidental, and where the motive for the lie was, apparently, altruistic). This mode of argumentation by Kant ought to give some pause to those who would give great weight to any alleged distinction between the moral and positive law in Kant. The metaphor of the positive law so permeates Kant's discussion of the moral law and the metaphysical foundations of morality that it is difficult to see how the categorical imperative can not have been infected by some degree of legalisms.

48. Lewis White Beck, *A Commentary on Kant's Critique of Practical Reason* (Chicago: University of Chicago Press, 1960), 160.

49. Ibid.

50. Arkes, *First Things*, 104–12.

51. Kant states in his *Metaphysik der Sitten*, 393: "For to sacrifice one's own happiness, one's true needs, in order to promote the happiness of others would be a self-contradictory maxim if made a universal law. Therefore, this duty is only a broad one; it has a latitude within which we may do more or less without being able to assign definite limits to it."

52. Kant states in "On Friendship," *Lectures on Ethics*, 208–9: "Is every man a possible friend for us? No. I can be a friend of mankind in general in the sense that I can bear good-will in my heart towards everyone, but to be the friend of everybody is impossible, for friendship is a particular friendship, and he who is a friend to everyone has no particular friend."

53. Compare with Chapter 4 of this book (in the case of Aristotle), and, in the case of Hume, see *An Inquiry Concerning the Principles of Morals* (Indianapolis: Bobbs-Merrill, 1981), 14–34; *A Treatise of Human Nature* (Oxford: Oxford University Press, 1978), 498–99.

54. Kant, *Metaphysik der Sitten*, 232.

55. Ibid., 230 (34).

56. Ibid.

57. Ibid., 234–35 (39–40).

58. Ibid.

59. Ibid., 234 (40).

60. Ibid.

61. According to E. Allan Farnsworth, *Contracts* (Boston: Little, Brown, 1982), 670–71: "The common law has been less receptive to claims of excuse based on events occurring after the making of the contract than it has been to claims of excuse based on facts that existed at the time of the agreement. In a seventeenth-century dictum that was to gain wide acceptance, the Court of King's Bench declared that: 'When the party by his own contract creates a duty or charge upon himself, he is bound to make it good, if he may, notwithstanding any accident by inevitable necessity, because he might have provided against it by his contract. And therefore if the lessee covenant to repair a house, though it be burnt by lightning, or thrown down by enemies, yet he ought to repair it.'" See *Paradine v. Jane*, Aleyn 26, 27 Eng. Rep. 897, 897 (K.B. 1647). This dictum seems very much in accord with Kant's strict notion of contract law—a notion that is not infected with notions of equity.

62. *Krell v. Henry*, [1903] 2 K.B. 740, (C.A.); Farnsworth, *Contracts*, 689.

63. 122 Eng. Rep. 309 (K.B. 1863); Farnsworth, *Contracts*, 673.

64. Farnsworth, *Contracts*, 674–75.

65. Ibid., 675.

66. Ibid., 676–77.

67. Uniform Commercial Code 2–615, Excuse by Failure of Presupposed Conditions. Farnsworth, *Contracts*, 677.

68. *Aluminum Co. of America v. Essex Group*, 499 F. Supp. 53 (W.D.Pa. 1980); Farnsworth, *Contracts*, 651.

69. Farnsworth, *Contracts*, 302–7.

70. Lord Hardwicke in *Earl of Chesterfield v. Janssen*, 2 Ves. Sen. 125, 155, 28 Eng. Rep. 82, 100 (1750); Farnsworth, *Contracts*, 304.

71. *Campbell Soup v. Wentz*, 172 F.2d 80, 83–84 (3d Cir. 1948).

72. UCC 2–302, Unconscionable Contract or Clause, provides: "If a court as a matter of law finds the contract or any clause of the contract to have been unconscionable at the time it was made the court may refuse to enforce the contract, or it may enforce the remainder of the contract without the unconscionable clause, or it may so limit the application of any unconscionable clause as to avoid any unconscionable result."

In commentary to this provision, the code drafters state: "This section is intended to make it possible for the courts to police explicitly against the contracts or clauses which they find to be unconscionable. In the past such policing has been accomplished by adverse construction of language, by manipulation of the rules of offer and acceptance or by determinations that the clause is contrary to public policy or to the dominant purpose of the contract." See UCC 2–302, Comment 1.

73. Farnsworth, *Contracts*, 307, 310.

74. In the English legal tradition, equitable remedies granted by the separate equitable courts were deemed as extraordinary exceptions intended to remedy defects in the outcomes from the competing jurisdiction of the law courts. Appeals to "conscience," or external considerations of justice or morality, while inappropriate in the separate law courts, were considered within the discretion of an equity court. See Farnsworth's discussion of the historical uses of equity in the contract-law area, in *Contracts*, 820–21.

75. Again, to repeat this distinction, this individuality is with respect to a rule or legal norm, but it is universal insofar as departing from the legal rule or norm is the only correct or just course of action that would be taken by a wise person possessing the virtue of epieikeia. See section 3 of Chapter 4 for a fuller discussion of this distinction.

4

Moving Beyond Law with Aristotle

It is not the province of the court to decide upon the justice or injustice, the policy or impolicy of these laws. The decision of that question belonged to the political or law-making power; to those who formed the sovereignty and framed the Constitution. The duty of the court is to interpret the instrument they have framed, with the best lights we can obtain on the subject, and to administer it as we find it, according to its true intent and meaning when it was adopted.[1]

The acknowledged absence of a remedy under ERISA's civil enforcement scheme for medical malpractice committed in connection with a plan benefit determination does not alter our conclusion. While we are not unmindful of the fact that our interpretation of the pre-emption clause leaves a gap in remedies within a statute intended to protect participants in employee benefit plans, the lack of an ERISA remedy does not affect a pre-emption analysis. Congress perhaps could not have predicted the interjection into the ERISA "system" of the medical utilization review process, but it enacted a pre-emption clause so broad and a statute so comprehensive that it would be incompatible with the language, structure and purpose of the statute to allow tort suits against entities so integrally connected with a plan.[2]

There can be no doubt that so far as procedure is concerned the rights of the patient are most carefully considered, and as every step in this case was taken in scrupulous compliance with the statute and after months of observation, there is no doubt that in that respect the plaintiff in error has had due process of law.[3]

A return to an earlier ethical understanding of law and justice in the philosophy of Aristotle can illuminate not only the defects in Dworkin's theory of jurisprudence but also the nature of the legal injustices we have examined. Of course, this return to Aristotle presupposes discarding a Kantian ethical framework, for the reasons already discussed in Chapter 3. In this return to Aristotle, use is not made of the extensive commentary by Aristotelian scholars who find the notion of natural law to be the core of his contribution in this area.[4]

The notion of natural law is simply not a major explanatory principle in Aristotle's ethical-political theory.[5] There is a notion of natural justice that is thought to be the same everywhere, in contrast to legal or conventional justice, but it is not characterized as some sort of separate legal order called natural law. Why a return to this notion of natural justice in Aristotle provides a suitable framework for understanding the injustices identified at the outset of my analysis is shown in a three-part argument that constitutes the remainder of this chapter.

The first part of the argument considers the nature of natural justice and its relation to legal justices and injustices. The second part of the argument considers the nature of legal justice and the role of custom. The third part and the culmination of this entire examination of legal injustices consider the nature and role of epieikeia, as a species of natural justice, in correcting defects in legal justice.[6]

1. The Nature of Natural Justice

The nature of natural justice is considered from three perspectives. The first and most important view of natural justice considers the nature of the relationship between natural justice and human sociability (friendship and community). The point of this first argument is that rejection of a rigid and excessive egalitarianism is inherent to any consideration of the relation of justice to friendship. The second view of natural justice involves the elaboration of its relationship to legal justice as a way of defining both natural justice and legal justice. Inherent in such an elaboration is a clarification of the difference between natural law and natural justice. The third view of natural justice is within a teleological framework that explains how it is that natural justice is, in fact, real when natural and legal injustices are so pervasive.

1.1 Natural Justice and Friendship.

Aristotle does not provide a theological grounding of natural justice in divine ideas. Nor does he ground natural justice in the positive law. Rather, natural justice is grounded in the associative bonds of the various friendships forming a natural political community. Moreover, the amount of natural justice is a function of the quality of the kind of friendship or association, and there are greater expectations of natural justice between closer relationships or among the more perfect forms of political association.

Accordingly, the level of perfection or virtue associated with this notion of natural justice has nothing whatsoever to do with lawlike imperatives or rules, whether arising from modern notions of the moral law or positive law; rather, this level of perfection or virtue arises naturally, out of the nature of the friendship. Conversely, where there is a lesser degree of friendship or more defective forms of political association, there is a lesser expectation of natural justice, and, by implication, a need to fill this gap with something else, which I will contend are legal and moral rules.[7]

> Friendship and justice seem . . . to be concerned with the same objects and exhibited between the same persons. For in every community there is thought to be some form of justice, and friendship too . . . And the extent of their association is the extent of their friendship, as it is the extent to which justice exists between them . . . for of friendships, too, some are more and others less truly friendships. And the claims of justice differ too; the duties of parents to children and those of brothers to each other are not the same, nor those of comrades and those of fellow-citizens, and so, too, with the other kinds of friendship. There is a difference, therefore, also between the acts that are unjust towards each of these classes of associates, and the injustice increases by being exhibited towards those who are friends in a fuller sense; e.g., it is a more terrible thing to defraud a comrade than a fellow citizen, more terrible not to help a brother than a stranger, and more terrible to wound a father than anyone else. And the demands of justice also naturally increase with the friendship, which implies that friendship and justice exist between the same persons and have an equal extension.[8]

> Each of the constitutions may be seen to involve friendship just in so far as it involves justice . . . But in the deviation forms [of political constitutions], as justice hardly exists, so too does friendship.[9]

Accordingly, natural justice, in this strong sense of justice grounded in friendship, exemplifies the manner in which people act in the absence of a legal coercion that compels them to act justly, according to the outward form of some legal rule.

Natural justice is not simple equality in the manner elaborated by Dworkin. Sometimes justice requires inequality, since not everyone is equal by nature, and it is just that things be distributed according to merit in a proportionate manner. Sometimes justice requires the imposition of an equality or a return to the conditions that obtained prior to a transaction that has injured one party. There are different kinds of justice, corresponding to the different kinds of associative bonds that naturally occur apart from the political organization of the state.

There is household justice between a husband and wife and between parents and children; there existed as well in Aristotle's time a different kind of justice between a master and a slave.[10] There is the justice expected between friends in the lowest form of friendships grounded in pleasure or utility, and there is the justice expected between the closest of friends in the highest form of friendship.[11] There is also a lesser form of justice that is expected between strangers.[12]

One of the ways in which this sense of natural justice has been lost in contemporary settings is the tendency of some persons, on the one hand, to view household justice in contractual terms and, on the other hand, to attempt to make their place of employment into a household.[13] Such imbalance is often a source of tension and, ultimately, injustice in these sorts of relationships.

The natural political community is small enough that its members can know one other's characters.[14] The natural political community arises naturally through the associative bonds of the various kinds of friendships described by Aristotle.[15] While some types of friendships have a greater excellence or virtue than others, all are coextensive with justice.[16] Of course, Aristotle specifically relates the extent and quality of the different types of friendships to the extent to which justice arises out of the friendship.[17] While he does not specifically make such an analysis, it is conceivable that the various kinds of justice are probably associated with the different types of friendship.

For example, a friendship of utility, one of the less perfect types of friendship, would probably emphasize commutative or distributive justice, more than it would the equitable. On the other hand, the highest form of friendship, where friends act for the sake of the advantage of each other, would probably emphasize equitable justice more than it would commutative or distributive. Nonetheless, Aristotle states without qualification that "friendship and justice seem . . . to be concerned with the same objects and exhibited between the same persons."[18]

Aristotle also observes that the various forms of political constitution involve friendship to the degree that they involve justice.[19] On the other hand, the perversion of these forms of constitution into tyranny, oligarchy, or democracy involves friendship and justice to a lesser degree. This difference is due to the fact that the just governments consider the common interest, whereas the perversions consider the interest of their governing factions.[20] Thus the democratic governs in the interest of the many over the minority, the oligarchy governs in the interest of the few, and the tyrant governs in the interest of one person.[21]

As a result, all persons in these perverse forms of constitution have a limited or partial notion of justice that is very imperfect (I will explore this concept in greater depth below).[22] For example, in democracies, the majority, who are poor, place equality of possessions over all else and seek redistribution of wealth from the rich.[23] On the other hand, aristocracies believe in equality only for the wealthy.[24] These partial notions of imperfect justice are contrasted to the shared notions of the good life established among the friends who are the members of a natural political community of virtue.[25] The extent of the presence and absence of friendship is the common denominator in Aristotle's diagnosis of the justice and injustice of various communities. Accordingly, any discussion of Aristotle's notion of natural justice that fails to recognize this association between friendship and justice makes possible the later confusions of natural justice with a natural legal order.

There is not a natural law in Aristotle enjoining persons to be friends. Rather, there is a mere recognition that natural justice arises out of friendship. Hence, natural justice is unlikely to arise and, arguably, cannot arise where there is not some form of friendship. It is significant that Aristotle further notes that the demands of justice seem to "naturally increase with friendship," and that it is "more terrible not to help a brother than a stranger."[26] While these notions may not appeal to a modern society that has arisen out of the Judeo-Christian tradition (this includes the so-called secular post-Enlightenment society that spurns its Judeo-Christian parentage), I find it hard to deny that these are, in fact, natural sentiments. Men may loudly proclaim adherence to abstract principles on the brotherhood of man, kingdom of ends, loving one's neighbor as oneself, but ultimately, the most natural behavior would seem to be that men behave more easily with justice with respect to persons they know and have some sort of association with.

As one raised in the Christian tradition, I reject that this is the way it ought to be. However, one must ground one's inquiry in solid, concrete experience and, based on this experience, I submit that Aristotle's implicit recognition is, at least, correct: namely, that whatever natural justice there is obtains between people having some sort of associative bond between one other. And it certainly explains the need for law in the first place, which Aristotle viewed as existing for men between whom there is natural injustice.

A feature not often properly understood concerning Aristotle's supposed support of "natural slavery" concerns the way the presence or absence of friendship of some sort distinguishes the so-called condition of natural slavery that is sanctioned by Aristotle from "conventional slavery," considered unjust by him, since it is purely based on coercion, with no element of friendship present. Some scholars have apparently been puzzled by a seeming inconsistency between the *Politics* I.6, 1255b13–14 passage, where Aristotle affirms that slaves and masters in a condition of natural slavery can be friends, and passages describing more conventional, nonnatural slave relationships in his ethical writings (*Nichomachean Ethics* [*EN*] VIII.11, 1161a32–34; *Eudemian Ethics* [*EE*] VII.10.1242a28–29), where Aristotle affirms the utter absence of any element of friendship between master and slave.[27]

But any reading of these passages in context makes it fairly obvious that there is no inconsistency, and that the distinction is simply that between natural and conventional slavery, the one involving friendship (and being natural and justified, for Aristotle), the other involving force (and therefore being unjustified). For example, in *EN* VIII.11, Aristotle is describing the less just political communities as involving less friendship, and he uses slavery as an example where such an absence of friendship exists. It ought to be obvious that he is talking about the unjustified, unnatural form of slavery here. When Aristotle's apparent justification of natural slavery is seen in this context, it takes a great deal of hypocrisy by modern thinkers to read this as a strong indorsement of slavery. Rather, Aristotle is condemning slavery, unless there is some element of friendship between the master and slave.

Since I accept Marx's point that the only real distinction between a chattel slave and a wage slave is the manner by which a laborer is exploited, having seen firsthand the exploitation of workers in supposedly freely contractable relationships, I find Aristotle's limitation of justifiable slave relationships to those involving friendship as one involving quite a bit of improvement over what often obtains in any kind of employer-employee relationship.

The legal form of the relationship ought to be less important than how naturally just is the relation between the parties. Modern thinkers are so caught up in abstract legalisms that they speak of Aristotle as if he were a John Calhoun and thereby fail to recognize how more moderate he is than they are. Modern capitalist employers often want to obtain as much surplus labor from their employees as possible, and therefore they try to get their workers to alienate as much as possible the entirety of their time (rather than a part of it) to work in the name of greater productivity and profits. Such exploitation is not naturally just; indeed, it meets Hegel's basic distinction between hired labor and slave labor: namely, a hired laborer alienates "individual products" of "particular physical and mental skills . . . for a limited period," whereas a slave alienates "the whole" of his or her time.[28]

The notion that hired labor is freely contractable and may be terminated at the will of either party ignores the fact that there often are absent viable alternative employment options. In a market involving disparate bargaining power between employer and employee, there are great incentives to exploit employees and render them into the functional equivalent of slaves by placing greater and greater time demands on them. I believe that a significant number of employees in supposedly free markets are treated more harshly and less justly than Aristotle's natural slaves. The degree of exploitation in a relationship is not always adequately characterized by the legal label, insofar as the conditions of chattel slaves and freely contracted labor have varied across cultures and eras, and even within the same society.[29] Modern scholars who simply condemn Aristotle without considering these distinctions are a bit hypocritical, in my estimation.

There are two notions that merit some emphasis in discussing the relationship between the degrees of natural justice in communities and the types of friendships composing the associative bonds of those communities. First, imperfect or partial notions of justice arise from treating unequals equally or from treating equals unequally.[30] The emergence of such notions is a result of rigid notions of equality that fail to consider or discern the particularities and differences in kind that merit various forms of discrimination between different kinds of relationships. There is a tension between the broadened notion of equity exemplified in Aristotle's epieikeia and rigid notions of justice reduced to equality, such as in Dworkin.

Second, political justice, of which natural justice and legal justice are the principal constituents, is premised on friendly associations between people who share a notion of the good life or human happiness. This shared notion of the good life involves shared amusements, recognizes the importance of leisure, and does not reduce the end of political or subsidiary associations to mere utility.[31] In other words, the end of a family is not mere procreation of children and heirs; the end of a commercial relationship is not merely profit; and the end of a political community is not merely achieving the greatest gross national product or trade surplus.

All of these instrumental ends have an end for the sake of which they are merely instrumental, and that end is human happiness. Accordingly, legislation, adjudication, and enforcement of laws that explicitly confine their scope to instrumental ends do not, by implication, form the type of legal system that Aristotle had in mind that would be compatible with a natural polity. That the theory and practice in the American legal system today does, in fact, repudiate any legal interpretation with a broader framework than the instrumental is well known, whether one calls oneself a conservative from the Chicago school or a liberal, such as Dworkin. Today, happiness is principally conceived as a private interest, with the public interest confined to regulating the "pursuit of happiness."

In considering the relation between community and natural justice, a final problem remains that is a bit more difficult than the preceding ones. To deal with this problem, it might be helpful to sketch the argument thus far: (1) It is natural to become friends with certain persons. (2) In friendship at its best, friends behave justly to each other by nature (and there are different levels and kinds of friendships, each with its different kind of justice). Implicit in the second statement is the notion that the just behavior between friends is right. (3) But friendships are, by nature, limited to a few persons. Accordingly, polities that exist principally, by nature, through friendships are sufficiently small and proximate to one another so that citizens may know one other's characters and share common ends, sacrifices, and amusements; they have a natural justice. The problem remains of how to extend the natural justice that arises between friends as constitutive of the natural community to the relations between strangers, thereby rendering such justice universal. The problem lies in making the particularity inherent in natural justice, such as in epieikeia, universal without committing the legalistic fallacy that universalizes an action in a manner that blurs its particularity. The fallacy consists in treating a particular as a universal.

Aristotle remarks in *Ethics* VIII.9 that greater justice is naturally expected between friends and associates than between strangers.[32] In *Rhetoric* I.13, he argues that there is a "natural justice and injustice that is common to all, even to those who have no association or covenant with each other."[33] The one instance he gives of the universal justice among strangers is an injunction against murder. The sparseness of his description of what is included in this type of natural justice (between strangers) may be contrasted with his rich description of the virtues of the various kinds of friendship, from the less perfect ones grounded in pleasure and utility (the only kind recognized by Dworkin) to the most perfect friendships, where one acts for the sake of the good of one's friend.

Apparently the justice appropriate for the encounter between strangers involves fewer requirements than that between friends. Such a distinction makes sense, since strangers often live in different geographic locales, have unknown characters, and do not necessarily have a shared notion of the good life; nor do they share in the sacrifices and amusements of a natural political community. Accordingly, from the fact that Aristotle recognized different kinds of justice—from the justice appropriate for a household to the justice appropriate to a community—one could infer that it is appropriate to recognize a different kind of justice between that accorded to strangers and that accorded to friends.

Supposing the validity of this inference, it follows that the legislator of an empire or nation state where most citizens are strangers to each other (something not considered by Aristotle) ought to legislate sparingly, particularly if the legislator is inclined to preserve the natural communities composing the empire and not polarize them into contending groups. Aristotle was also very respectful of natural differences in kind, particularly in regard to the framing of a constitution. Thus he opened his criticism of Plato in *Politics* II.2 by remarking that there ought not be too great a unity in a state, lest the different kinds of associations composing the state be weakened and destroyed, thereby destroying the underlying constituents of the state itself.[34]

None of these speculations about an empire or nation state are to be found explicitly in Aristotle, who, unfortunately, only grappled with the nature of small political organizations. But the point of this chapter is to indicate that Aristotle's failure to consider the difficult problem of extending his model of the natural political community to artificial national states and empires held together by conquest and the force of law—on the model of Rome and the United States—does not relieve the modern era of the responsibility of building upon his solid, albeit incomplete foundations.

Insofar as natural justice is natural because of its origins in friendship, it becomes important to understand the way in which a small political community is primarily constituted, through friendship, by nature, and to a lesser degree constituted artificially by laws. A natural political community does not refer to the nation state or Dworkin's community of principle (or liberal community). Rather, the natural political community is just that: the grouping of various associations or friendships sharing their common pursuit of a happy and good life.[35]

Such a natural political community cannot be constituted exclusively (or fabricated) by laws. Contrary to the pretensions of some modern legislators, political activists, and judges, friendships cannot be coerced through extensive legislation or litigation. Indeed, such legalistic activism acts against such natural bonding between people, by polarizing groups into victims and those who owe them certain duties. Rather, such a natural community arises through the forming of friendships between persons pursuing the common ends requisite for their happiness and flourishing. The forming of friendships is a natural human activity—no extensive metaphysical sophistication is required to acknowledge this—except, perhaps, for those pathological humans who attempt to live a Hobbesian life. That the art of legislation plays a role, albeit a subsidiary one, in habituating citizens in the direction of certain preferred customs is not denied, but neither is the more important role played by nature.

Throughout Dworkin's discussion of community and its relationship to justice, he does not make one acknowledgment or criticism of Aristotle. To be sure, Dworkin and Aristotle essentially agree on one point: namely, in

Dworkin's way of putting it, that the legitimacy for collective community action through the laws resides in the associative bonds of community, not in the justice between strangers or by contract.[36] In Aristotelian terms, natural justice and legal justice are components of political justice, which is coextensive with the natural bonds of friendship.[37]

Despite this area of essential agreement, however, there are substantial differences between Dworkin's and Aristotle's conceptions of justice and law. Where Dworkin emphasizes the potential conflict between justice and the friendship of natural communities because of the narrow range of such associations,[38] Aristotle emphasizes the grounding of justice in friendship.[39] Where Dworkin emphasizes a notion of justice reduced to a rigid egalitarianism,[40] Aristotle recognizes the complexity of different mixes of equality and inequality in different kinds of justice associated with different kinds of friendships.[41] Finally, Dworkin's notion of the community of principle is much more artificial than Aristotle's notion of the natural community or polity.

This artificiality is apparent from Dworkin's explicit acknowledgment of the origin of the notion of the community of principle in Rousseau's general will.[42] This artificiality is also apparent when the key characteristics of Aristotle's communities are compared with those of Dworkin's community of principle. Aristotle's community is constituted by friends who live together in the same geographic locale, know one other's characters, have a shared notion of the good life, have common amusements,[43] and yet are not a unity, in the sense that Aristotle finds and criticizes in Plato's notion of community.[44] By contrast, Dworkin's community of principle is exemplified by a hypothetical ideal judge with perfect knowledge and discernment: Hercules.[45] The only commonality making it a community are its shared principles of equality, due process, and fairness, and the implicit notion that it consists of judges, legislators, and lawyers.[46] There is no notion of living together, sharing amusements, or even knowing each other. The only bond tying it together are its liberal principles. Such an artificial community can apply the coercion of the law with indifference and apparent impartiality against natural communities, because in that artificial community, there is no notion of a shared life or a stake in living together of the sort that obtains in Aristotle's natural communities.

The lawyers composing Dworkin's elite community of principle are almost like shamans for an ostensibly secular society where the law has replaced the deity.[47] There is no sense, just as there is none for the Olympian gods or the demigod Hercules, that they truly share in the struggles of everyone else.

The notion that someone who is a stranger to a natural community can render justice in that community is the result of such an artificial construct as the community of principle. By contrast, there is a sense of having a shared stake in living together in a natural community that is absent from Dworkin's community of principle.

1.2 Natural Justice and Legal Justice.

Aristotle does not so much define legal justice as contrast it with natural justice. Having considered Aristotle's rooting of natural justice in friendship and political association, we are better prepared to grapple with the artificial component in the political community: its laws. This subsection will focus on why legal justice is less perfect than natural justice, and why it may be characterized as artificial. From these considerations, the framework will then exist for explaining in detail why natural justice is not to be confused with natural law notions.

Law's domain is not imperial, but is restricted to those areas where natural justice does not obtain—where there is a breakdown of the associative bonds of friendship in the natural community. So-called legal justice for Aristotle is, accordingly, a form of justice that is less than perfect and even inferior to natural justice.[48]

"Of political justice part is natural, part legal—natural, that which everywhere has the same force and does not exist by people's thinking this or that; legal, that which is originally indifferent, but when it has been laid down is not indifferent, e.g. that a prisoner's ransom shall be a mina, or that a goat and not two sheep shall be sacrificed."[49]

"Things are just either by nature or by law."[50]

"Natural justice, then, is better than legal."[51]

Thus, adherence to legal justice by itself can never approximate or reach the level of natural justice. Rather, natural justice and legal justice coexist in different realms, the one natural and superior, the other artificial and inferior.[52]

If artificial laws cannot constitute natural justice, but this natural justice is, instead, grounded in friendships, the questions remain: To what areas is it appropriate to limit law, and what is the nature of the legal justice that is to be expected in these areas? Although Aristotle never explicitly raises or answers these questions, his clear distinction between legal justice and natural justice is fully compatible with such inquiries. While it is probably easier to identify occasions where legal justice is needed or has gone too far after the fact, defining these limitations in advance is about as difficult as detailing a physician's diagnostic techniques in a formula—a possibly impossible task.

To use a simple example, a breakdown in the natural justice of a natural community occurs when there is a murder, and natural justice exists in that community to the extent that there are no murders in it. In the event there is a murder, the best possible legal justice (as opposed to a defective legal justice) punishes the murderer by finding him, convicting him (and not someone else), and executing him. However, legal justice cannot bring the victim back to life. Only natural justice, by avoiding the murder in the first place, has any amount of perfection to it.

Legal justice is contractual, or conventional, or established by legislation.[53] Although man is by nature a political animal,[54] and the political community is prior in nature to the individuals, families, and other associations that make it up,[55] such a community is also constituted artificially by the laws.[56] The act of legislation is more the act of a craft or art than something natural.[57] However, a legislator should consider the nature of the customs of the political community for which he is constituting the laws.[58] Indeed, the aim of laws should be that of disposing men to fulfill their cooperative nature, that is, to dispose and habituate men to natural justice.[59] That role for legal justice does not, however, blur the fundamental distinction between legal justice and natural justice as a difference in kind and degree.[60]

Aristotle does not devote an excessive amount of attention to defining law, the issue of choice in the stale controversy between positivism and natural law partisans.[61] The fact that Aristotle does not, apparently, take the problem of defining law to be an important question, but rather focuses on natural justice and its relation to legal justice, might be seen by some as a defect. But for our purposes, Aristotle's neglect of the traditional jurisprudential question that attempts a precise definition of law opens up the inquiry to areas previously closed off by the more narrow jurisprudential question. When one acts merely to conform one's behavior indifferently to a rule, whether it be legislated, adjudicated, or customary, one is not acting in the same manner in which one would act if one were acting out of one's friendship with another person. Accordingly, precisely defining what Aristotle would include in the various types of rules, or norms, or laws is beside the point when the question concerns the status of natural justice and its relation to laws or norms—however broadly or narrowly defined. It is in this context that one must approach Aristotle's sometimes broad use of law.

Aristotle takes it for granted that law is conventional and that justice is natural.[62] As a convention or norm, law encompasses the written and unwritten laws, the legislative enactments, adjudications, and customary practices of communities. Sometimes, from the context of his examples, it is clear that Aristotle is using law in an adjudicative sense, whereas on other occasions, he is using it in the broadest sense, to encompass custom. The various senses in which he uses law are not important for his purposes or for our purposes. It is significant that a philosopher who ordinarily takes such great pains to define his terms so blatantly ignores the modern preoccupation with the problem of defining law. Rather, it is more important for Aristotle to contrast law to natural justice and show the ways in which political justice must make room for natural justice to mitigate legal justice.

Accordingly, Aristotle's notion of law as convention should not be taken to exclude an ontological characterization of law (or convention) as artificial when he contrasts law to natural justice. Indeed, the contrast of law to natural justice cannot be adequately explained without resort to the nature/art distinction implicit in such a contrast. A natural justice grounded in something natural, such as friendship, is different in kind from and superior to an artificial legal justice grounded in force. The difference is precisely one of the sort articulated by Aristotle between the natural, as an internal cause of movement and change, and the artificial, as an external and violent cause of change.

"Acts just and unjust being as we have described them, a man acts unjustly or justly whenever he does such acts voluntarily; when involuntarily, he acts neither unjustly nor justly, except in an incidental way, for he does things that happen to be just or unjust."[63]

Although Aristotle does not explicitly say so, the written law is an accidental or violent cause of outwardly just behavior, and, in this way, the written law may be deemed artificial in contrast to natural justice. Even the customary law can be an accidental cause of just behavior, at least until custom has so habituated citizens to voluntarily choose to act justly that the custom has become a natural cause of just behavior. When considered in this way, it is only natural justice that is properly just, in the fullest and most natural sense, and the artificiality of so-called legal justice becomes manifest. But taking these inferential steps to conclude that legal justice may be characterized as artificial requires linking the Aristotelian understanding of natural causes as being voluntary and artificial causes as being accidental.

Accordingly, the focus adopted and urged by my endeavor to understand legal injustices is Aristotle's focus: namely, the relation of legal justice to natural justice, and not an excessive preoccupation with defining Aristotle's notion of law. But even if Aristotle's notion of law is broader than the contemporary notion of law generally presupposed throughout much of my analysis of legal injustices, I can still analogize from his fundamental distinction between legal justice and natural justice.

Thus I can equally evaluate and criticize a narrow conception of the positive law and a broad conception of law that encompasses custom—within the Aristotelian framework that contrasts natural justice to legal justice. There is no ontological necessity that requires me to adhere strictly to a broad Aristotelian notion of law whenever I use his distinction between legal justice and natural justice, especially in view of the fact that defining law is not a significant issue for Aristotle. Thus I can legitimately criticize either custom or the positive law or both within his framework, and, similarly, I can disregard any distinction between the positive and moral law. Indeed, in the passages where Aristotle specifically draws the distinction between natural justice and legal justice and the role of epieikeia, he uses adjudicative and legislative examples to illustrate legal justice.[64]

This lack of concern with defining law is why Aristotle's shedding of Platonic metaphysics makes his notion of natural justice much less legalistic than that of traditional natural law theory. At one level, conceiving justice as natural justice is conceiving it as an internal tendency in political organizations, a principle of change and stability in polities. At another level, conceiving of justice as natural justice is understanding its genesis out of various levels of friendship and recognizing this as involving a teleological argument.

Thus natural justice corresponds fairly closely with the ways in which people actually behave and speak, even if such a notion of natural justice does not correspond to the Christian ideal of a universal love toward everyone. As such, natural justice is neither the natural law nor moral law, since it is not something that can be articulated in a universal rule; rather, it is natural in the fullest teleological sense of *natural*. That is, what is natural in natural justice is the teleological explanation of its relationship to friendship. And by contrasting natural justice to legal justice as being more perfect and different in kind, Aristotle is implicitly suggesting that law, however it is defined, is artificial, at least when compared with the natural justice arising out of friendships.[65]

There is a tangible, concrete reality to Aristotle's notion of natural justice not present in the notion of natural law, for two reasons. First, the Aristotelian notion of a natural justice, when properly understood to exclude a Platonic interpretation, corresponds to the way ordinary persons speak about justice. Second, the Aristotelian notion of a natural justice is grounded in something very concrete, tangible, and natural: human friendship.[66] Accordingly, when properly understood in this way, Aristotle's notion of natural justice cannot be confused with a separate legal order of rules arising out of divine ideas. Indeed, it is not even clear that its notions could be expressed as imperatives or rules. Rather, it more properly is viewed as a causal explanation of the natural way in which humans behave justly and cooperatively when they are friends—in the absence of artificial rules.

Bernard Yack apparently refers to Aristotle's notion of natural justice simply as political justice. This serves to clarify even further that natural or political justice is not to be equated with natural law. Indeed, Yack sharply contrasts Aristotle's notion of political justice with what Yack calls legalistic views of justice, as exemplified in Rawls, Dworkin, and natural law thinkers. For Yack, Aristotelian political justice is more "open-ended" and "indeterminate" than such "legalistic conceptions" of justice, because it does not conceive of justice as involving the discernment and application of the right norm, rule, or principle to different particular cases. That is, natural justice is not legal justice and cannot be comprehended in the same way, in terms of norms or principles that supply right answers to legal cases.

> Rawls identifies determinate standards against which to measure the justice of our social and political institutions, by asking which principles of justice rational individuals would choose if they were constrained to reason fairly by a "veil of ignorance" that concealed from them their personal identity and characteristics. Ronald Dworkin offers a path to "right answers" about questions of justice, when he insists that our legal and political institutions, when viewed as a coherent whole, contain implicit principles of justice that allow us to resolve even the most difficult legal cases.[67]

Yack considers modern and contemporary views of justice to be more legalistic or adjudicatory than Aristotle's views. The predominant (or "normal") view

> conceives of justice, on the model of legal adjudication, primarily as a matter of applying general norms to particular cases. Normal models of justice answer questions about the justice of laws and other familiar norms by seeking to identify a body of extralegal norms against which to measure them. . . . As such, they extend a legalist or adjudicatory understanding of justice beyond the sphere of legal judgment, by encouraging us to treat competing claims about the justice of established norms and practices as if they could be ad-

judicated, like competing legal claims, with reference to a body of shared and commonly recognized norms.[68]

While I agree that proponents of natural law and Rawlsian and Dworkian theories of jurisprudence tend to invoke legalistic notions of justice and that this involvement distinguishes them from Aristotle, I am not sure that the distinction lies primarily in the indeterminacy of Aristotelian notions of justice. I do not believe that Aristotle was a relativist. However, to the extent that Yack is properly emphasizing the cooperative component of justice that is natural, calling it "political justice," and that he is viewing such political justice as arising out of naturally cooperative or friendly actions, as opposed to arising out of compliance with moral codifications of rules, he has hit on the proper distinction between what he calls the normal model of justice and Aristotle's notion. And I further concur with Yack, if *indeterminate* and *open-ended* merely mean that Aristotle is not concerned with finding a so-called just rule or norm, so long as this indeterminacy does not extend so far that there is not a single just outcome in a particular case.

In other words, there is a difference between Solomon's decree and trying to come up with a universal rule to justify the decree, as if it would be used as a legal precedent. Aristotle is indeterminate, open-ended, and indifferent with regard to the lawyer's preoccupation with articulating the appropriate universal rule. But Aristotle is not open-ended in the sense of finding a contrary decree to that rendered by Solomon as just. While there are conceivably significant differences between Yack's interpretation and that offered here, his interpretation appears to be very similar to my own.

A rather simple but credible analogy between natural justice and health may be usefully made, at this juncture. The natural justice of the natural political community is analogous to the health of the human body, whereas legal justice is analogous to the art of medicine. That is, health is to justice as medicine is to law, and health is to medicine as justice ought to be for law.

HEALTH   :   JUSTICE
medicine   :   law

Accordingly, natural justice ought to be viewed as having as much ontological significance as health. Few would dispute that health is a meaningful notion communicated between most persons and recognized as such by most sane persons. Of course, if some were to speak of a notion of natural medicine instead of health as the state by which one evaluated the effectiveness of the art of medicine, this would probably confuse the discussion, to some degree. But it would not be an intellectual advance to deny the relevance of health in any discussions of the art of medicine, as a result of this unfortunate linguistic confusion involving natural medicine.

But if medicine were viewed as a self-contained system, where the health of the patient was irrelevant and the evaluation of medicine was conducted exclusively in terms of the degree to which a physician followed certain procedures, the result would be analogous to what has happened to much of modern jurisprudence. Such a result might be relatively harmless, were it not for the hubris of such a jurisprudence, a hubris that justifies the expansive use of law, just as if physicians were to maintain that human health could be completely fabricated through medicine.

At this point, the preceding arguments may be summarized as follows: The notion of natural justice is not to be confused with natural law or looked upon as a remarkable metaphysical abstraction. Aristotle simply contends that natural justice arises out of the natural bonds of friendship. As such, natural justice is analogous to right-handedness being superior to left-handedness, "for the most part"—a teleological analogy from biology. As such, natural justice is not a divine dictate. Rather, natural justice requires, as a necessary condition, some form of friendship.

Such natural justice can never be fabricated by an artificial legal justice. Indeed, just as drug overdoses and side effects often make nature the best healer of certain health conditions, reserving medicine and surgery for the real breakdowns, so legal systems are best viewed as tools of limited scope, due to their pernicious side effects.

Natural justice refers to the ways in which persons who are involved in common associations, or in the various forms of friendship articulated by Aristotle, act toward one another. Thus, to deny ontological significance to natural justice in the Aristotelian sense is, ultimately, to deny ontological significance to the ways in which friends behave toward one another. But friendship is all too common and natural a phenomenon that few would be willing to deny. Accordingly, when natural justice is properly understood in the Aristotelian sense, it has a plausibility that natural justice understood as natural law or as a universal and transcendent Form otherwise lacks.

There is a further philosophical reason for shedding Aristotle of the natural law baggage. Natural law theory makes positivism conceivable and inevitable. But positivism is untenable, because it rejects the commonsensical notion that one ought to be able to conduct a moral evaluation of the law. Positivism retains its credibility because of the lack of credibility of natural law theory, which has become a convenient straw man for positivists: anyone advocating a moral view of the law is cast as someone advocating the importation of theology into jurisprudence, or must at least explain that that is not what they are doing.

Natural law theory made positivism possible by asking the wrong question—what is law—and making this question the predominant concern of jurisprudence, rather than the question considered by Aristotle of the relation of natural justice to legal justice. A recovery of Aristotle's notion of nature and art is emphatically not a return to moral evaluation of the law on the basis of the Platonism of natural law theory.

At this point, I move beyond at least the letter of the Aristotelian text to argue that in the area of jurisprudential explanation, it is a category mistake either to speak of legal justice as somehow having the potential to achieve natural justice by itself or to conceive of legal justice as existing without some minimal degree of natural justice. That is, while legal justice is not to be confused with natural justice, nonetheless, legal justice requires some minimal level of natural justice in order to exist at all.

Just as a person can be so far down the road of sickness that no amount of drugs or surgery will help that person, so, too, can a natural political community be so ravaged with natural injustices that no amount of laws will cure the plague. Conversely, a natural political community with a slight degree of natural injustices can be harmed to a greater degree if the wrong dose or wrong set of laws (the wrong prescription) is enacted. A failure to recognize this category mistake results in the confusions that fail to confine law to its appropriate ends. Put more simply, it is a category mistake to argue that law by itself may ever achieve natural justice, since naked law is nothing more than coercion, and such an argument is, accordingly, nothing more than a euphemistic version of Thrasymachus's "might makes right" argument.

The exclusive sanction for law is political power in an imperfect world where the potential for natural justice, as natural as it is, has not been actualized. There is no moral sanction for the law. Indeed, it is a category mistake to confound the legal order with the moral order, the order of violence with the order of right and natural sociability. There is a difference that cannot be reconciled between doing something because one is forced to do it by a rule and doing something because of one's regard for a friend (because one wants to do what is best for the friend). The former is violent, and the latter is voluntary and natural. Only by redefining the moral order as a separate legal order apart from this natural sociability can it be possible to confuse the issue by purporting to find some moral sanction for the law.

Hadley Arkes attempts a justification of law's coercion (or force) through the necessity of "first principles" of morality, upon which he argues that law must be grounded: "This is the 'first principle' that expresses the logical connection between morals and law. Once we establish that 'X is wrong,' the logical implication is to remove X from the domain of personal taste or private choice. We may forbid X, then, for everyone, with the force of law."[69]

While I am sympathetic to such an attempt, I believe that justifying law's coercion ultimately involves justifying the power of some official charged with enacting, interpreting, or enforcing that law. And insofar as officials are corruptible, I find it difficult to be convinced of the moral force of law in practice, however much I might be convinced in theory that there is a moral necessity underlying the first principle that might, conceivably, justify it.

Iredell Jenkins justifies our "obedience" to a limited notion of law, where law is only a "supplement" to the social order. In such limited circumstances, law is the most effective, and the coerciveness and expansionist tendencies inherent in the law are tempered by "lived relationships" shared between citizens and officials.[70] The shift of emphasis from justifying law's *coercion* to that of justifying *obedience* to the law is not insignificant, and one that may contribute to solving my dilemma.

Traditional natural law theory tries to provide a sanction for the positive law, to the extent that it conforms to the moral law (or nature). But the positive law can never even minimally conform to the so-called moral law: even when it functions as intended, the positive law is imperfect, from a moral standpoint (for example, killing a murderer is less perfect than having a society in which the murder does not occur in the first place). This is because law is inherently violent and coercive. The only justification for law is the protection of persons and their property from violence by means of the violence of the law, when there is not sufficient natural justice (that is, when the natural community is weak).

Because law is inherently violent, so-called legal justice is the most imperfect form of justice, akin to the so-called just war (probably an oxymoron). Every law requires a sanction or penalty—imprisonment, confiscation, fining, taxing—and an enforcer. An increase of laws provides an ever greater number of pretexts for unscrupulous busybodies to twist laws to harass others, with the illusion that there is some moral sanction for this harassment.

1.3 Teleological Considerations.

Aristotle's notion of natural justice did not create in nature a second legal order from which the positive law was stipulated. The shadow of Plato cloaks much of natural law thinking, making it, arguably, anachronistic to view Aristotle as the father of natural law in the way that natural law has come to be known. Aristotle's notion of nature and natural is not analogous to Plato's grounding of law in the divine, or to his theory of the unchangeable and eternal forms.[71] Aristotle's notion of nature is a teleological principle explaining the change that natural substances undergo.[72] As such, nature is a principle of internal change or stability.[73]

In contrast, the artificial is a principle of change through accidental causes.[74] A natural substance undergoing change has a potency toward its nature, which may be actualized through this internal teleological principle of change. The changes in an artificial thing arise through external sources, rather than through some inner tendency.[75] The natural exists always, or for the most part.[76] Thus, exceptions from the natural are possible.[77]

Accordingly, Fred Miller places great weight on Aristotle's analogy of natural justice to Aristotle's statement of an alleged superiority of the right hand over the left hand.[78] Aristotle asserts the superiority of the right hand over the left by nature, even though, by practice, we may become ambidextrous, and he makes an analogy between this relationship and the natural superiority that natural justice has over legal justice, notwithstanding the pervasiveness of the less perfect form of legal justice.

> It is evident which sort of thing, among things capable of being otherwise, is by nature, and which is not, but is legal and conventional, assuming that both are equally changeable. And in all other things, the same distinction will apply; by nature, the right hand is stronger, yet it is possible that all men should come to be ambidextrous. The things which are just by virtue of convention and expediency are like measures; for wine and corn measures are not everywhere equal, but larger in wholesale and smaller in retail markets. Similarly, the things which are just not by nature but by human enactment are not everywhere the same, since constitutions are not the same, though there is but one that is everywhere by nature the best.[79]

> Things are just by nature or by law. But we must not regard the natural as being something which cannot by any possibility change; for even the things which are by nature partake of change. I mean, for instance, if we were all to practice always throwing with the left hand, we should become ambidextrous. But still by nature left is left, and the right is none the less naturally superior to the left hand, even if we do everything with the left as we do with the right. Nor because things change does it follow that they are not by nature. But if for the most part and for the greater length of time the left continues thus to be

left and the right right, that is by nature. The same is the case with things just by nature. Do not suppose that, if things change owing to our use, there is not therefore a natural justice; because there is. As to what we establish for ourselves and practice, that is thereby just, and we call it just according to law. Natural justice, then, is better than legal. But what we are in search of is political justice. Now the politically just is the legal, not the natural.[80]

Miller explains this analogy by analyzing Aristotle's discussion of right-handedness in various biological writings, where Aristotle uses teleological explanations of right-handedness.[81] Miller states that Aristotle argues that the right side is superior to the left "*because* it contains the origin of movement" (emphasis added), making the right necessary and useful to living things.[82] Miller notes further how Aristotle also supplies a material cause for the superiority of the right over the left, through heat.

Later in this chapter, I will argue that natural sociability is the material cause of natural justice, or epieikeia. Unlike Aristotle's obsolete biological explanation of the superiority of right over left, I argue that there is a high degree of plausibility, indeed a necessity, to grounding natural justice in human sociability, and that a failure to recognize this necessity and the inherent limitations of legal justice is, accordingly, a source of many legal injustices.

The import of this emphasis on teleological explanations analogized to concrete biological examples reveals the incongruity of traditional natural law notions with that of natural justice. It is anachronistic to view Aristotle's notions of natural justice and legal justice in traditional natural law terms, because such natural law interpretations inevitably have to minimize the degree of Aristotle's break from Plato's metaphysics.

More important for our purposes, under a Platonic natural law reading of Aristotle, there is little room for recognizing the inherent tension between the particularity of natural justice from the universality of the rules in legal justice. All that is retained of Aristotle in such a reading is the sense of the superiority of the natural over the legal, but in a framework contrasting two levels of universals: the legal and the natural. The sense of just how epieikeia works in such a framework is inevitably lost.[83]

Nonetheless, there are two sorts of problems involved in using Aristotle's grounding of natural justice in the natural political community as a model for the purposes of this inquiry: namely, the investigation of the origins of injustice in legal systems. The first problem is that all kinds of injustices arise in natural communities. Given the small scale of Aristotle's natural communities, there is also the problem of extending whatever justice exists in such natural communities to strangers and other natural communities.

The first concern, that injustices arise in natural communities, can be handled fairly easily. That a natural community is a necessary condition of natural justice in no wise makes it a sufficient condition of natural justice. Whatever justice might arise naturally between persons through the associative bond of friendship arises only where such a bond exists to some degree. Stated in this manner, it is almost a tautology. When natural justice is understood not as some abstract metaphysical notion of natural law theory, but, rather, as a concrete manifestation of the principle that there is a justice that arises naturally in the relationships of friends, it proves to be a rather unremarkable notion. The fact that injustices arise in such natural communities in no wise makes such a recognition more remarkable.

The second concern is a bit more difficult: namely, the problem of extending whatever justice there is in such small, natural communities to strangers or to different natural communities.[84] That the extension of justice is or ought to be the preeminent role of the legal system in no way makes the problem any less difficult, given the inherent limitations of the legal system already briefly discussed. The legal system simply cannot constitute a natural community (and this is a source of Dworkin's shortcomings). Aristotle defines the natural political community as requiring more than the provision of markets and the affording of protection from crime.[85] Rather, the natural political community within which equity naturally arises as a limitation on the defects of the legal system is one where families choose to live together out of friendship and share a self-sufficing (happy and honorable) life—with shared amusements and common sacrifices.

In sum, such natural friendships require a shared vision of the good life—something that the most recent liberal theoreticians emphatically reject. And yet, Aristotle also argues that such a natural political community is not to be viewed as a single unity, but as a plurality of different kinds of men, since similars do not constitute such a union. Indeed, Aristotle argues that too great a unity may destroy the natural bonds of the natural political community.[86]

That legal systems cannot establish political communities with the same degree of associative bonds that ground natural justice in the natural political communities is a very important point that requires a bit more elaboration, given its centrality to my argument. David Keyt argues that Hobbes gives a better account than does Aristotle of whether the "political community is a natural or artificial entity," since "in Aristotle's view man does not realize his nature by nature."[87] The nub of Keyt's argument is to question why Aristotle needs an art of politics or laws to habituate men to become good, if it is man's nature to be good. Keyt submits "that the bonds of justice that unite the members of a polis, unlike the bonds of instinct that unite the bees in a colony, are the bonds of (practical) reason, not the bonds of nature, and that the polis is an artificial rather than a natural entity."[88] If Keyt is right, then much of my preceding analysis is in error, and natural justice is, indeed, the metaphysical fiction the positivists say it is.

There are three basic replies to such a criticism. First, Keyt ignores a very fundamental component of Aristotelian teleology and metaphysics: namely, that of the distinction between being in act and potency. That something potentially has a nature by which it is perfected in no wise entails that it will fully actualize that nature in complete perfection.

Second, one merely has to appeal to concrete experience to support Aristotle's notion that the natural political community arises out of friendships, and friendships may not be constituted artificially, but arise naturally. I suppose one may accept the fact of experience that there is such a thing as friendship and that it arises naturally rather than artificially. However, the quarrel still might remain if someone were to deny that any aspect of friendship goes into the creation of political associations. This claim, because it could appear extreme, might be replaced with the more moderate view that natural associations or friendships, although present in the formation of political communities, are not the principal constituents. That this more moderate claim mirrors historical facts in the case of the modern nation state is fairly indisputable. I would certainly concur with Keyt that the modern nation state is held together mostly through bare coercion—but this fact does not warrant an argument that the modern nation state is at the pinnacle of teleological perfection, nor that man's nature is somehow irrelevant to assessing the perversity of the nation state by virtue of the bare fact of the nation state's existence.

By ending the analysis with the bare fact that the state exists and is predominantly artificial, Keyt effectively places the state beyond any moral criticism for not being in accord with man's natural needs. Indeed, the very viability of embarking on such a moral critique of the state is rendered more difficult, to the extent that Aristotelian teleological notions of human perfection and nature are jettisoned.

The criticism may be rebutted thirdly, and most trenchantly, by appealing to an analogy between health and natural justice, on the one hand, and the corresponding arts of medicine and the laws, on the other. The fact that a natural phenomenon such as health sometimes requires the intervention of the art of medicine does not mean that health is not a natural phenomenon, nor that it is completely fabricated through the art of medicine. Similarly, the fact that natural justice (and the natural community in which it is grounded) sometimes requires the intervention of laws does not mean that there are no such things as a natural community and natural justice, nor does it mean that a natural community and natural justice are completely fabricated by the art of law.

Moreover, the unfortunate accident that most persons in human history as well as in contemporary times have been unhealthy more often than healthy because of wars, diseases, poor nutrition, crime, or lack of exercise does not mean that the teleological notion of health is a meaningless artifact of language. Similarly, the pervasiveness of legal injustices in no way undercuts the intelligibility of a teleological notion of perfection such as natural justice. Accordingly, the pervasiveness of legal injustices throughout recorded history does not diminish the intelligibility of natural justice in the expressions of ordinary persons.

2. Ethos, or Custom

Having shown the relation of natural justice to legal justice and the central role of friendship in defining natural justice, we will next consider the role of custom in two very important senses. The first sense will explore why the inflexibility of the written law often renders it inferior to the customary law, even as custom and the written law are sometimes both viewed as law in the broadest possible sense. The second sense will explore the role of custom in serving as a bridge between the separate categories of natural justice and legal justice.

In doing so, we must take care not to confuse custom with nature, which is easy enough to do, since custom is the result of habitual practices that can occur for the most part, and, for Aristotle, the natural occurs always or for the most part. Customs can be perverse or natural and can render the written laws either onerous or just. As such, custom does not define the ideal so much as provide the means for reaching the ideal—that is, it provides the means for reforming perverse legal systems so that there is room for natural justice to breathe. While nature cannot be understood without custom, nature and custom must not be collapsed together.

2.1 The False Question on the Rule of Law, Custom, or Man.

While there is merit in the contention, advanced by the theorists of critical legal studies, that the legal system inherently reflects the interests of the powerful, the contention does not warrant an expansion of the legal system to promote leftist interests.[89] Rather, the merits of the contention lead to the opposite conclusion: namely, that the legal system's coercive role should be limited, and that the end of order and natural justice should be encouraged through natural cooperation (friendship) and custom rather than through naked force.

The law, in the absence of natural justice, is about as morally empty as a gun. If a murderer is attacking you, you might be able to use the gun to stop the murderer. But it may also be the case that the gun is used by the murderer against you, or that the person assumed to be a murderer is not a murderer at all.

Since no ideal form of government exists, laws, for the most part, reflect the interests of those who are or have been politically powerful. The politically powerful are not just those whose interests are represented by officials, but also those whose viewpoints predominate in the media. Law is coercion sanctioned by the sovereign power, whether that sovereign power is one, few, or the many. It never reflects the interests of everyone; it reflects only the interests of those who litigate or who control or influence the legislative process. This particular argument is not Aristotelian, but it is based upon speculations within an Aristotelian framework.

> The claim to be governed by laws, rather than by individual men and women, is one of the most popular and enduring boasts of republican rhetoric. Liberal republicans portray the rule of law as a set of hedges that blocks and channels the cruel fury of mobs and monarchs . . . Radical republicans portray the rule of law as the fair and impartial exercise of authority that one expects from a responsible and well-educated citizenry. . . . Both groups loudly proclaim the need to ensure that the community's laws rule supreme over the wills of particular individuals. . . . But republican boasts about the rule of law are very easy to undermine and ridicule . . . [as] laws are made, interpreted, and enforced by particular individuals, individuals who use their power to impose their understanding of a community's standards of mutual accountability on others. To insist that we are governed by laws, rather than by particular individuals and groups, merely conceals the political power of these individuals and groups by protecting it from direct challenge and criticism.[90]

A strong case can be made that Aristotle was far from a naive republican and had no illusions about the efficacy of law in limiting abuses by powerful persons. Indeed, a reading of Aristotle that does not interpret him as a naive republican is compatible with, and indeed a consequence of the recognition that natural justice is different in kind from and superior to legal justice.

Aristotle explores the question of whether it is better to be ruled by a man or by the law. The fact that he considers the question itself or considers some of the problems attendant to rule by man makes him something other than a naive republican. He identifies the risks and problems of both. The problem with rule by man: "He who bids man rule adds an element of the beast; for desire is a wild beast, and passion perverts the minds of rulers, even when they are the best of men."[91]

The problem with rule by the law: "The laws speak only in general terms, and cannot provide for circumstances. . . . The law is reason unaffected by desire. We are told that a patient should call in a physician; he will not get better if he is doctored out of a book."[92] He concludes that "a man may be a safer ruler than the written law, but not safer than the customary law."[93] For example, the practice of releasing an obviously dangerous criminal (such as a child murderer) at the completion of his sentence illustrates the stupidity of too rigid a notion of rule by law. Keeping an obviously violent criminal behind bars is somehow deemed a greater threat to the so-called rule of law than releasing him to prey upon the community.

While custom here is not necessarily coextensive with epieikeia, the description of custom in Aristotle's consideration of the question posed is very much like his description of epieikeia in his ethical writings, where he describes epieikeia as a virtue, or feature of natural justice, which corrects defects in legal justice because of the generality of legal rules, rules that would be overly harsh if rigidly applied in the circumstances.[94] Of course, this similarity in descriptions does not permit us to collapse the two very different notions of custom and epieikeia together. But it does serve to emphasize that even if Aristotle backs away from endorsing out-and-out rule by man here, custom and epieikeia are features possessed by men and not the written law.

The fact that he refers to the customary law here does not undercut this point, given Aristotle's sometimes broad and sometimes narrow uses of *nomoi*. It is clear by the context of comparing customary law to written law here that the written law corresponds more to contemporary notions of the positive law, and the customary law is as broad as are the habits of citizens in a society. When epieikeia has become a habit or custom, that is clearly a superior situation to one in which the customs are not always at the level of epieikeia. This is why custom and epieikeia must not be collapsed.

There may be perverse communities in which the customs are perverse and harsh—the very opposite of epieikeia. Although Aristotle does not say so here, it is clear to me that he emphasizes custom because this implicitly leaves room for epieikeia. In contrast, if he had emphasized rule by the written law, this would leave no room for epieikeia.

At bottom, Aristotle is presupposing in this passage that custom, like epieikeia, arises out of the natural political community and the ordinary ways, outside of the law, in which the natural community interacts. Thus custom, to the extent that it exemplifies epieikeia (and only to that extent) potentially mitigates both the arbitrary rule of a man and the rigid inflexibility of written law.[95] The notion that law, in the absence of custom, somehow suffices to limit the rule of man does not accurately reflect the subtlety of Aristotle's reflections in this area.

2.2 Custom's Role in Mediating Between the Law and Justice.

Aristotle notes that since enactments must be universal, it is impossible that everything be set down in writing, particularly when actions are required.[96] This statement of what should be common sense might seem extraordinary today, for anyone visiting a law library. The number of volumes of federal cases between 1970 and 1980 equals the number of volumes for the 180 years prior to that. And that between 1980 and 1990 dwarfs the number of volumes between 1970 and 1980. The numbers of statutes, regulations, and federal agencies since the 1930s, 1960s, 1970s, and 1980s similarly indicate this almost exponential growth. Dworkin's title *Law's Empire* certainly describes the current arrangement.

Related to Aristotle's notion that everything cannot be written down in legal prescriptions is his notion of custom.[97] Society cannot function without custom.[98] The administration of existing laws cannot work very well without customs indicating a disposition to respect and obey the laws. Aristotle notes that lightly changing laws can defeat any customary respect or obedience toward law.[99] This is because obedience and respect for the law is a custom, and customs are habits of a community, cultivated over time.[100]

Law has no power to command habitual obedience, except by customs developed over time.[101] Consequently, extending the range of law to such an extent that no single person could comprehend it and its enforcement was selective would, likewise, defeat any habit of respect and obedience toward the legal order. The legal order then would become a set of traps for the unwary and political tools to dispose of rivals, rather than a pedagogical expression of the shared goods of society.

The justice or injustice of a law cannot be evaluated apart from the natural justice and customs of the political community. Accordingly, a constitution established by law that is not democratic may be administered democratically, owing to the habits and education (that is, the customs) of the citizenry.[102] Conversely, a constitution established by law inclining to democracy may be administered in an oligarchical spirit, where the habits and education of the citizenry undermine the laws.[103] Custom affects what laws are enacted, the ways in which laws are obeyed or enforced, the extent of a society's reliance on professionalized lawyers to resolve disputes, and the degree to which citizens in a society are to retain control over their lives or defer to governmental power. Just as laws may be just or perverse, so, too, may customs be just or perverse. Indeed, customs ultimately render the laws just or perverse.

Customs, to the extent that they may be perverse, may be unnatural, in the sense of being contrary to the natural sociability of men that is requisite for human happiness and well-being. Although the natural in one sense is that which occurs always or for the most part, the natural must not be confused with or collapsed into the customary. In another sense, the natural is the potential in humans for sociability and happiness, even if that potential may not seem to be actualized with the type of frequency one ordinarily associates with something occurring always or for the most part.

If one fails to incorporate the act-potency distinction as an essential feature of one's notion of the natural, one runs the danger of reducing the natural to that which is customary, in the sense of occurring always or for the most part—an unacceptable reduction. While legal reforms cannot ignore prevailing customs, this does not mean that customs cannot or should not be changed, in part through the laws, in part through education, and in part through the natural sociability of men (as a potency).

As certain functions of citizenship become professionalized, such as the functions of politician or lawyer, they often become obstacles to the establishment of customs of participation in the political process. High crime rates, high rates of litigation, the alienation of modern voters from the political process, and the general disaffection with politics are all symptoms of a weakening of the unwritten customs that are required to make society and its laws function as intended. Aristotle emphasized that customs have more weight and relate to more important matters than the written laws.

Custom turns things into nature.[104] Moral character derives from custom. Accordingly, natural justice requires the habits of just relationships between citizens over time. While some customs can be reduced to written laws and written laws can be enacted to combat other customs, the efficacy of laws ultimately turns on the customs of the political community. As the role of law expands into areas previously occupied by custom, this expansion can, in turn, indicate a weakening of custom. However, there are not enough police and prisons for a society to function where law displaces custom as the basis for habitual cooperation between citizens.

The art of legislation is conceived by Aristotle as having the role of inducing the development of certain customs.[105] As such, the law cannot replace custom. Rather, law has the pedagogical role of disposing the morally weaker persons in a society to act contrary to their habits of vice and to develop a virtuous habit over time. As such, the law is like a medical prescription for a mildly sick patient: by itself, it can never revive a terminally ill patient. The law must be tailored to the customs of the community. Where legislators ignore these customs, they not only undercut their own specific designs, but ultimately they circumvent respect for the law itself.

Custom, although it encompasses the unwritten practices involved in interpretations of the law by its elite practitioners, is, obviously, broader than Dworkin's community of principle. Custom is broader than the common law, although much of common law is undoubtedly the result of writing down in legal opinions what has become customary. Consideration of custom in the traditional jurisprudential debate about the nature of law does not consider custom within the broader Aristotelian question of its role in habituating communities toward virtuous or perverse ends.

Rather, the traditional jurisprudential question concerns whether law is restricted to legislation, a view advocated by Bentham, or may also include the judge-made common law, viewed as custom. This notion of custom is certainly a very narrow view, probably arising from the narrowness of the question of traditional jurisprudence that limits its concerns to the nature of law.[106]

By contrast, for Aristotle, nature in general is a causal explanation of internal change or self-movement toward an end in a substance, and the artificial is an accidental, or external cause of change or movement in a substance. In ethics, nature explains voluntary virtuous actions toward a good, whereas something artificial, like the laws, causes involuntary action through external violence or coercion to induce the development of habits of virtue. Accordingly, custom is the bridge between the artificial and the natural. It is a bridge by which habits repeated over time result in customs favorable to virtue and the natural, or vice versa.

Murphy gives two examples of the ways in which custom can misinterpret the legislator's intention: "The equal rights guaranteed by the Fourteenth Amendment become interpreted as separate but equal; the *Brown* decision forcing integration of public schools sent white students to private schools."[107]

The Fourteenth Amendment was adopted in the Reconstruction era, immediately after a bloody Civil War, as part of an effort to afford African Americans equal protection and due process of law. But the equal-protection clause of the Fourteenth Amendment was initially interpreted, under prevailing customs, as permitting discrimination against African Americans by educating them in separate schools, as long as the schools were of equal quality to the schools attended by Caucasian Americans.

When the *Brown* decision held "separate but equal" to violate the equal-protection clause of the Fourteenth Amendment, the efforts to forcibly integrate the public schools were, in effect, undercut by custom, because most white students either left the public schools for private schools or moved to the suburbs. In one case, the law was interpreted consistent with custom, and in the latter circumstance, the law attempted to change custom. But ultimately, custom got the better of the law and was more important than law in determining the actual justice or injustice of the outcome.

In one sense, it is the custom of the people more than the nature of their laws that ultimately determines the harshness of their legal system. Yet on the other hand, excessive changes in laws, and, by implication, an overexpansion of the legislative function in a society, can adversely affect the customs required for just functioning of the legal system. The interplay of these two seemingly conflicting principles—the notion, on the one hand, that custom is more important than law, and yet, on the other hand, that law can adversely affect custom—contains the core of Aristotle's treatment of custom in his ethical and political writings.[108]

While man is by nature political and has a potential to form friendships, and while such friendships are coextensive with the virtue of justice, none of the moral excellences (including justice) arise in us by nature or contrary to nature. Instead, all moral excellences require the cultivation of habits of virtue.[109] And the cultivation of this inherent potential for virtue through the development of habits of virtue is the role of legislators.[110] Namely, legislators make citizens good by helping them form habits or customs.[111] Indeed, the effect of a legal system on the customs of its citizens is what distinguishes a good constitution from a bad constitution.

Yet, the customs of the citizens can affect the nature of a constitution, making a good one bad and vice versa. This would seem to indicate that while Aristotle places a significant emphasis on the art of legislation, he nonetheless recognizes that it is subsidiary, as an art, to nature, and that cus-

tom is the bridge between law and nature. As such, custom is neither exclusively natural nor artificial, but has an element of both the natural and the
artificial in it, just as does the political community that it defines.

3. Epieikeia

We now turn to epieikeia, that intangible virtue that is most often translated
as equity and that corrects for the harshness arising out of the universality
of legal rules. We will consider the topic of epieikeia from five vantage points.
From the first, we will establish the degree to which epieikeia is different
from contemporary notions of legal equity and the extralegal principle of
equality. This will enable us to explore more clearly, as our second point,
the principal ontological characteristic of epieikeia, that is, its particularity.
The third area examined is the epistemology of epieikeia, manifested in the
distinction between the wisdom that can grasp the particularity of natural
justice and the knowledge that only comprehends universals. The fourth
area explored is the relationship between epieikeia and mercy and friendship. The fifth and final perspective involves an attempt to make an even
sharper distinction between epieikeia and legalistic bodies of rules—even
those with so-called equity as their motive. This five-part argument will, hopefully, provide the constructive framework and an alternative to the inadequate jurisprudential approaches epitomized by Dworkin and the positivists.

3.1 Epieikeia Contrasted to Legal Equity and Equality.

Sometimes justice requires a flexibility and mercy (a forgiveness of certain
facts) that correct legal justice by means of a notion of equity that is much
broader than the traditional notion of equity in Anglo-Saxon law. The latter
notion more closely approximates fairness as a proportion than it does forgiveness and making exceptions. Accordingly, there are three striking features in the following passages describing Aristotelian epieikeia: (1) the absence of any notion of fairness, equality, or impartiality in his description of
this virtue, (2) his emphasis on forgiveness, not insisting on one's rights, and
taking less than what one is owed, (3) his emphasis on the act of judging
and distinguishing forgivable from unforgivable acts, or important from
unimportant facts.

"What is called judgement, in virtue of which men are said to be forgiving
and to have judgement, is the right discrimination of the equitable. This is

shown by the fact that we say the equitable man is above all others a man of forgiveness and identify equity with forgiveness about certain facts."[112]

"After this, we must enquire into equity. What is it? And what is its field and sphere? Equity and the equitable man is he who is inclined to take less than his legal rights."[113]

> Equity must be applied to forgivable actions; and it must make us distinguish between wrongdoings on the one hand, and mistakes, or misfortunes, on the other. (A misfortune is an act, not due to wickedness, that has unexpected results; a mistake is an act, also not due to turpitude, that has results that might have been expected; a wrongdoing has results that might have been expected, but *is* due to turpitude.) Equity bids us be merciful to the weakness of human nature; to think less about the laws than about the man who framed them, and less about what he said than about what he meant; not to consider the actions of the accused so much as his choice, nor this or that detail so much as the whole story; to ask not what a man is now but what he has always or for the most part been. It bids us remember benefits rather than injuries, and benefits received rather than benefits conferred; to be patient when we are wronged; to settle a dispute by negotiation and not by force; to prefer arbitration to litigation . . . [114]

In contrast, there is an entirely different emphasis in the modern definition of equity that follows. There is no mention of forgiveness, mercy, or making exceptions at all. In fact, the very opposite is emphasized, by means of the notions of impartiality and fairness (the latter of which is practically a synonym for impartiality). It would take quite a leap to argue that forgiveness and making exceptions with respect to certain rules amounted to the same thing as impartiality.

As defined in the *American Heritage Desk Dictionary*, the first two meanings of the word *equity* are (1) the condition or quality of being just, impartial, and fair, (2) something that is just, impartial, and fair.

In 30 *Corpus Juris Secundum* Equity, p. 517, section 109, it is stated: "It has frequently been stated that equality is equity. The maxim is one of broad application, and should never be departed from or in any wise rejected unless it is clearly not intended to apply. It is applicable to burdens as well as to rights, and means that, in the absence of relations or conditions requiring a different result, equity will treat all members of a class as on an equal footing, and will distribute benefits or impose burdens and charges either equally or in proportion to the several interests, and without preferences."[115]

The forgiveness and mercy of epieikeia is so different from the impartiality of contemporary senses of *equity* that their underlying notions of justice must ultimately be recognized as very different.

This is why epieikeia for Aristotle is not a separate set of legalistic rules supplementing laws, as is the case for the equity of Anglo-American law. Instead, it involves the correction of the harshness arising out of the universality of legal rules, through the exercise of practical wisdom by persons (not rules) who ignore the legal rule in particular circumstances, because the object of this practical wisdom is something particular.

> What creates the problem is that the equitable is just, but not the legally just but a correction of legal justice. The reason is that all law is universal but about some things it is not possible to make a universal statement which will be correct. In those cases, then, in which it is necessary to speak universally, but not possible to do so correctly, the law takes the usual case, though it is not ignorant of the possibility of error. And it is none the less correct; for the error is not in the law nor in the legislator but in the nature of the thing, since the matter of practical affairs is of this kind from the start. When the law speaks universally, then, and a case arises on it which is not covered by a universal statement, then it is right, when the legislator fails us and has erred by over-simplicity, to correct the omission—to say what the legislator himself would have said had he been present, and would have put into his law if he had known. Hence the equitable is just, and better than one kind of justice—not better than absolute justice but better than the error that arises from the absoluteness of the statement. And this is the nature of the equitable, a correction of law where it is defective owing to its universality. In fact this is the reason why all things are not determined by law, viz. that about some things it is impossible to lay down a law, so that a decree is needed.[116]

For this reason, there is a sense in which the kind of judgment involved in epieikeia has to be different from that involved in the modern notion of equity. The former emphasizes a departure from a general rule in consideration of particular ends, whereas the latter emphasizes adherence to a general rule with utter indifference to any particular ends.

> Now all the states we have considered converge, as might be expected, on the same point; for when we speak of judgement and understanding and practical wisdom and comprehension we credit the

same people with possessing judgement and comprehension and with having practical wisdom and understanding. For all these faculties deal with ultimates; i.e. with particulars; and being a man of understanding and of good judgement or of forgiveness consists in being able to judge about the things with which practical wisdom is concerned; for the equities are common to all good men in relation to other men. Now all things which have to be done are included among particulars or ultimates; for not only must the man of practical wisdom know particular facts, but understanding and judgement are also concerned with things to be done, and these are ultimates. And comprehension is concerned with the ultimates in both directions; for both the primary definitions and the ultimates are objects of comprehension and not of argument, and in demonstrations comprehension grasps the unchangeable and primary definitions, while in practical reasoning it grasps the last and contingent fact;, i.e. the second proposition. For these are the starting-points of that for the sake of which, since the universals are reached from the particulars; of these therefore we must have perception, and this is comprehension. . . . Therefore, we ought to attend to the undemonstrated sayings and opinions of experienced and older people or of people of practical wisdom not less than to demonstrations; for because experience has given them an eye they see aright.[117]

In the above Aristotelian formulation, epieikeia is defined as a practical wisdom that cannot be taught, because its object consists of particular circumstances and substantive ends in the realm of action. The just results achieved through epieikeia cannot be articulated as universal precedents on the basis of which the just action can be replicated. In the above Aristotelian formulation, it is abundantly clear that epieikeia cannot be codified into a body of universal rules.

This may be contrasted with the following illustrations, taken from a modern legal dictionary, of the various manifestations of equity as exemplified in legalistic rules. The notion of equity as a separate body of legalistic rules supplementing another body of legal rules arose out of the separate ecclesiastical jurisdictions (or courts of equity) that competed with the law courts of the king in medieval England. Where one could not obtain an "adequate remedy at law," one turned to the equity courts for redress.[118]

Because of this competition for causes of action between the two jurisdictions, the equity courts were more prone to invent new rules not recognized by the courts of law.[119] Hence arose the notions of equitable assignment, equitable conversion, equitable defense, equitable distribution, equitable lien, equitable mortgage, equitable ownership, equitable redemption, and equitable relief, which are defined below for illustrative purposes. Gradually, the equity courts became as legalistic as the common-law courts, developing their own separate jurisprudential rules and deference to precedent. The notion of separate equitable and legal jurisdictions was preserved throughout the nineteenth century in American courts, and only recently were the two jurisdictions merged, so that the same court could apply both sets of rules.

"While a court of equity is a forum for the administration of justice, 'equity' is not synonymous in meaning with 'justice' or 'natural justice,' administered without fixed rules, although the terms have sometimes been so used. On the contrary, equity is a separate but incomplete system of jurisprudence, administered side by side with the common law, having its own fixed precedents and principles, now scarcely more elastic than those of the law. The formalism distinguishing law and equity is largely historical."[120]

The fourth sense of *equity,* as defined in the *American Heritage Desk Dictionary,* is: (a) justice applied in circumstances not covered by civil or common law, (b) a system of rules and principles supplementing civil and common law and overriding such law in cases where a fair or just solution cannot be provided, (c) a right or claim considered appropriate for a court of equity.

Black's Law Dictionary (fifth edition) defines *equitable assignment* as an assignment that, though invalid at law, will be recognized and enforced in equity. *Black's* also defines the following terms:

Equitable conversion: A doctrine commonly applied when death intervenes between the signing of an agreement to sell real estate and the date of transfer of title, resulting in treating land as personalty and personalty as land under certain circumstances.

Equitable defense: Formerly, a defense that was only available in a court of equity. With the procedural merger of law and equity, however, equitable defenses can be raised along with legal defenses in the same action.

Equitable distribution: No-fault divorce statutes in certain states (for example, New Jersey) grant courts the power to distribute equitably upon divorce all property legally and beneficially acquired during marriage by husband and wife, or either of them, whether legal title lies in their joint or individual names.

Equitable lien: A right, not existing at law, to have specific property applied in whole or in part to payment of a particular debt or class of debts.

Equitable mortgage: Any agreement to post certain property as security before the security agreement is formalized.

Equitable ownership: The ownership interest of one who has equitable as contrasted with legal ownership of property, as in the case of a trust beneficiary.

Equitable redemption: The act or process by which a mortgagor redeems his property after payment of the mortgage debt. The purchase of the equity of redemption after foreclosure has commenced.

Equitable relief: That species of relief sought in a court with equity powers as, for example, in the case of one seeking an injunction or specific performance instead of money damages.

In another so-called equitable procedure, the state of Michigan took possession of an automobile jointly owned by a husband and wife, calling the auto a "public nuisance." The justification for this action was that the husband had used it when with a prostitute, even though the wife had not known about the illegal use of the vehicle. This case (*Bennis v. Michigan*) was termed a "nuisance abatement proceeding."[121]

That the creative fashioning of new legal rules is not the same thing as Aristotle's notion of epieikeia ought to be fairly obvious, at this point. The creative invention of new rules through flexible interpretation and the related notion of judicial discretion are fundamentally different from the kind of wisdom that can recognize when rules ought to be ignored completely. Impartiality and equality are compatible with the judgment that emphasizes a regard for generalizable rules, but are utterly incompatible with the type of judgment that has for its objects particular substantive ends involving the good for particular humans rather than for the realm of universal rules.

As is argued later, a notion of justice that reduces itself to a rigid egalitarianism or impartiality loses a great deal in the process. Namely, it reduces all justice to an inflexible (and therefore inequitable) legalistic justice. Likewise, a justice that reduces itself to rules that may be rationally justified becomes harsh and inequitable in the Aristotelian sense, because it fails to acknowledge the role and importance of a less articulate practical wisdom in rendering the rules more just. This notion of practical wisdom cannot be accommodated in the Anglo-American legalistic set of rules called equity. Equity is not merely a competition between the rules of the courts with equitable jurisdictions and those with legal jurisdictions recognized in medieval England. In short, equity, in the proper Aristotelian sense, cannot be summarized in a general rule and is not simply a notion of equality or impartiality—particularly where impartiality is incompatible with forgiveness of errors and mercy.[122]

Accordingly, equity, a central and essential ingredient of Aristotle's notion of natural justice, is not present in legal justice and not present in the

Dworkian notion of justice as simple equality. Equity is, in fact, essential to
a true sense of natural justice. Moreover, in the absence of this notion, the
very idea of natural justice becomes a paradoxical, reified abstraction, open
to ridicule by positivists. This notion of equity cannot be adequately understood apart from an understanding of the natural political community and
of the degree to which equity depends on the strength of the associative
bonds in a natural political community. These bonds are the habits developed over time, that is to say, the customs of a community that dispose it to
act with equity and natural justice.

Indeed, this vigorous and enlivened notion of equity, arising from the virtuous dispositions and associative bonds of a natural political community,
distinguishes it from the narrower equity arising from the jurisdictional dif-
ferentiations of the Anglo-American courts or medieval law and jurisprudence. Equity is not only exercised by officials in adjudication of disputes,
but also between members of a natural political community.[123] In one very
broad sense, people are equitable if they are "patient when they are wronged,
settle disputes by litigation rather than by force, prefer arbitration to litigation."[124] An equitable person is someone who "tends to take less than his
share though he has the law on his side."[125]

In another sense more specific to legal justice, equity is a "correction of
legal justice" and is superior to legal justice.[126] This latter sense of equity tai-
lors legal justice to the particular or individual, out of recognition that the
universality or generality of a legal rule may, indeed, render legal justice inequitable and an affront to natural justice. "And this is the nature of the equitable, a correction of law where it is defective owing to its universality."[127]

3.2 The Ontology of Epieikeia: Its Particularity.

Nothing could be more contrary to Dworkin's notion of integrity than
epieikeia. It may be recalled that integrity was Dworkin's notion that legal
rules must be interpreted coherently with his principle of equal concern
(justice reduced to equality). Of course, if epieikeia were reducible to a rigid
egalitarianism, Dworkin's notion of integrity would be compatible with
epieikeia.

But insistence on equality is not the central concern of epieikeia, and, indeed, epieikeia can involve a certain equitable inequality.[128] If, as in Dworkin,
concern for equality answered all questions about legal justice, then there
would be no room and no need for the flexibility and particularity inherent
in Aristotelian epieikeia.

In one sense, Dworkin's doctrine might appear to be an advance over that of the positivists, insofar as he is willing to go beyond the rule as expressly legislated by the legislator. That is, to say, he considers another principle, namely, equality. But ultimately, Dworkin's doctrine is less accommodating to the flexibility inherent in Aristotelian epieikeia than are the views of a positivist such as H. L. A. Hart. At least Hart recognizes so-called hard cases, where the adjudication of legal rules is unclear and subject to disagreement because of legislative gaps in the law.[129] In such hard cases, Hart argues for some minimal level of discretionary judgment in adjudicative decisions.

But Dworkin rejects such discretion, because his egalitarian principle of integrity ultimately fills any gaps in the law. In this latter sense, the allowance for discretion by a traditional positivist, such as Hart, might appear closer to the spirit of flexibility underlying epieikeia. At the same time, however, Hart limits such discretion to so-called gaps in the law where the legislature failed to address the specific question being adjudicated, a limitation not necessarily applicable to epieikeia.

Hart's notion of discretion, given its relativism or indeterminacy, also differs from epieikeia insofar as epieikeia does not imply that there are many right answers, but only that the correct answer is particular and not derivable from a universal. Otherwise the particularity of epieikeia cannot be the object of practical wisdom, which it is in Aristotle, but merely one alternative opinion among many. Moreover, epieikeia is broader than having discretion to deal with so-called gaps in the law, since legislators can be morally wrong and enact unjust laws. And epieikeia is narrower than such discretion, to the extent that it is a virtue or perfection of practical wisdom that results in a singular correct outcome, and not a mere opinion.

For Dworkin, universal rules enacted by legislators, and extralegal principles of integrity adjudicated by Herculean judges (the community of principle), are sufficient to determine the outcomes of all legal disputes. Accordingly, there is no room for epieikeia at all in Dworkin—unless one somehow can argue that epieikeia is reducible to equality—a position emphatically rejected here. Epieikeia is not mere tolerance, to the extent that tolerance is indifferent to moral content and is relativistic.

At any rate, there is only room for epieikeia where one acknowledges that the realm of human action is not completely comprehensible through universal rules. As first intimated in the section in Chapter 2 where I criticized Dworkin's emphasis on interpretation, the following three positions are very different:

1. Dworkin's integrity: holding that there is a single interpretation or universal rule that ought to be applied in a given situation;

2. Hart's discretion: holding that there are sometimes alternative interpretations or universal rules that may be applied to a given situation where no single rule has been stipulated by whatever group has sovereign authority; and

3. Aristotle's epieikeia: holding that there is a single correct course of action in a given situation, but that this course of action is not necessarily exemplified in a single interpretation or universal rule, but may, in fact, require a departure from or an exception to a universal rule.

What distinguishes the latter from the first two positions is that epieikeia is concerned with substantive ends or the realm of human action, to the exclusion of any concern with rationalizing the substantive ends into a rule that can be generalized as a precedent.[130] On the other hand, the first two positions, as much as they differ from each other, differ to a greater extent from the third position in their disregard of substantive ends, a disregard exemplified by their exclusive focus on the interpretive level.[131]

Accordingly, there is little room for the broadened Aristotelian notion of epieikeia in either Hart's or Dworkin's jurisprudential theories, and deciding which of the two contemporary thinkers does the most damage to epieikeia is difficult. With Hart's approach, as law develops and more rules are legislated over time to fill any gaps in the law, any role for discretion, arguably, diminishes or disappears. For this reason, according to Roger A. Shiner, Dworkin conceives his debate with Hart on the issue of discretion and hard cases as a merely historical or factual dispute. Dworkin analogizes gaps in the law to holes in a constrictive doughnut, holes that Dworkin believes have been filled with his extralegislative interpretative principles of equality.

But the essence of Aristotle's notion of epieikeia, as very aptly explained by Roger A. Shiner, is not about filling in gaps in the law or about whether such gaps exist. Indeed, Dworkin and Hart are engaged in a misleading and poorly conceived debate by focusing on the question of gaps in the law. That very focus greatly narrows the range of flexibility required, by restricting the emphasis to the level of legal interpretation. This excludes any consideration of the interaction of law with substantive ends at the level of human action, which is inherently particular. As a result, this focus makes the legal system appear more rational and objective than it really is.

Shiner convincingly argues that Aristotle's notion of epieikeia differs from the assumptions underlying the debate between Dworkin and Hart on the adjudication of hard cases because Aristotle, unlike Dworkin and Hart, prop-

erly considers the nature of the subject matter and the ontology of equitable
judgment.

> The element which uniquely distinguishes Aristotle's discussion of
> equity is the emphasis on . . . "matter," on the subject-matter itself of
> equitable judgment. The emphasis is explicit only in the *NE* (cf.
> 1137b17–19). The mistake, Aristotle says, is really in neither the law
> nor the legislator, but "in the nature of the business" . . . "for from
> the very start such is the matter of practical affairs." . . . This dis-
> tinction in the kind of truth attainable by each kind of science re-
> flects the nature of the subject-matter of each kind of science, a fea-
> ture of the . . . "matter," with which the scientist or the practical
> agent has to work. It is the mark of an educated man, Aristotle tells
> us in a famous passage, to look for precision in each class of things
> just so far as the nature of the subject permits (*NE* 1094b23–5). . . .
> Decrees and flexible rules are necessary because of the subject-mat-
> ter, not because of inefficiency and poor craftsmanship. . . . Practical
> wisdom consists generally in judging correctly about the particular
> case when, because of the "matter" of practical judgment, there are
> no absolutely universal truths to determine judgment as to what
> shall be done. Equity consists also in correct judgment about a par-
> ticular case in the face of an absence of universal truth.[132]

Thus, epieikeia is necessary in adjudications not because of legislative omis-
sions (or gaps in the law), but because the very nature of justice and its subject matter, from an ontological standpoint, are particular and, therefore,
not adequately comprehended in either universal legal rules or universal
principles for interpreting such rules (such as Dworkin's principle of equal
concern).

The particularity at the root of Aristotle's notion of justice makes the centrality of epieikeia understandable. Fred Miller Jr. has recently described
Aristotle's notion of justice as that of a "moderate individualism." It is individualistic, for Miller, because the common good for Aristotle requires that
the just polity "must promote the common advantage of its members, in the
sense of the *mutual* advantage rather than at the overall advantage. That is,
it must aim at the virtue and happiness of *each and every* citizen, not at a collective goal attained by the polis as a whole but not by its members, or in
which some members partake to the exclusion of others."[133]

Miller elaborates further that this "political individualism reflects a deep
metaphysical commitment to the individual." He quotes Edward Zeller to

emphasize that this is the "fundamental point of divergence of Aristotle from Plato:

"'In politics as in metaphysics the central point with Plato is the Universal, with Aristotle the Individual. The former demands that the whole should realise its ends without regard to the interests of the individuals: the latter that it should be reared upon the satisfaction of all individual interests that have a true title to be regarded.'"[134]

One can fully agree with Miller's and Zeller's interpretation of Aristotle's notion of justice as being individualistic and particular in this sense, without necessarily buying in to Miller's reconstruction of Aristotle as "entailing" a theory of "natural rights," however distinct those natural rights are from modern, post-Enlightenment theories of natural right. Indeed, a fully elaborated understanding of Aristotle's notion of epieikeia, as argued for in this book, makes this particularistic view of justice fully visible, thus rendering Miller's natural rights reconstruction of Aristotle largely unnecessary.

Moreover, there are dangers attendant to a natural right reconstruction of Aristotle, to the degree that Aristotle becomes so transmuted into the contemporary legalistic-rights paradigm that epieikeia becomes obscured from view. To the extent that epieikeia is a notion that ought to be recovered as a framework for bringing into relief contemporary legal injustices that would not be fully visible as unjust within a natural right framework, I have scrupulously avoided such natural right reconstructions of Aristotle in the present study.[135] That said, my primary reason for elaborating on Miller's views here is to provide another vantage point for seeing the central role that epieikeia plays in rendering political justice so particular and individualistic (in the senses described above) in Aristotle.

As I have intimated throughout this book, emphasizing the particularity of epieikeia is not the pathway to indeterminate results or moral relativism. It must be remembered that epieikeia is a virtue, and, as such, its complete perfection in act results in a single correct course of conduct or a decree, albeit not one necessarily universalizable into other circumstances that are only superficially similar. Indeed, the very evolution of the law through outright legislative reform, or the resort to "legal fictions" or "public policy" rationales by judges are all imperfect, tacit, and often belated recognitions of the need for even weakened notions of epieikeia, where legal injustices are initially tolerated for only so long, based upon the rigid application of a legal rule that does not fit a situation until the system changes itself. The notion is masked and distorted by appeals to the need for some judicial discretion or, on the contrary, for greater deference to legislative bodies. Both of these distort what is really at stake, as far as justice is concerned, because they limit themselves to procedural ends (Lon Fuller's prudential art of law concerns), rather than the substantive ends of justice.

At any rate, epieikeia is only indeterminate with respect to the governing legal norm to which it requires an exception. Epieikeia is not indeterminate with regard to the just outcome that it demands. Indeed, Aristotle also emphasizes that "the principles of equity are permanent and changeless" as features of natural justice.[136] This passage is fully compatible with the other discussions of epieikeia in Aristotle's writings that describe epieikeia as "a correction of law where it is defective owing to its universality," as a readiness to forgive, and as a part of political and natural justice.[137]

Although it is these latter features of epieikeia that I have chosen to emphasize, I have repeatedly distinguished the universality and necessity of acting in conformity with epieikeia from the universality of the legal rule from which epieikeia carves out an exception. Arguing against grounding justice in abstract rules because of their rigid universality is very different from holding that it is universally just to make exceptions to the universality of such rules.

3.3 Epistemology of Epieikeia: Wisdom Versus Knowledge.

Corresponding to an ontology that emphasizes the particular over the universal legal rule is an epistemology of practical judgment.[138] Aristotle remarks that young men can become geometricians and mathematicians, since these deal with universals, whereas it takes the experience of an older man to attain the practical wisdom required to discern the particulars required for epieikeia.[139] Indeed, insofar as the practical judgment required for epieikeia is concerned ultimately with particulars rather than universals, it is concerned with objects not of knowledge, but of perception. Aristotle distinguishes the type of perception involved in epieikeia from the perception of sensible qualities, arguing that the perception involved in epieikeia is akin to that through which one perceives that a particular figure is a triangle. As such, it is not subject to demonstration, but is a judgment that grasps the particulars underlying actions and relationships between men. This particularity inherent in epieikeia is why it cannot be reduced to some abstract formula, whether conceived as legal rules or as principles.

One consequence of this particularity is that adjudication involves more than the mere application of the law to a particular set of facts. The contemporary focus on the question of the nature of the law and its interpretation is less central to Aristotle; his concern is the broader question of what is just in the circumstances. As such, a narrow technical knowledge of what is the law is less important than practical wisdom.

> [In *Politics* 1253a38 and *EN* 1134b31] Aristotle describes adjudication as the determination of justice or injustice rather than as the determination of whether laws have been broken. If Aristotle simply identified law and justice, then we could ignore this distinction since the determination of injustice and of whether a law had been broken would be identical. . . .
>
> Adjudicators can no more than individual actors know justice simply by referring to laws, whether written or unwritten. Ideally, adjudicators must be "living [*empsuxon*] justice" (*EN* 1132a20), since they should know what a just individual would do in a particular situation in order to render the best judgment.
>
> Adjudication thus demands something more than the application of general rules to particular cases. It requires prudential rather than technical judgment. . . . The most important qualification for an Aristotelian adjudicator then is a just disposition—that is why an ideal adjudicator is "living justice"—rather than the special knowledge of the law we demand of judges. Given this understanding of adjudication, it should not be surprising that Aristotle expresses little interest in modern ideas about the separation of law and politics through the creation of an independent and politically neutral judiciary.[140]

Such wisdom cannot be inculcated into a professional class, but can only result from living a life of virtue, as if one were part of the community rather than indifferent and impartial to it. This sense of justice and adjudication does not carry with it the aridity of modern notions of impartiality.

3.4 Epieikeia: Forgiveness and Friendship.

Accordingly, there is another sense of Aristotelian equity that broadens it even further. This is the notion that it is a part of equity to forgive.[141] As Aristotle himself puts it: "What is called judgement, in virtue of which men are said to be forgiving and to have judgment, is the right discrimination of the equitable [that is, epieikeia]. This is shown by the fact that we say the equitable man is above all others a man of forgiveness and identify equity [epieikeia] with forgiveness about certain facts."[142]

Such forgiveness is not the mercy of an impartial professional judge or a technical expert on what the law is; it is, rather, a virtue cultivated by living in the community. It encompasses all citizens, whether or not they are acting in official adjudicative capacities. And this forgiveness looks not merely to the specific transgression—the fact that a person has broken a given law, with its penalties—but distinguishes wrongdoing from mistakes and misfortunes, and takes into consideration the history of a person in the context of the good he or she has done as compared against the present infraction.[143]

Such equitableness is certainly not the equality associated with impartiality, the notion of no man being above the law and all being treated alike, with rigid equality. For two contemporary examples in which legislators, officials, and judges acted with a harshness completely incompatible with epieikeia, one only has to look at the *Harmelin* case discussed in Chapters 1 and 2, in which a nonviolent first-time drug offender was sentenced to life in prison without possibility of parole, or the prosecution and imprisonment of persons for making improvements on land classified as a wetland by the Army Corps of Engineers.

The very idea of imprisoning persons for such petty offenses, when murderers receive lighter sentences or remain unpunished, is revolting to any natural sense of justice. The very idea that prosecutors first target a person and then manipulate the law so that it can apply to that person's actions, as happened in the prosecution of Senator D'Amato's brother, exemplifies a complete absence of epieikeia in the sense discussed in this section. Just as revolting is the use of entrapment by the government to induce persons to commit crimes so that they can then be prosecuted.

Epieikeia supplies a contextual understanding that distinguishes the essential from the petty and trivial. Prosecuting owners of unregistered guns for defending themselves from muggers is another example of the kind of thinking that fails to supply the contextual grasp of practical circumstances supplied by epieikeia. But the response of such prosecutors is that an example must be made, or that no exceptions can be made to the law, which must be enforced rigidly in every case.

The complex federal criminal sentencing guidelines were established to assure greater uniformity in sentences between similar defendants, by replacing the judge's discretion with rules. The rules apply numerical weights to various criteria. The rules are so complex that they have been likened to the tax code. To determine the sentence on any particular individual requires parsing through numerous cross-references to different criteria and mathematical formulas throughout the guidelines.

While the guidelines have often forced judges to exact draconian penalties in the name of this uniformity, numerous critics have documented that they have not resulted in the uniformity in sentencing that was their original impetus, precisely because of their complexity. Their very complexity makes them subject to interpretation and manipulation by police and prosecutors. For example, since the sentencing guidelines are based upon the elements of the crime for which a criminal defendant has been charged, rather than limited to a consideration of the actual conduct of the defendant, prosecutors will typically pile on multiple count indictments for the same conduct. This increases the prosecutor's bargaining leverage, so that the act of filing a single false statement to the government can implicate a number of different statutory crimes, each with its own cumulative offense. Nothing illustrates better than these guidelines the difference between rule-based and egalitarian approaches to justice and the mercy that is the essence of epieikeia.

"'Instead of looking at the person in front of us whose liberty we're about to take away and making arguments about his characteristics, we look at the code and pick up issues to argue there, creating this incredible body of arcane case law,' said Dick Reeves, a federal public defender in New Haven, Connecticut."[144]

Accordingly, very little consideration has been made of the incompatibility between egalitarianism and mercy, but this is because mercy is always particularized to an individual, whereas egalitarianism always involves a measuring of an individual against a universal principle—making sure that individual gets no more nor less than anyone else. Insistence on one's rights, coupled with a rigid egalitarianism, is contrary to the natural sociability at the root of epieikeia.

A contemporary illustration of the absence of the type of epieikeia in the broad Aristotelian sense is the way in which the AIDS problem has been handled since the 1980s. The ACLU and various gay political organizations, as well as certain public-health officials co-opted by these groups, have regarded the privacy interest of persons with AIDS as a higher priority than saving lives.[145] Accordingly, in the 1980s there was vigorous and successful opposition to testing of the donated blood supply and contact tracing so that persons infected would reveal those with whom they had slept.[146] As a result of the delay in testing the blood supplies, numerous hemophiliacs became infected with AIDS. In New York, "with the backing of Gov. Mario Cuomo, [the late] State Health Commissioner David Axelrod refused to classify AIDS as a sexually transmitted disease. As a result, the testing and partner notification that applied to syphilis and gonorrhea [did] not apply to HIV" in New York.[147]

This absurd situation epitomizes the absence of the broadened notion of equity considered essential by Aristotle to the presence of natural justice in a society.[148] People who are friends or have some minimal degree of cooperative association with others do not stand on ceremony to protect abstract notions of their privacy when the lives of those with whom they ought to be associated are potentially adversely affected by their insistence on privacy—even if by legal right they might have a claim of privacy.

That equity, in great part, distinguishes a defective legal justice from natural justice reveals the connection between equity (or natural justice) and friendship. Such an equity, apparently, cannot be readily exercised where men are strangers, but arises naturally where the community is naturally constituted through friendships (I will discuss this in greater detail below). Accordingly, equity arises out of man's natural sociability and is not an artificially constructed set of rules arising out of the legal order.

Where the legal order is stronger than the natural political community, equity is necessarily weakened. Where the legal order is confined to its proper role (which has not yet been completely defined here but is reserved for the final chapter), the full force of equity is able to mitigate the defects in legal justice. Thus equity, not procedural due process, is the ultimate protection against abuses of legal authority. This means that the equitable character of prosecutors, judges, and jurors, plaintiffs and defense attorneys is more significant than the specific rules in the legal system, as far as attaining just ends is concerned. A draconian system administered by equitable persons can conceivably be less harsh than a so-called democratic system administered by professional lawyers.[149]

According to Edward Banfield, social workers in welfare bureaucracies historically performed a valuable function in the exercise of discretion in the dispensation of welfare benefits to the poor, by distinguishing between the truly poor and those who were only technically poor (that is, "welfare cheats").[150] He argued that this discretion, when appropriately exercised, could mitigate against some of the inevitable evils of a welfare system that would otherwise spawn dependency and facilitate the breakup of families. The alternative of a rigidly administered regime of complex rules would otherwise careen between two evils, on the one hand providing insufficient levels of benefits to those who truly needed welfare, and on the other hand providing excessive benefits to those who technically met the eligibility requirements but were undeserving.

Banfield's insight is particularly revealing, but for a reason probably unrecognized by him. Public welfare—that is, welfare through governmental largesse as opposed to private charity—has the inevitable tendency of undermining such discretion, as welfare takes on the trappings of a legal entitlement. A few years after Banfield's article appeared in the *Public Interest,* the Supreme Court significantly impaired the type of discretion that Banfield was talking about by doing what all legal systems inevitably seem to do, that is, it replaced discretion with strict legal rules. In *Goldberg v. Kelly,* the court held that procedural due process required that all welfare beneficiaries be entitled to an evidentiary hearing prior to the termination of benefits.[151]

This result is consistent with the insight of Alexis de Tocqueville that public charity, as distinct from private charity, tends to become a legalistic right or entitlement, and in this way it severs whatever possibility exists of fostering social connections between rich and poor. Envy becomes codified in the law as a right and grievance, ending any possibility of the kind of flexibility that is only truly possible in voluntary giving between persons who have maintained some type of social connection with each other.[152]

The next stage is the legislative expansion of welfare benefits, and then their legislative retrenchment. In both cases, the inevitable result is the arbitrariness, paradoxically, which, Banfield argues, can only be alleviated through discretion.[153] Namely, the truly poor often do not get enough, and those who are welfare cheaters but know how to play the system get too much, imposing unacceptable costs on the system.

It is, indeed, ironical that governmental action in dispensing welfare benefits and other entitlements is often as coercive and legalistic as it is in the collection of revenues. Where a person exercising the virtue of liberality by voluntarily giving money to the needy in his or her community will merely cease giving money to a fraud, in the public welfare realm, when the entitlement-program costs are rising too fast or it is just that time in the political cycle to demagogue the issue, the government will inevitably spend a hundred dollars to save every nickel and embark upon criminal prosecutions of any deep pocket involved in the dispensation of welfare benefits.

The current campaign against doctors and Medicare providers for defrauding Medicare by allegedly overbilling for certain procedures is just one example. It is commonly known that Medicare systematically under-reimburses for the costs of medical care, that the Medicare cost-reimbursement rules are as complicated and ambiguous as are the tax code, and that there are incentives under the False Claims Act for the government to blur any distinction between a supposedly fraudulent charge and one that involves a mere billing error.[154] Under such an ambiguous and draconian welfare scheme, there is clearly no room for the flexibility, mercy, and social connection between giver and recipient exemplified by epieikeia.

The mean-spiritedness inherent in the governmental dispensation of ben-

efits, which inevitably involves a legalistic regime, is best illustrated with a
couple of examples. Even when Congress purports to use the tax code to
help the poor, its complexity enables the Internal Revenue Service to make
it difficult for qualifying poor persons to obtain the desired tax relief. For example, a young mother earning $5,700 annually, who also lived with her re-
tired mother over the age of sixty-five (who had a yearly pension of $7,200)
had to hire a lawyer on a pro bono basis to convince the IRS that she was
entitled to the $1,500 "earned income credit" refund it sent her. After fight-
ing with the IRS for over two years, she filed a petition in the U.S. Tax Court,
a venue ordinarily too expensive for poor persons and that she was able to
afford only because her attorney had agreed to represent her on a pro bono
basis. While the case was pending in the tax court, the IRS assessed her with
a $1,500 billing, plus interest and penalties. The IRS settled with her a month
before the scheduled Tax Court trial date, possibly to avoid a precedent that
would bind the IRS with other taxpayers in her situation.[155]

For another example, suppose, in a hypothetical welfare system, that a single mother obtained more benefits than one who was married, and suppose
an intact poor family cheated by fraudulently claiming that the father was absent so that they could obtain benefits necessary to maintain less than minimally acceptable standards of health and nutrition for their children. In addition, suppose that a single mother with children cheated by receiving a
slightly higher welfare benefit of sixty dollars greater per month than what
the welfare criteria allowed, and that this sixty dollars was the difference between feeding her family at a minimally nutritious level and letting one of
her children suffer from malnutrition.

Let us further suppose that in this same welfare system, a medical-school
student from an upper middle class family technically qualified for some
welfare benefits by ceasing to be declared as a dependant to his family. Finally, let us suppose that it was easier to prosecute and prove that the single
mother or the intact family cheated the system than it was to prosecute the
medical student, because the medical student was technically not a welfare
cheat, from a legal standpoint.

Compare this hypothetical story to the story of Jean Valjean and Inspector Javert from *Les Misérables*. It may be recalled that Valjean was sentenced
to be a galley slave for stealing a loaf of bread to feed a hungry child, and
when he escaped from the galleys, he stole silver candlesticks from a kindly
bishop who had provided him shelter and a meal. Jean reformed himself after the example of the bishop and became a highly respected member of
the middle class under an assumed identity.[156] But then police inspector

Javert, the ultimate caricature of a legal positivist, pursued Valjean with a relentless energy, because Valjean was an escaped convict, and the law had to be enforced strictly and without exception.

Those who are moved by this tale, as I am, will recognize in Jean Valjean the welfare mother who cheats the system for sixty extra dollars to feed her family, or the intact family that cheats the system by receiving benefits while staying intact. They also will be able to distinguish the Valjeans from the cheats meriting censure, such as the undeserving medical student. But a legal regime of public benefits cannot make this distinction.[157] Unfortunately, there are many candidates for the unseemly role of Inspector Javert as there are few for the forgiving bishop.

In fact, it has been reported that many welfare recipients also secretly work to make ends meet, because welfare benefits are insufficient to keep a family above the poverty line. Welfare case workers take this form of "welfare fraud" far too seriously, and rather perversely refer to it as SLAM (Suspected of Living Above Their Means).[158] When rigid rules intersect with reality, just barely living above an arbitrarily set poverty line is deemed to be living beyond one's means.

We will return to *United States v. D'Amato,* where the Second Circuit reversed the conviction of Armand D'Amato for mail fraud to further distinguish the mercy and social connections underlying epieikeia from the harshness of notions of egalitarianism and current legal practice.[159] An officer of Unisys had employed Armand to lobby his brother, Senator D'Amato, on behalf of Unisys. To avoid adverse publicity, the written contract and billing provided that Armand was to write reports on various congressional activities of interest to Unisys. However, the undisputed oral understanding between Armand and Unisys was that Unisys employees would write the reports and that Armand's real role was to lobby his brother. After press reports of this relationship, the federal prosecutors with jurisdiction decided that they did not approve of this lobbying, but could not find a criminal statute that prohibited such actions. Accordingly, they stretched the mail fraud statute very broadly and successfully prosecuted Armand for allegedly defrauding Unisys when he mailed his billings for his services.

Some might react that it was unfair that Unisys and Armand should benefit from Armand's filial relationship to a powerful senator and that therefore, Armand's conduct ought to be illegal. This sensibility is, indeed, probably what impelled the prosecutors to manipulate the mail fraud statute. On the other hand, the circuit judge upheld the rule of law by reversing Armand's conviction based on a strict and narrow reading of the mail fraud statute, a highly defensible position from a legal standpoint, because Armand's conduct did not fall within the elements of the crime as defined by the statute.

To some, Armand and Unisys, arguably, lacked epieikeia in their capitalizing on Armand's filial relationship—taking more than their due. Just as some would probably argue that people possessing special talents would lack epieikeia were they to take "more than their due." But this approach reduces epieikeia to a rigid egalitarian principle, and thereby undermines its core meanings that recognize flexibility and the natural human relationships where such flexibility is often most exhibited.

More important, epieikeia is not an envious quality that critically regards the fact that others take more than they are due. Rather, in the interests of harmonious relations, epieikeia will restrain itself from litigating even where it might have a claim, and thereby take less than it is due. Even if a conflict-of-interest statute existed to proscribe Armand's lobbying his brother, why should some, and not other natural human relationships be criminalized, based purely on the presence or absence of a textual prohibition? Why should statutory language, by itself, have the magic of transmuting conduct into something punishable by imprisonment? Are there not degrees of shameworthy or immoral conduct that ought not be subject to the criminal law, simply because lobbying one's brother ought not get the enforcement emphasis that, say, kidnapping and murdering children should get? Why should the range of illegal conduct be extended beyond fraud, bribery, murder, into every other possible human relationship—from that of lobbying one's brother to, for example, sexual harassment? Why is there this natural impetus in a legalistic culture to extend the realm of law (that is, criminal sanctions and civil liability) to cover every possible relation that some might disapprove of? What would be wrong with letting the democratic political process and exposure in the press constrain such activities as lobbying one's brother?

On the other hand, in the current environment, public exposure might not necessarily constrain such conduct. As things are today, a person who ought to be shamed by such exposure is able to successfully defend him or herself with the legalistic reduction that his or her conduct is moral because it is not illegal.

At any rate, legislators lack epieikeia when they unduly expand the range of law and criminalize new areas of conduct through the mere stroke of a pen, something that did not happen in the D'Amato case, but that some readers might want to happen as a result of the case. Voting Armand's brother out of office—or, for that matter, initiating a shareholder suit to recover damages on behalf of the corporation—are two less drastic remedies in the circumstances.

And yet, even under the supposedly more permissive standards for bringing a civil case, the appellate court noted that there was not enough of a case against Armand to survive a motion to dismiss prior to discovery. In other words, there was less settlement or extortion value to a civil case against Armand than there was under the criminal case. That is a sobering thought for those who only express concerns about the abuses of civil litigation in our system, under the assumption that governmental prosecutors who are lawyers within the same culture and training as civil litigators are somehow going to behave differently and with greater restraint.

With regard to the prosecutor's conduct, the prosecution of Armand is a classic example of the absence of epieikeia in an all too common form exemplified repeatedly throughout our system. Critics of our legal system's excesses most commonly point to the extortion value of otherwise unmeritorious civil litigation, because losers in civil litigation do not have to bear the costs of litigation. But this same culture has too often infected public prosecutors, who interpret statutes as broadly as do plaintiffs' attorneys, in the knowledge that the costs of fighting them severely disadvantage any criminal defendant.

This notion of relying on prosecutorial leverage is at the root of the commonly accepted practice called plea bargaining, a practice that may be a necessary evil in the current legalistic environment, where technical violations of due process are sufficient to free and reduce the sentence of a dangerous criminal. But plea bargaining is also used against innocent persons, an unacceptable cost of a system that does not effectively work. On its face, stretching and manipulating statutory language so that one might prosecute a person, while fully ethical within the legalistic canons of ethical rules promulgated by the bar, exemplifies what I am trying to portray as the most egregious example of the absence of epieikeia.

A more appropriate exercise of prosecutorial discretion involves the restraint from prosecuting otherwise technically illegal conduct in the interests of natural justice. For example, where two teenagers technically violate the statutory rape laws but decline to abort their child and end up marrying each other, a prosecutor exercising discretion with epieikeia in mind would decline to prosecute. But the notion of a discretion connoting mercy is apparently too nonneutral in this age of legal positivism. As much as some might disapprove of Armand's conduct from a moral standpoint, the ability to recognize that it did not merit the harsh rigors of our prison system is the kind of recognition central to one who possesses epieikeia.

The appellate judge's reversal of D'Amato's conviction was explicitly based on the rule of law, and therefore it might be seen by some as an argument against the notion of epieikeia amplified within this book. But this misconceives my purpose. I am not arguing against law, but against its inappropriate expansion and rigid interpretation at the expense of a merciful notion of epieikeia and natural justice. In this case, Judge Winter narrowly interpreted a criminal statute in a manner that limited the reach of law. But he only reached this outcome because Armand had first been inappropriately convicted under a broad interpretation of law's empire. He did not reach this result out of mercy, and, in fact, he would have been at the very least subject to severe criticism had his opinion been couched in terms that invoked mercy, because this would have raised questions about his impartiality.

Had D'Amato plea-bargained his sentence, as happened in the case of Michael Milken and a host of other persons, or had there been, in fact, a criminal statute prohibiting lobbying one's brother, the rigid and narrow rule of law would have reached a far different result. For criminality to turn exclusively on the mere changing of a few words in a statute is what is problematical with our system. Why should words and language have such magical import where imprisonment and fines are at stake?

There are very good reasons that legislative bodies should be reluctant to enact laws, notwithstanding the view that legislatures are somehow superior to judges because of the time taken in hearings, fact finding, and debate before enacting new laws.[160] Laws may have noble-sounding aims and yet achieve paradoxical results when applied, because of the inherent limitations of language. What ought to be permitted as an exception to a prohibition in one set of circumstances, or even in most circumstances, is often not apparent to even the wisest lawmaker.

What natural justice would require as exceptions to a general rule is sometimes difficult to foresee in the abstract, in the absence of the context provided by specific facts. Indeed, efforts to legislate, whether by courts or by legislators, cannot avoid the legalistic fallacy, because that is what the craft of legislation entails: drafting generalized rules based on contingencies not immediately at hand. More important, when the realm of law is expanded to apply to areas previously subject to the moral restraints of epieikeia and natural justice, as imperfect as these restraints might be, it is often not recognized that the price for this legal expansionism involves entrusting some governmental official or private plaintiff's attorney with the coercive power to interfere or extort in a new area. When law itself is reduced by this expansionism to become the only legitimate moral restraint, such trust is dangerous precisely because legal language is so malleable in the hands of professional lawyers who would recoil at the notion of epieikeia. This malleability is often the difference between a neutral, clever, and truly arbitrary discretion and the type of accommodating and merciful discretion that constitutes epieikeia. And this distinction arises precisely because natural justice and not the legal text informs epieikeia.

For a concrete illustration of this distinction between discretion and epieikeia, I will turn to what might appear as a strong potential argument against my position. Mary Ann Glendon blames judicial discretion for the inequitable distributions of the economic burdens of divorce on the custodial parent, usually the mother, in the case of American family law in the early 1980s. She contrasts the effect of this discretion on the settlement outcomes for child support in an American context with the apparently more adequate and predictable approach in Sweden and West Germany at the time.

Namely, standardized support tables established the framework for more reasonable settlements between divorcing parents in Sweden and Germany. When Glendon wrote this criticism of discretion, in 1987, she expressed some hope that the situation would improve in the United States as a result of federal legislation in 1984 requiring each state to establish standardized tables for child support by October 1987.[161] In the Family Support Act of 1988, Congress provided that states receiving federal welfare funds had to substantially limit the discretion of judges in applying child-support guidelines. At this point, it is not at all clear that the elimination of this discretion has in any way more equitably shifted the economic burdens from custodial mothers after a divorce, and there is often anecdotal evidence of its harshness when applied against noncustodial parents who are as poor as the custodial parent.[162]

To the extent that discretion, and not broader cultural issues, is at the root of the problem, I argue that replacing the current professional family law judges, who serve potentially indefinite terms, with a jury of peers might result in a more appropriate exercise of discretion consistent with epieikeia. Such a jury of peers would necessarily have a limited term, include persons who know the family, who have been mothers or fathers, and, preferably, have been the primary care givers in raising their own children.

3.5 Epieikeia: Not a Body of Rules.

In a classic illustration of the legalist fallacy, Justice William O. Douglas, writing for the majority in *Terminiello v. Chicago*, struck down the conviction of Terminiello for disturbing the peace, based on the purported vagueness of the local ordinance under which he was convicted.[163] According to Douglas,

the ordinance conflicted with the free-speech notions of the First Amendment, because any person with views outside the norm could "invite dispute"
and risk conviction under the statute. To support this holding, Douglas relied on a single, isolated jury instruction by the trial court interpreting the
ordinance's words, "breach of the peace," as including speech that "stirs the
public to anger" or "invites dispute."

But in the factual record summarized in Justice Jackson's dissenting opinion, it appeared that Terminiello did, in fact, breach the peace with his
speech, and that the local police actually applied the ordinance with considerable restraint in the circumstances. The police escorted Terminiello
and his followers to the auditorium and kept back the angry mob, even while
Terminiello incited his own followers with fascistic and anti-Semitic rhetoric.
When some of Terminiello's opponents became violent, the police did not
immediately silence Terminiello but instead removed those who were violent. Only after matters got completely out of hand did the police finally remove Terminiello from the premises.

What is significant is the fact that Douglas ignored what actually happened
according to the record before the court and instead focused on the hypothetical possibility that in other circumstances not before the court, the
statute could be misapplied. It is also significant that Justice Jackson's dissent appeared to involve less restraint than that actually exercised by the local police, in that he would have countenanced the silencing of Terminiello's
speech as soon as Terminiello's opponents started rioting. The removed, almost Olympian distance between the verbal interplay at the Supreme Court
and what actually happened reveals the difference between a jurisprudence
that views legal rules and principles as the appropriate product of adjudication, particularly by higher courts, and a jurisprudence that leaves a role
for epieikeia by limiting the role of professional lawyers. The Supreme Court
does not render justice, something that only can be rendered with factual
particularity; rather, it legislates universal legal rules and principles.

The recent case of *R. A. V. v. City of St. Paul, Minnesota,* although bearing
some similarity to *Terminiello,* illustrates, in a slightly different way, the consequences of a legal system that views legal rules and principles, rather than
justice, as its aim.[164] Although the opinions in *R. A. V.* are substantially longer,
more abstract, and convoluted than those in *Terminiello,* what is most striking are the indications as to how and why the particular case was before the
Supreme Court. St. Paul enacted a Bias-Motivated Crime Ordinance, which
explicitly criminalized the display of burning crosses, Nazi swastikas, and
anything else that a person knew would arouse anger or resentment in others on the basis of race, color, creed, religion, or gender. While all nine jus-

tices agreed that the statute was unconstitutional, they squabbled in four separate opinions as to the rationale for their judgment. Unlike *Terminiello,* the statute was likely enacted, and the prosecution of R. A. V. for cross burning pursuant to the newly enacted statute was likely undertaken with a view to obtaining a Supreme Court opinion.

By prosecuting the least sympathetic defendant under the statute, a racist cross burner, and obtaining a Supreme Court sanction of the underlying statute, the door would be open to later prosecutions testing the limits of the statute against anyone viewed as offending the sensibilities of any person of a different gender, race, creed, and so on. Given the rather loose usage of such labels as racist or sexist to silence opposing viewpoints in the so-called political-correctness movement during this period, this was not an unreasonable legal strategy.

The Supreme Court had earlier sanctioned in the *Meritor Savings Bank, FSB v. Vinson* case a subjective standard opening the doors to sexual harassment litigation predicated on whether the person alleging harassment viewed the alleged harasser's behavior as offensive. Indeed, three of the justices (White, Blackmun, and O'Connor) viewed the rationale of five of the justices (Scalia, Rhenquist, Kennedy, Souter, and Thomas) for invalidating the St. Paul ordinance as threatening to the underpinnings of the *Vinson* sexual harassment case.[165] Moreover, both Justice Scalia and Justice Blackmun indicated some consciousness of this posturing, to the degree that Blackmun accused Scalia of erroneously crafting his opinion with political correctness in mind when political correctness was not at issue: a cross burner was being prosecuted, not some person erroneously labeled as biased because they had a different viewpoint from someone claiming to speak in the name of tolerance and diversity. But there was a sense in which political correctness was at issue in this case. I remember the media reporting on this case as involving a major test of political correctness. The Supreme Court does not exist in a sequestered bubble.

Scalia pointed out that the cross burner could have been prosecuted under a local statute that was not directed, as was the antibias statute, against particular biases or viewpoints. Indeed, Scalia emphasized that provocative speech or "fighting words" expressed in favor of racial and sexual tolerance were not prosecutable under the antibias ordinance, while the statute specifically barred fighting words that might be labeled by some as racist or sexist. "One could hold up a sign saying, for example, that all 'anti-Catholic bigots' are misbegotten; but not that all 'papists' are, for that would insult and provoke violence 'on the basis of religion.'"

The lengthy arguments were like shadowboxing, and they were primarily about what might happen in other cases based on the supposedly different principles being articulated for the same outcome—that the ordinance was unconstitutional. Unlike *Terminiello,* the issue of the statute, and its potential applications beyond the facts being adjudicated, was apparently the central issue before much of the court. The reach of the St. Paul ordinance and not cross burning was the issue, whereas in *Terminiello,* at least in the case of Justice Jackson, a great deal of consideration was placed on the facts of the case.

In *St. Paul,* portentous distinctions were drawn between restrictions on speech based on "subject matter" and restrictions on speech based on "viewpoint," restrictions on "political speech" as opposed to "fighting words" under the so-called categorical approach to the First Amendment; the distinction between statutory "overbreadth" and "underbreadth" analysis, and more such reified abstractions.

At this point, it should be clear how abstract principles formulated by legal combatants have displaced natural justice. If epieikeia had been exhibited, the cross-burner case would never have reached the Supreme Court; the local prosecutor would only have sought to prosecute cross burners, and not persons who happened to be labeled as biased by others because of their different viewpoints. And persons would not falsely accuse others of being racists or sexists in contexts where the term did not apply.

Where the restraints of epieikeia are absent, litigation strategies and legal argument displace natural justice, and the contextual meanings of words that merely express a different viewpoint become less distinguishable from words that truly do offend and provoke violence. In this context, where an expansion of law may truly have been at issue, a justice exemplifying epieikeia would have been as out of place as a pacifist in the midst of a war. Justice Douglas's concerns in *Terminiello* bore fruit in *St. Paul* in a manner unanticipated by him, as a result of the very legal expansionism exhibited by his earlier opinion.

And subsequent history certainly indicates that the viability of sexual harassment law after *St. Paul* was not eroded at all, contrary to the concerns of Justice Blackmun. Indeed, the *Vinson* standard for mounting a sexual harassment claim was reaffirmed in *Harris v. Forklift Systems, Inc.,* a few years after *St. Paul,* as a subjective standard from the standpoint of the person (usually a woman) alleging harassment. Namely, if a reasonable woman in like circumstances felt that the alleged behavior constituted unwelcome harassment, then that was sufficient to mount a sexual harassment claim.[166]

Some readers might view the *Vinson* and *Harris* sexual harassment legal standards as exemplifying the type of particularized and subjective rule required by epieikeia. But this totally misconceives the genesis of these legal standards and the nature of epieikeia. As in *Terminiello,* the court in *Vinson* and in *Harris* focused less on the factual conduct at issue and more on the appropriate legal standard, remanding to the trial court for the application of the new standard. As a result of this estrangement from the facts, the court in *Vinson* in all seriousness justified its legal standard for sexual harassment claims by mounting a distinction between "unwelcome" sexual advances and "voluntary" participation in sex by the woman alleging harassment. That is, a person alleging harassment could somehow voluntarily participate in sex and yet find that participation to be unwelcome.

While much has been made by some critics of the *Vinson* standard on the difference between *voluntary* and *unwelcome,* it is arguable that many of the same types of facts relevant to a finding of voluntary behavior would also be relevant to a determination of how unwelcome the alleged behavior really was. More significantly, the essence of epieikeia cannot be exemplified in any type of legal rule. Rather, it is in the application of the legal rule whereby epieikeia is or is not exemplified, and in the application of *Vinson* and *Harris,* there certainly has been little restraint shown by the plaintiff's bar. But that is not necessarily a problem with the legal standards articulated for sexual harassment in these cases and is more indicative of a problem with the community of lawyers and the small but expanding subset of the population that retains lawyers in such matters. Those who would criticize *Vinson* and *Harris* as somehow spawning the abuses of sexual harassment litigation, because these rules do not provide so-called bright-line rules are, in a sense, presupposing that society is an empty vessel that only functions because of legal rules.

But this overestimates the importance of law and underestimates the importance of those tacit levels of cooperation attained between those still fortunately large segments of society that fail to resort habitually to the legal system. The misapplications of *Vinson* and *Harris* result from a legal culture where legal combatants apply the standard for sexual harassment as part of a growth industry. Lawyers test its limits and thereby effectively expand the range of conduct governed by the standard (even if unintended). They may even get a new legal rule established as a result of this activity.

What is inequitable, in the sense of epieikeia, is not the rule, but this absence of restraint in the application of the rule. But there is also a sense in which the critics of *Vinson* are correct, insofar as *Vinson* expanded the realm of law into an area previously handled informally, through cultural restraints on gross behavior. As these restraints became less acceptable to a significant minority with the advent of the so-called sexual revolution of the 1960s, some found it necessary to fill the void with litigation.

As a result, even as the First Amendment protects cross burners and anti-Semitic speakers, sexual harassment law entangles in its web a six-year-old boy for kissing a little girl at school, a writing professor for quoting a belly dancer's description of her technique as an illustration of colorful language, and an employee who refused to attend sexual harassment training sponsored by his employer.[167] And the same logic applied to religious speech in the work place prompted the Equal Employment Opportunity Commission to propose religious harassment guidelines that would expand federal antidiscrimination law in the work place in a manner that would have chilled religious expression.

Although these proposed guidelines were withdrawn after an avalanche of protests from the religious community, the issue is far from over, and eventually employers will consult with attorneys on the hair-splitting rules to be applied. They will have to conduct training sessions to indoctrinate employees on these rules, and the plaintiff's bar will have a new moneymaking area.

It strains one's credulity to believe that Congress anticipated such a use of the Civil Rights law when it originally enacted the provisions stating that "it shall be an unlawful employment practice for an employer (1) to fail or refuse to hire or to discharge an individual, or otherwise discriminate against any individual with respect to his compensation, terms, conditions, or privileges of employment, because of such individual's race, color, religion, sex, or national origin." But the conventional criticism that such expansionism would cease if courts merely deferred to the strict legislative language is no answer and is contrary to the notions of epieikeia. The problem, rather, is with the notion of appellate review itself, the notion that courts ought to focus their attention on precedent, and that appellate courts should properly only deal with arcane matters of law (and not fact). I wish it were that simple.

For every example of appellate courts abetting legal injustices through expansive interpretations of laws contrary to legislative intent, there are just as many examples of legal injustices arising through strict deference to legislative enactment. One only need point to the *Dred Scott* case or the ERISA preemption case briefly discussed in Chapter 1. It may be recalled that the freedom of an escaped slave in *Dred Scott* turned on the Supreme Court's deference to the legislative branch. In *Corcoran,* the appellate court's refusal to afford a state law remedy against an employer health benefit plan for denying coverage for extended hospitalization recommended by the attending physician to a mother in a high-risk pregnancy turned on the fact that the health plan was not individual insurance purchased by the mother, but was provided by her employer and was therefore subject to ERISA, the federal law governing employee benefit plans. Congress failed to anticipate the pervasive use of medical utilization review panels when it enacted ERISA. The appellate court indicated that it knew Congress would have likely mandated a different result if it had known that medical utilization review panels would deny benefits in such circumstances. Yet the appellate court strictly followed the letter of what Congress had enacted and effectively denied a legal remedy to this mother.

The way out of this conundrum is for appellate courts to function more like courts of equity, in the traditional sense, rather than limiting themselves to questions of law. Where justice is the product of a court, and not lawmaking, the facts have to take precedence. This means throwing stare decisis and the whole legalist fallacy out the door. The idea of articulating a new legal standard and then remanding to a lower court should be replaced with the notion of truly trying to test the real meaning of that standard with the facts at issue. Appellate judges would have to work harder, but we would probably get far better results, since their job would change to that of rendering justice rather than constructing abstract rules based on hypothetical impacts having nothing to do with the facts before them. But this will not happen until our society critically examines the problem at its roots: namely, professional lawyers make larger sums of money by expanding law into new practice areas.

That equity could be considered a mere "legal fiction" by some is a testament to the narrowing of the notion of equity to a set of legal rules and practices made possible by the grounding of natural justice in another level of the legal order. As noted before in the consideration of the relation between epieikeia and custom, it is incorrect to view equity as a mere legal fiction. It can be customary to act with epieikeia, as it can be customary to act without epieikeia. The entire notion of legal fiction is a vanity born of viewing everything of ontological significance as either arising out of the legal order or as possessing no ontological significance whatsoever. This is, indeed, another way of articulating the legalistic fallacy discussed in the introductory chapter.

It is the notion that only law has any ontological significance in considering jurisprudential problems, even if this means that law, in the interest of universality, is divorced from its particular consequences on individual persons. It is very important to retain the Aristotelian conception of equity as being something apart from the legal notion that corrects a defect in legal justice. By viewing equity as a mere species of the legal order, one is just one step removed from regarding equity as a legal fiction. This is just another illustration of the confusions resulting from an expansion of the legal order into that of natural justice.

The notion that bodies of rules constitute the sum total of what counts for just behavior underlies the attitude of many lawyers I have known and worked with, particularly with respect to their understanding of the so-called ethical rules of the profession. For these lawyers, so-called ethical behavior is mere conformity to so-called ethical rules promulgated by bar associations and adopted by the judiciary. There is clearly no room for epieikeia here. Thus, such so-called ethical rules become a lowest common denominator, where anything not in violation of the rules is deemed ethical by many practitioners. This confusion is, at bottom, the same confusion that reduces or collapses legal justice and natural justice into one another, by failing to recognize that natural justice is not a justice of rules and imperatives, but consists of the actions that would naturally occur between friends. For the most part, just as most mothers in nature do not require a rule book for the care of their children, most natural friendships are not artificially constituted through prescriptive rules but contain a natural cooperative element not reducible to rules. Indeed, prescriptive rules would likely destroy such natural friendships.

In Europe, for at least the last thousand years, the nation state has used law to legitimize its monopoly over the instruments of coercion and violence in communities. As a part of this process, a narrow notion of equity, as a legal principle, competed with epieikeia as a natural principle. With the monopoly over force came an effort to assert a monopoly over equity. Initially, in England, equity was a separate ecclesiastical jurisdiction dealing with matters of family law, trusts and estates, and forms of relief (for example, injunctive) that were not recognized as remedies in the king's law courts.[168] Equity was a separate jurisdiction in the legal system with its own remedies, procedures, and causes of actions.

Gradually, in the United States, the separate equity courts were merged into the law courts, with the old equitable remedies recognized as systems of legal rules indistinguishable from other legal rules in the legal system. As such, bankruptcy, the law of estates and trusts, pension law (ERISA), and any type of judicial relief other than monetary damages are recognized as equitable.

In addition, judicial opinions use the term *equity* in the sense of the "clean hands" doctrine—that is, one cannot avail oneself of equitable relief without clean hands. For example, one cannot seek bankruptcy protection if one is merely using bankruptcy to defraud creditors by transferring one's assets into the title of other related parties within one year before seeking bankruptcy protection. If one performs a fraudulent transfer one year and one day before one's bankruptcy petition, one has clean hands, whereas if one performs the fraudulent transfer within one year one does not, and therefore cannot protect the transferred asset from one's creditors through the equitable jurisdiction of bankruptcy.[169] Hopefully, this example neatly illustrates one way in which legalisms have contaminated the notion of equity.

Inherent in the evolution away from epieikeia as a form of natural justice into equity as a form of legal justice is the confining of equity to the actions of officials or to actions taken before official bodies. Gone is the notion that refraining from litigating one's so-called legal rights is equitable. In fact, under the clean-hands doctrine, one cannot assert the so-called equitable defense of laches if one has slept on one's rights. Under laches, whether or not there is a statute of limitations defense, one cannot sue someone else where a considerable length of time has elapsed. Under this legal perversion of equity, equity requires that one not sleep on one's rights.

The illegitimacy of vigilantism, or taking justice into one's own hands outside the law courts, may also be, arguably, viewed as an attack by the nation state against competing sources of justice. The notion that the only form of justice is legal justice is inherent in such a notion. While vigilantism can often be unjust, so can the law. There are justified and unjustified versions of vigilantism. For example, the American courts have often given stiffer prison sentences to persons who shot their attackers because they possessed unregistered handguns than they have to their would-be muggers.[170] Women defending themselves with violence from domestic abuse have been imprisoned for murdering their husbands if they were not in imminent danger of attack from their husbands, notwithstanding the absence of any protection by the police from future threatened attacks by their husbands.

I suspect that the judges and prosecutors involved in these cases would have acted differently if their own family member had been involved. But that merely illustrates the difference between natural justice and legal justice: equity in the truest sense and a bogus impartiality. In the modern sense, as illustrated by judicial opinions, equity has taken on the meaning of treating a person with impartiality or equality.

This notion of equity is distinct from an epieikeia viewed as the natural actions that would be taken by a friend to correct an injustice in the legal system. An impartial and universal type of equity is, indeed, diametrically opposed to an epieikeia grounded in natural justice. Confining equity to official actions ultimately leads to the narrower notion of equity as impartiality. Broadening equity to encompass the epieikeia of a natural community necessarily involves some partiality and particularity.

There is a recent example of epieikeia in the community serving as a corrective to the absence of epieikeia in the officials charged with enforcing the law. A criminal who had abducted a child fifteen years earlier was let out of prison on parole, whereupon he kidnapped another eleven-year-old boy.[171] The boy's mother went to the District of Columbia police for assistance within two hours after her son had disappeared. The police told her that since her son was over age six and under age eighty-five and not on medication or physically or mentally disabled, the case would be classified as noncritical. After the police took no action to search for the boy, the desperate mother corralled members of the community (including criminals from a halfway house) to search for the boy. The volunteer searchers found the boy and the kidnapper, rescued the boy, and apprehended the kidnapper. The police response was to investigate their handling of the case through an examination of whether their internal procedures had been followed for such cases.

A community that confines epieikeia or equity to its legal officials and legal justice ultimately stifles justice. In the above incident, people who cared for each other as members of the same community ultimately did a better job of rendering justice than did those who were impartially following legalistic procedures.

Thus the notion of procedural due process as somehow safeguarding miscarriages of justice by protecting against officials lacking in epieikeia betrays a fundamental misunderstanding of both the dependence of legal justice on natural justice and the crucial role of epieikeia in correcting defects in legal justice. The bonds of community, the sense of sharing one's life in a community, these are the foundations of epieikeia, not procedures in the legal system. It is not compliance with procedures that assure against conviction of an innocent man, but the character of the official that determines this outcome. Prosecutors who know the rules can convict an innocent person by apparently following every procedural safeguard. Conversely, the defense attorney for a guilty person, particularly if the criminal is wealthy, can manipulate procedural due process to achieve an unjust result, just as crooks can use procedural due process in civil cases to harass others.[172]

A legal system that pretends to rely on procedural due process alone to assure that justice is done is built on a deception. One only has to consider the *Buck v. Bell* case discussed in Chapter 1 to see the emptiness of moral content in due process alone. It may be recalled that in *Buck v. Bell,* the Supreme Court upheld the forcible sterilization of a "feeble-minded" mother because she had been afforded all the due process and equal protection provided by the laws as enacted by the Virginia legislature.

The decade-long persecution of Thereza Imanishi-Kari and David Baltimore on unfounded charges of "scientific fraud" is a good example for testing some of the major themes advanced in this chapter. Imanishi-Kari was initially accused of scientific fraud by a fellow researcher at Tufts University, in work that had been supervised by Nobel laureate David Baltimore. Two university committees and a National Institute of Health panel initially exonerated her. However, Congressman Dingell was dissatisfied with this outcome and called for hearings, where public attacks were made upon both Imanishi-Kari and Baltimore, who had consistently defended her. The Secret Service then got involved in investigating her, and different charges of misconduct were launched, charges that were later determined to have resulted from the lack of scientific sophistication on the part of the investigators.[173]

Imanishi-Kari was barred from receiving federal research grants after a hearing in which she had no opportunity to cross-examine her accusers. At the time of this adjudication, there was no provision for an appeal of such a decision. However, as a result of criticisms by some within and outside the scientific community, the rules were changed and an appeals panel was established. Ultimately, both Imanishi-Kari and Baltimore were exonerated by this appeals board, which established procedural due process safeguards and rules of evidence that had not been used in the earlier investigations.

For some, this happy result (the exoneration of a person who had been unjustly adjudicated as guilty of misconduct) would seem to vindicate the lawyers and the importance of procedural rules of due process.[174] But this assumes that the correct and just application of these newly established procedural rules for adjudicating scientific misconduct cases will be replicated in a just manner in subsequent cases, where there might be less external scrutiny of the proceedings.

I am not so sanguine, insofar as any given set of rules (even the improved ones that have been newly established) are subject to interpretation and manipulation. Mean-spirited whistle-blowers, jealous of their colleagues, and full-time investigators will learn these procedural rules and find loopholes for finding new ways to accomplish the same persecutions that were inflicted over a protracted period on Imanishi-Kari. Eventually these procedural loopholes will be exposed and reformed with new procedural due process rules, which, in turn, will have their own set of loopholes for the mean-spirited to exploit.

What I find more alarming, however, is that this apparently fortunate result (in this case—after ten years of persecution) has set the stage for institutionalizing a new area for litigiousness, an area that apparently had previously involved greater flexibility and informality. A larger bureaucracy is being set up to investigate and adjudicate cases of scientific misconduct, and this bureaucracy, I fear, will ultimately generate a greater workload for it-self.[175]

How this new atmosphere of legal expansionism will ultimately affect the scientific community and the very nature of the scientific enterprise—even with these supposed new protections—is highly problematical. This might seem absurd, but recent legal history in other areas would indicate that the next stage of legal expansionism might involve self-protective scientists find-ing it prudent to consult attorneys at various stages of their research, par-ticularly at the publication stage.

When the technical vocabulary beloved by lawyers and philosophers is a circumlocution for the ways in which ordinary persons speak about and rec-ognize a phenomenon such as health or natural justice, this added level of technical language is fine, so long as it does not conceal the underlying sit-uation. Where there is a fundamental yet unrecognized disconnection be-tween a technical vocabulary and ordinary language, the immediate pre-sumption of assuming that the ordinary language is incorrect ought to be set aside, at least long enough to be certain that the technical vocabulary is truly an advance in understanding.

This critical reservation of judgment is particularly warranted where the technical vocabulary is advanced by a group that has a self-interest in the tech-nical vocabulary's legitimacy. This is what has happened to the notion of pro-cedural due process, the bedrock legal surrogate for the notion of epieikeia advanced in my analysis of legal injustices. Analysis of a case where officials have lacked epieikeia cannot be exclusively considered in terms of procedural due process without losing something that is often recognized by laypersons as indicative of corruption, but that cannot be legally challenged unless it is recast in formulaic terms of some failure to follow procedural due process. This fact also serves to screen the official from ultimate accountability for a lack of epieikeia, since the issue is reserved to a consideration of procedures.

The notion of procedural due process is also dangerous to the extent that it deludes persons into believing that procedures by themselves are an in-sulation against official abuses of power. Practicing lawyers tacitly recognize this as a language game in which, if one is contending against the govern-ment, one has to somehow find the magic procedural due process formu-lation that fits a situation that ordinary language would already recognize as an obvious breach of natural justice.

These observations are not intended to condemn procedural due pro-cess. Rather, my intent is to emphasize that the analysis of miscarriages of justice does not always neatly fit within procedural due process terms alone, particularly since this language game often conceals more about the situation than it reveals.

3.6 Summary

1. Epieikeia is not a set of rules, and its subject matter is particular.
2. Epieikeia involves not knowledge (or demonstration), but practical wisdom.
3. Epieikeia is a perfection or virtue and, as such, is not indeterminate with respect to a course of action, but only with respect to general rules.
4. Epieikeia is merciful and forgiving.
5. Epieikeia is not merely adjudicative, but is the framework for a just legal system that encompasses the actions of all citizens—and not merely officials.
6. Epieikeia is not morally neutral, like the notions of discretion and tolerance.
7. Epieikeia is not reducible to equality or impartiality.
8. Epieikeia is flexible and indeterminate with respect to the law through its departure from the otherwise rigid universality of a legal rule, in order to deal more adequately with the particularity of human action and associations in a naturally just way.
9. Epieikeia arises out of the unique relationship between natural justice and friendships.
10. Epieikeia contravenes the notion that Aristotle was the founder of the republican notion of "no man before the law," or that law is somehow a protection against official abuses of power. The protection comes from epieikeia, not the law.
11. Epieikeia cannot be taught or reduced to legal or moral rules (whether legislated by humans or arising from divine ideas), and it certainly cannot be professionalized.

Conclusion

The notion of a natural justice that is grounded in human association and that has as much ontological reality as does health, notwithstanding the pervasiveness of injustice, has to become the fundamental framework of any

workable ethical-legal-political theory. The notion that custom is the in-be-
tween state mediating for better or worse between an artificial and imperfect
legal order and natural justice, is, likewise an important ingredient in such
a framework, but one that nonetheless does not complete that framework.
The notion of epieikeia as correcting legal injustices arising out of both the
written and customary law has to be the essential ingredient to diagnosing
what is wrong with any legal order.

However, the inadequacies of the Aristotelian model of natural justice
must also be recognized. Although it is not clear that Aristotle is completely
comfortable with his position on slavery, he does offer a weak justification
of slavery as being both a conventional and natural social phenomenon.[176]
That this use of his method should give one pause in placing too great a reliance on it for the construction of a complete moral or political philosophy
is all too apparent. Nonetheless, there is a great plausibility to Aristotle's
model of natural justice that cannot be denied, and it ought to serve as a
starting point for further reflection.

He assumes that there is a notion of natural justice arising out of the associative bonds of community, that the associative bonds of community are
as natural as friendships we encounter every day, and that this natural justice is different in kind from and superior to legal justice. These assumptions mirror the ways in which ordinary persons understand the functioning
and malfunctioning of legal systems. That these positions are reflected in
the way the language is used carries with it some ontological significance.

Once the plausibility of his model is accepted, the problem of why it is im-
practical to make it universal also becomes apparent. As often is the case
with many ordinary persons, Aristotle notes that it is natural to treat friends
with greater justice than strangers. The just treatment of friends and mistrust of strangers is, indeed, natural. While one cannot assert that such disparate treatment is morally correct, this imperfection is not a basis for
rejecting the limits of natural sociability as a relevant consideration in developing a basis for conducting a moral evaluation of the relation of law to
justice. Something can be gained from examining the just relationships that
obtain between friends with a view to not interfering with these natural relations. There is a moral worth to such friendships, even if they are not universal and even if they are not in compliance with categorical imperatives.

The notion that morality can only be built upon a Kantian metaphysical
foundation must be discarded if any further progress in morality and jurisprudence in a practical way is ever to occur. Recognizing the importance
of natural sociability would be a step in the direction of at least supplementing equality as our principal value with the value of epieikeia, and

maybe, as a result, we would find it easier to live with each other. Once it was recognized that natural associations were important for achieving some level of justice, however imperfect and incomplete, the problem of rendering such natural justice universal, that is, the problem of dealing with the parochialism of natural justice, could be dealt with in a sensitive manner. The legal system would not be regarded as a means of reengineering natural associations. Instead, the legal system would restrict the range of the law of the nation state to gross injustices committed by the natural community. In other words, the nation state would have to cease its attempt to monopolize justice into legal justice. How such a balance between natural justice and legal justice might be achieved, given the present enervated state of natural justice, is the subject of the next chapter.

Notes

1. *Dred Scott v. Sandford,* 60 U.S. (19 How.) 393 (1856). J. Taney, justifying his decision to deny freedom to an escaped slave.

2. *Corcoran v. United HealthCare, Inc.,* 15 E.B.C. 1793, 1805 (5th Cir. 1992), justifying the absence of a remedy for wrongful denial of coverage to a mother by an insurer in a high-risk pregnancy that resulted in the infant's death.

3. *Buck v. Bell,* 274 U.S. 200, 207 (1927). J. Holmes, justifying forced sterilization of a poor woman who was allegedly mentally retarded.

4. Marcus Tullius Cicero, *Laws,* trans. C. W. Keyes (Cambridge: Harvard University Press, 1928); Saint Augustine, *On Free Choice of the Will,* trans. Anna S. Benjamin and L. H. Hackstaff (New York: Library of Liberal Arts, 1964), sections I.5, 13; Aquinas, *Summa Theologica,* I-II, qu. 90–97, qu. 100, qu. 105.

5. It is only, arguably, referred to in the *Rhetoric* I.13, 1373b3–6, and in *Politics* I.6, 1255b4–15. Fred D. Miller Jr., "Aristotle on Natural Law and Justice," *A Companion to Aristotle's Politics,* eds. David Keyt and Fred D. Miller Jr. (Cambridge: Basil Blackwell, 1991), 279–80. Even if one labels it "natural law," such a natural law is different from that of Cicero, Augustine, and Aquinas. For a contrary view, see W. von Leyden, *Aristotle on Equality and Justice* (New York: St. Martin's Press, 1985), 87–90; Leo Strauss, *Natural Right and History* (Chicago: University of Chicago Press, 1953).

Recent efforts, such as those of Fred D. Miller Jr. in *Nature, Justice, and Rights in Aristotle's Politics* (Oxford: Oxford University Press, 1995), to "reconstruct" Aristotle as a "proto-liberal" who carries implicitly and latently within his notion of natural justice the roots of late medieval and modern notions of natural right are scrupulously avoided in the following discussion. Although (as a contemporary American) I cannot avoid being sympathetic to such "reconstructions," it is easy, sometimes, to lose sight of what Aristotle might have had to say to us within his own framework. Indeed, for reasons that will, hopefully, become clear by the end of this chapter, legalistic constructions such as the notion of natural rights can obscure the relationship of epieikeia and Aristotle's notion of political friendship to his notion of natural justice.

However, I believe that Miller's reconstruction largely avoids such problems, because his reconstruction of the conceivable Aristotelian roots of natural rights pertains to a notion of natural right that is sufficiently distinct from contemporary notions of natural rights.

6. Before launching into the major arguments in this chapter, I will make a brief nod to

political correctness by noting that I do not subscribe to Aristotle's views on women, children, or slaves. As it should be fairly obvious that his views on these matters are not essential features of his thought and affect in no way the selective uses of his ideas within this study, I will dispense with any extended apologetic on these issues.

7. While legal rules or the positive law form the focus of my examination of legal injustices, it is not necessary for me to distinguish between the moral and positive law in Aristotle, since he does not recognize such a Kantian distinction.

8. Aristotle, *Nichomachean Ethics* (hereafter *EN*) VIII.9, 1159b25–1160a8.

9. Aristotle, *EN* VIII.11, 1161a10–11, 1161a30.

10. Aristotle, *Politics* I.6, 1255a4–1255b15.

11. Aristotle, *EN* VIII.9–VIII.13, 1159b25–1163a23.

12. Aristotle, *EN* VIII.9, 1160a1–10; *Rhetoric* I.13, 1373b6–10.

13. The modern employment relationship often has elements of both the commercial one of utility and the master-slave relationship.

14. Aristotle, *EN* IX.10, 1170b20–1171a20; *Politics* I.2, 1252a24–1252b10; III.9, 1280a7–1281a10; VII.4,1325b34–1326b25.

15. Aristotle, *EN* IX, 1163b28–1172a15; *Politics* I.2, 1252a24–1252a39.

16. Aristotle, *EN* VIII.9, 1159b25–1160a30.

17. Ibid.; *EN* VIII.11, 1161a10–1161b10.

18. Aristotle, *EN* VIII.9, 1159b25–27.

19. Aristotle, *EN* VIII.11, 1161a10–1161b10.

20. Ibid.; Aristotle, *Politics* III.6–9, 1278b6–1281a10.

21. Aristotle, *EN* VIII.11, 1161a10–1161b10; *Politics* III.6–9, 1278b6–1281a10.

22. Aristotle, *Politics* III.9, 1280a6–1281a10.

23. Ibid.

24. Ibid.

25. Ibid.

26. Aristotle, *EN* VIII.9, 1160a3–8.

27. Nicholas D. Smith, "Aristotle's Theory of Natural Slavery," in *A Companion to Aristotle's Politics*, eds. Keyt and Miller, 146.

28. See, for example, Georg Wilhelm Friedrich Hegel, *Philosophy of Right*, trans. T. M. Knox (Oxford: Clarendon, 1967), section 67.

29. David Brion Davis, "At the Heart of Slavery," *New York Review of Books*, 17 October 1996, 51:

> Yet the condition of slavery itself has not always been the most abject form of servitude, and is not necessarily so today. Some contract labor, though technically free, is more oppressive than many types of conventional bondage. One thinks, for example, of the Chinese "coolies" who were transported in the mid-nineteenth century across the Pacific to the coast of Peru, where they died in appalling numbers from the lethal effects of shoveling sea-bird excrement for the world's fertilizer market. . . . In ancient Babylonia and Rome, as in the medieval Islamic world and sub-Saharan Africa, chosen slaves served as soldiers, business agents, and high administrators.

30. Aristotle, *Politics* III.9, 1280a8–35.

31. Aristotle, *Politics* III.9, 1280b29–1281a2.

32. Aristotle, *EN* VIII.9, 1160a1–8.

33. Aristotle, *Rhetoric* I.13, 1373b5–8.

34. Aristotle, *Politics* II.2, 1261a13–25.

35. Aristotle, *Politics* III.9, 1280a7–1281a10; *EN* IX.9, 1169b3–1170b19.

36. Dworkin, *Law's Empire*, 205.

37. Aristotle, *EN* V.7, VIII.9, VIII.11; *Politics* I.2, III.9.

38. Dworkin, *Law's Empire*, 202.

39. Aristotle, *EN* VIII.9, 11.

40. Dworkin, "What Is Equality? Part 3: The Place of Liberty," 1–54; Dworkin, "What Is Equality? Part 4: Political Equality," 1–30; Dworkin, *Law's Empire*, chapter 2, 136–49.

41. Aristotle, *EN* V.1–5, VIII, IX; *Politics* III.9.

42. Dworkin, *Law's Empire*, 189.

43. Aristotle, *EN* IX; *Politics* III.9.

44. Aristotle, *Politics* II.2.

45. Dworkin, *Law's Empire*, 225, 239.

46. Ibid.

47. Carl Schmitt, *Political Theology*, trans. George Schwabb (Cambridge: MIT Press, 1988), 36–37.

48. Aristotle, *EN* V.7, 1134b18–1135a5, V.9, 1136b35; *Magna Moralia* I.33.

49. Aristotle, *EN* V.7, 1134b18–23.

50. Aristotle, *Magna Moralia* I.33, 1194b30.

51. Ibid., 1195a5.

52. Ibid.; Aristotle, *EN* V.10, 1137b6–12.

53. For example, see Aristotle, *EN* V.7, 1134b30–33.

54. Aristotle, *Politics* I.2, 1253a2–10.

55. Ibid., 1253a18–28.

56. Ibid., 1252a24–1253a39.

57. Aristotle, *Politics* VII.4, 1326a1–5.

58. Aristotle, *Politics* VII.13, 1332a39–1332b11; *EN* II.1, 1103b1–5.

59. Aristotle, *EN* II.1, 1103b1–5.

60. Aristotle, *EN* V.7, 1134b18–1135a15; V.9, 1137b33–35; V.10, 1137b8–10, 1137b24–29; *Magna Moralia* I.33, 1193b1–5, 1194b30–1195a8.

61. In *Problems of a Political Animal*, 178, Yack elaborates at some length on the implications of Aristotle's disregard of this traditional question of jurisprudence, finding this omission in Aristotle to be not a defect, but a basis for comparison with the current jurisprudential dogmas.

62. In *Problems of a Political Animal*, 179, Yack notes both Aristotle's broad use of *nomos* and, more important, Aristotle's apparent indifference to attempts to precisely define it.

63. Aristotle, *EN* V.8, 1135a16–18.

64. For example, see Aristotle, *EN* V.10, 1137a32–1137b32. These and other passages are quoted and interpreted in section 3 of this chapter.

65. Compare Aristotle, *Physics* II.1; *Ethics* V.7, 1134b18–1135a5; V.9, 1136a35 with *Rhetoric* I.13, 1373b3–6.

66. Aristotle, *EN* VIII.9, 11, 1159b25–1169a8, 1161a10–1161b1.

67. Yack, *Problems of a Political Animal*, 129.

68. Ibid., 130–31.

69. Arkes, *First Things*, 162.

70. Iredell Jenkins, *Social Order and the Limits of Law*, 192–13.

71. Miller, "Aristotle on Natural Law and Justice," 289.

72. Sarah Waterlow, *Nature, Change, and Agency in Aristotle's Physics* (Oxford: Oxford University Press, 1982).

73. Aristotle, *Physics* II.1, 192b8–23.

74. Ibid.

75. Ibid.

76. Aristotle, *Physics* II.8, 198b34–36.

77. Ibid.

78. Miller, "Aristotle on Natural Law and Justice," 289; Aristotle, *EN* V.7, 1134b33–1135a1; *Magna Moralia* I.33.

79. Aristotle, *EN* V.7, 1134b30–1135a5.

80. Aristotle, *Magna Moralia* I.33, 1194b30–1195a7.

81. Miller, "Aristotle on Natural Law and Justice," 289–92.

82. Ibid., 290–92.

83. To render Aristotle's analogy more compelling for contemporary readers, I would suggest replacing his references to right and left with *healthy* and *unhealthy*, since health is a teleological notion that has retained intelligibility. Namely, there is such a state as being healthy, notwithstanding the failure of many people in attaining or maintaining health because of poor diet, war, and diseases. To deny any ontological significance to the notion of health, or the superiority of a state of health to being unhealthy, ought to be an obvious absurdity. Accordingly, I return to the health analogy throughout this chapter, to reenforce particular teleological arguments.

84. Lawrence M. Friedman treats this problem with a great deal of sensitivity to what is being lost in the process of the expansion of the modern nation state and its legal framework. Lawrence M. Friedman, *Total Justice* (New York: Russell Sage Foundation, 1994).

85. Aristotle, *Politics* III.9, 1280b30–35.

86. Aristotle, *Politics* II.2, 1261a10–1261b15.

87. David Keyt, "Three Basic Theorems in Aristotle's *Politics*," in *A Companion to Aristotle's Politics*, eds. Keyt and Miller, 118–41.

88. Ibid., 135.

89. Roberto Mangabeira Unger, *The Critical Legal Studies Movement* (Cambridge: Harvard University Press, 1983).

90. Yack, *Problems of a Political Animal*, 175–6. Yack argues convincingly against traditional interpretations of Aristotle that interpret him as a naive republican.

91. Aristotle, *Politics* III.16, 1287a28–31.

92. Aristotle, *Politics* III.16, 1287a31–33.

93. Aristotle, *Politics* III.16, 1287b5–7. The written law is that which is legislated by officials. While some might argue that the English common law accords with Aristotle's notion of ethos or custom, the analogy is far too narrow. The common law was promulgated by judges, whereas custom connotes the habits of a natural political community as a whole and is not just limited to the influence of these habits in the adjudications of certain officials.

94. Aristotle, *EN* V.10, 1137b10–28; see following discussion of epieikeia in section 3 of this chapter.

95. For a discussion of the role of custom in interpreting, misinterpreting, and mitigating the law, see especially James Bernard Murphy's recent tract; "Nature, Custom, and Stipulation in Law and Jurisprudence," *Review of Metaphysics* 43 (1990): 751–90.

96. Aristotle, *Politics* II.8, 1269a10–12.

97. *Politics* II.8, 1269a10–27; IV.5, 1292b10–20; VII.13, 1232a38–1232b11; *Ethics* II.1, 1103a14–1103b25; Murphy, "Nature, Custom, and Stipulation in Law and Jurisprudence," 751–90; see n. 134.

98. A recent study combines sociology, game theory, and economic theory in some case studies to illustrate and model the ways in which disputes are settled based on customary nonlegal norms. Robert C. Ellickson, *Order Without Law: How Neighbors Settle Disputes* (Cambridge: Harvard University Press, 1991).

99. Aristotle, *Politics* II.8, 1269a10–27.

100. Ibid.

101. Ibid.

102. Aristotle, *Politics* IV.5, 1292b10–17.

103. Ibid.

104. Aristotle, *EN* II.1, 1103a14–1103b25; *Politics* VII.13, 1332a38–b11.

105. Ibid.

106. For a discussion of this debate within the positivist framework, see Postema, *Bentham and*

the Common Law Tradition. For a broader understanding of custom than that of Postema, albeit one that views the common law as part of custom, see Murphy, "Nature, Custom, and Stipulation in Law and Jurisprudence," 751–90.

107. Murphy, "Nature, Custom, and Stipulation in Law and Jurisprudence," 789.

108. Mary Ann Glendon, in a comparative study of the relation of custom and law in various European countries and the United States, on the questions of abortion and divorce, noted how the incidence of abortions, for example, was significantly lower, and the enforcement of child-support burdens was emphasized more, in European countries with very liberal abortion and divorce laws, but that had different customs concerning sexual mores and child-support obligations. And, more important, they had a different view of the role of law—where law was less polarizing than in the United States, and yet also was more pedagogical—as a source of shared moral expectations. Glendon, Abortion and Divorce in Western Law.

In a similar vein, various criminological studies have indicated that "informal social controls," exemplified in the unwritten customs of a society involving families, religion, and communal relationships, are often more significant than the nature of the laws themselves in discriminating between societies with high and low crime rates. See, for example, W. Timothy Austin, "Crime and Custom in an Orderly Society: The Singapore Prototype," *Criminology* 25 (1987): 279–92; Freda Adler, *Nations Not Obsessed with Crime* (Littleton, Colo.: Rothman, 1983).

109. Aristotle, *EN* II.1, 1103a14–1103b25.

110. Ibid.

111. This is why the use of entrapment by police and prosecutors to enforce laws is such a perversion of justice. Moreover, the notion that laws have a moral and educational aim does not mean that legislators should be busybodies. Nor does this imply that laws by themselves can morally constitute the social order. The primary point of this section—that custom is, ultimately, more important than the number and type of laws—does not, however, mean that laws are or ought to be morally neutral, a myth of positivism.

112. Aristotle, *EN* VI.11, 1143a19–24.

113. Aristotle, *Magna Moralia* II.1, 1198b25–27.

114. Aristotle, *Rhetoric* I.13, 1374b4–21.

115. *Pearcy v. Citizens Bank and Trust Co. of Bloomington,* 96 N.E.2d 918, 927 (Ind. 1951), quoting with approval the legal encyclopedia, 30A *Corpus Juris Secundum.* Numerous other cases make the same point that "equality is equity." See, for example: *Underwood v. Phillips Petroleum Co.,* 155 F.2d 372 (10th Cir. 1946); *Buhl v. Kavanagh,* 118 F.2d 315 (6th Cir. 1941); *Woodlawn Federal Savings and Loan Association v. Williams,* 187 So. 177 (Ala. 1939); *Wasson v. Pledger,* 96 S.W.2d 8 (Ark. 1936); *Century Indemnity Co. v. Kofsky,* 161 A. 101 (Conn. 1932); *Mordt v. Robinson,* 156 So. 535 (Fla. 1934); *Williams Bros. Lumber Co. v. Anderson,* 78 S.E.2d 612 (Ga. 1953); *Shepherd v. Dougan,* 76 P.2d 442 (Idaho 543); *Maccabees v. City of Ashland,* 109 S.W.2d 29 (Ky. 1937); *Smith v. Whitman,* 189 A.2d 15 (N.J. 1963); *Mikels v. Cowie Cut Stone Co.,* 171 N.E. 251 (Ohio App. 1929); *Nash v. Gardner,* 101 S.E.2d 283 (S.C. 1957); *Davis v. Carothers,* 335 S.W.2d 631 (Tex. Civ. App., Waco, 1969), *dismissed by agreement; Rich v. Stephens,* 11 P.2d 295 (Utah 1932); *Price v. Price,* 7 S.E.2d 510 (W.Va. 1940).

116. Aristotle, *EN* V.10, 1137b10–28.

117. Aristotle, *EN* VI.11, 1143a25–1143b14.

118. The law of trusts and estates arose out of the equity jurisdiction exercised by ecclesiastic officials. Inheritance taxes were avoided by having a churchman hold one's lands in trust. Various so-called forms of equitable relief, such as injunctions, arose to supplement the inadequacies of courts of law under the king, which only awarded damages. The standard legal encyclopedia, 30A *Corpus Juris Secundum,* section 3 (1992), 162, summarizes the development of equity in English law:

> English equity as a system administered by a tribunal apart from the established courts
> made its first appearance in the reign of Edward I, according to some authorities, its ori-

gin being due to the inability, and to a limited extent the unwillingness, of the common-law courts to entertain and give relief in every case, and thus meet all the requirements of justice. . . . The growing powers of chancery as a judicial tribunal [initially] met with much opposition, owing to an apparent disposition on their part to entrench on the jurisdiction of courts of law. . . . The doctrine of stare decisis became an established part of equity jurisprudence. Thenceforth, equity ceased to be a mere corrective agency and became a definite system of jurisprudence occupying the field side by side with the common law, each with a distinct jurisdiction, and, therefore, necessarily there also grew up, not only two distinct systems of practice in these courts, but also two distinct systems of substantive jurisprudence, that in the court of chancery being the system which we call "equity." Much of the English equitable jurisprudence was taken from the Roman civil law.

119. This historical understanding of how the notion of epieikeia was changed and perverted into a legal framework of so-called equitable rules is important to preclude setting up epieikeia into a straw man by attacking the inflexibility and injustice of the Chancery Courts in England. For a discussion of Bentham's reforms of the inflexible legal rules of equity in the Chancery Courts, see Postema, *Bentham and the Common Law Tradition*.

120. A *Corpus Juris Secundum*, section 2, 159.

121. *Bennis v. Michigan*, 116 S.Ct. 994 (1996).

122. The difference between equity reduced to equality and equity as a correction of the law where, by reason of its universality, it is deficient ought to be fairly obvious. Treating persons with equality is not departing from a universal legal principle, but rather is a submission to the rule of equality—a principle enacted in statutes and expounded in case law. Yet, without any analysis, the court in *Pearcy v. Citizens Bank and Trust Co. of Bloomington* quoted Aristotle's notion of equity as a correction of defects arising from the universal application of a legal rule, and treated this notion as if it was not incompatible with the notion that equity was equality.

123. Yack, *Problems of a Political Animal*, 194: "Aristotelian equity is, in the end, a characteristic we expect of just individuals (*NE* 1138a3) rather than a set of rules."

124. Aristotle, *Rhetoric* I.13, 1374b4–21.

125. Ibid.

126. Aristotle, *EN* V.10, 1137b11–12.

127. Aristotle, *EN* V.10, 1137b26–27.

128. See discussion in von Leyden, *Aristotle on Equality and Justice*, 1–10.

129. H. L. A. Hart, *The Concept of Law*, chapter 7. For a brilliant discussion of Hart, Dworkin, and Aristotle, for which I am greatly indebted in the next few paragraphs, see Roger A. Shiner, "Aristotle's Theory of Equity," in *Justice, Law, and Method in Plato and Aristotle*, ed. Spiro Panagiotou (Edmonton, Canada: Academic Printing and Publishing, 1987), 173–91.

130. Of course, epieikeia is universal, in the sense of there being one correct outcome—that being the exercise of the virtue of epieikeia by making an exception to a universal norm to render particular justice in the circumstances. See, for example, *Rhetoric* I.15, 1375a31, where Aristotle says that "the principles of equity are permanent and changeless."

131. Roger Shiner does not sufficiently distinguish these alternatives in a way that makes it clear that flexibility in Aristotelian epieikeia is not a recipe for moral relativism. This omission in Shiner's essay may in part be due to the fact that Aristotle himself does not emphasize the sense in which the flexibility of epieikeia is not completely open-ended, because he probably takes it for granted that no one would read him that broadly.

132. Shiner, "Aristotle's Theory of Equity," 184.

133. Fred D. Miller Jr., "Aristotle and the Origins of Natural Rights," *Review of Metaphysics* 49 (June 1996): 877. Aristotle's "individualistic" notion of justice is "moderate" for Miller (as op-

posed to an "extreme individualism") because it acknowledges that the "individual good includes other-regarding morally virtuous activity, for example, acts of courage, generosity, friendship, and justice." Miller also stipulates that his characterization of Aristotle's notion of justice as individualistic does not carry with it broader contemporary notions of individualism that assume that "the good varies from individual to individual."

134. Miller, "Aristotle and the Origins of Natural Rights," quoting Edward Zeller, *Aristotle and the Earlier Peripatetics,* trans. B. F. C. Costelloe and J. H. Muirhead (London: Longmans, Green, 1897), 2:224–26.

135. This exclusion in no wise passes on the ultimate merits of such reconstructions on their own terms. I am merely making the point that a natural right reconstruction of Aristotle is ill-suited to the present aims of this particular study—without at all pronouncing upon the usefulness of such reconstructions in dealing with other problems.

136. Aristotle, *Rhetoric* I.15, 1375a31.

137. See, for example, Aristotle, *EN* 1121b24, 1137a31–1138a3, 1143a20; *Magna Moralia,* 1198b24–35, *Rhetoric* 1372b18, 1374a25–b23. Fred D. Miller ducks the issue of reconciling the two senses of epieikeia in the manner offered here by viewing the reference to epieikeia as a "universal" feature of justice, in a more popular sense of the term than Aristotle's more technical senses in the other references cited. See Miller, "Aristotle on Natural Law and Justice," 284–85. However, I do not see the need for any "reconciliation" here, for the reasons explained in the body of my text.

138. Roger A. Shiner's essay clearly elucidates the relationship between the ontology and epistemology underlying and explaining the breadth of the flexibility at work in Aristotle's notion of epieikeia. The only significant omission in Shiner's essay is a discussion of the centrality of the relationship between epieikeia and friendship, or the natural sociability associated with natural justice and that constitutes a political community. Accordingly, Shiner's emphasis is on the adjudicative manifestations of epieikeia; it thereby fails to acknowledge adequately the role of epieikeia by citizens who are not acting as officials.

139. This discussion of the epistemology of epieikeia is based on Aristotle, *EN* VI.8, 11, 1142a23–30, 1143a25–b14.

140. Yack, *Problems of a Political Animal,* 188–89.

141. The sense of *forgiving* here is not a Christianized sense, but the sense of one who judges "rightly" what is "truly equitable." I am grateful to criticisms of Professor Daniel Robinson for properly pointing out to me the need to clarify my usage here.

142. Aristotle, *EN* VI.11, 1143a19–24.

143. Aristotle, *Rhetoric* I.13.

144. Flaherty and Biskupic, "Rules Often Impose Toughest Penalties on Poor, Minorities."

145. Nat Henthoff, "The AIDS Establishment's Conspiracy of Silence," *Washington Post,* 1 October 1994, A23.

146. Ibid.

147. Ibid.

148. Arguably, parallel to epieikeia acting as a corrective to legal injustices is the similar virtue of liberality that acts as a corrective to distributive injustices in the private market.

149. Aristotle, *Politics* IV.5, 1292b11–17: "It should, however, be remembered that in many states the constitution which is established by law, although not democratic, owing to the education and habits of the people may be administered democratically, and conversely in other states the established constitution may incline to democracy, but may be administered in an oligarchical spirit."

150. Edward C. Banfield, "Welfare: A Crisis Without 'Solutions,'" *Public Interest* 16 (Summer 1969): 89–101.

151. *Goldberg v. Kelly,* 397 U.S. 254 (1970).

152. De Tocqueville, "Memoir on Pauperism," 102, 114.

153. I say "paradoxical" here because most legalist scholars, judges, and lawyers tend to view "discretion" as the very core of arbitrariness.

154. For a documented example of the systematic underpayment of medical costs by Medicare, see *United Wire, Metal and Mach. Health and Welfare Fund v. Morristown Memorial Hospital*, 995 F.2d 1179 (3d Cir. 1993). See also Holman W. Jenkins Jr., "Who's Scamming Whom?" *Wall Street Journal*, 5 August 1997, A19; George Anders and Laurie McGinley, "Surgical Strike, A New Brand of Crime Now Stirs the Feds: Health-Care Fraud."

155. Bob Kamman, "Tax Czars vs. the Poor," *Wall Street Journal*, 17 January 1997, A12.

156. How many counts for fraud would be applied against Valjean if he filed a tax form under this assumed name in our contemporary system?

157. This inability—to distinguish between those (1) truly in need and entitled to a benefit (2) merely technically entitled to that benefit (3) truly in need and not technically entitled to that benefit—is the essential problem with affirmative action. In the first category are lower-class African American males from the inner city. In the middle category are upper-middle-class African Americans and women. In the third category are lower-class and lower-middle-class whites and some recent poor immigrants who are not part of a protected minority. Most of the beneficiaries of affirmative action are in the second category. There are few in the first category, and none that qualify in the third category.

158. Vobejda and Havemann, "Welfare Clients Already Work Off the Books."

159. *United States v. D'Amato*, 39 F.3d 1249 (2d Cir. 1994).

160. Of course, this idealized view ignores the crafty parliamentary maneuvers used by seasoned legislators to get their pet projects voted upon without sufficient deliberation.

161. Glendon, *Abortion and Divorce in Western Law*, 86–87.

162. See, for example, Thomas L. Hanson et al., "Trends in Child Support Outcomes," in *Demography* (Washington, D.C., November 1996): 15–16: "The percentage of women with child support awards declined by about 12 percent during the 1980s, and average award amounts and receipts decreased by about 20 percent," largely as a result of declines in fathers' incomes.

See also, for example, William P. O'Hare, "A New Look at Poverty in America," *Population Bulletin* (Washington, D.C., September 1996): 17–18: "But in reality, only about 18 percent of poor single-parent families received any child support payments in 1994. . . . Furthermore, while many fathers deliberately evade their child support obligations, others simply earn too little to be able to pay it."

163. *Terminiello v. Chicago*, 337 U.S. 1 (1948).

164. *R. A. V. v. City of St. Paul, Minnesota*, 505 U.S. 377 (1992).

165. In reality, *Vinson* is still good law, but this does not belie the recognition of the inconsistency.

166. *Meritor Savings Bank, FSB v. Vinson*, 447 U.S. 57 (1986); *Harris v. Forklift Systems, Inc.*, 126 L.Ed.2d 295 (1993).

167. Greenfield, "Sexual Harasser?" See also Jeremy Rabkin, "New Checks on Campus Sexual-Harassment Cops," *Wall Street Journal*, 19 October 1994, A21; Henthoff, "'I Would Prefer Not To': The Man Who Refused to go to Sexual-Harassment Prevention Class."

168. Separation of church and state prior to the triumph of Henry VIII over the church meant having two equal centers of power in competition with each other that, arguably, checked each other.

Since the Enlightenment, separation of church and state has tended to mean the subordination of religion to the state, to the point of Dworkin's notion that it is illegitimate for religion to even enter into the public realm at all. Without attempting to unpack what this all means, it is interesting to note that this change occurred coincident with the change in meaning of equity over the same period.

169. Indeed, in the area of employee benefit litigation, the Supreme Court recently sharply distinguished between "equitable" and "legal" relief available against nonfiduciaries who knowingly participated in a breach of fiduciary duty with respect to an employee benefit plan. Legal relief permits compensatory damages, whereas equitable relief is limited to injunctive and similar such remedies, according to the court—based on a historical conventionalist approach to interpretation. The point here is to merely illustrate how the term *equity* has become infected with legalisms. See *Mertens v. Hewitt Association*, 113 S.Ct. 2063, 2068–69 (1993).

170. Bovard, *Lost Rights*, 221.

171. Avis Thomas-Lester, "Abduction Suspect Paroled in '79 Case: Kidnapped Boy's Mother Questions Role of Judicial System, D.C. Police," *Washington Post*, 3 October 1994, A1.

172. For example, squatters can occupy apartments for eighteen months in some jurisdictions, in the knowledge that the procedural burdens are on the landlords to eject them and that this cannot start for eighteen months.

173. Some responsible commentators have pointed to "institutional incentives to find more fraud rather than less" on the part of the National Institute of Health and to the fact that "Mr. Dingell's subcommittee engaged in political grandstanding at the scientists' expense." Editorial, *Washington Post*, 30 June 1996, C6.

174. Rick Weiss, "Proposed Shifts in Misconduct Reviews Unsettle Many Scientists," *Washington Post*, 30 June 1996, A6.

175. See Weiss, "Proposed Shifts in Misconduct Reviews Unsettle Many Scientists":
> Even though scientific exploration is inherently susceptible to honest mistakes that run the risk of being misinterpreted as fraud, the new system will rely to an unprecedented degree on strict legal principles. As a result, it will increasingly force scientists to deal with creatures they've never been comfortable with: lawyers and politicians. . . . Until recently . . . scientists were largely left alone. If questions arose about the veracity of their findings or their published reports, the issue was resolved over coffee, at the lab bench, or— in extreme cases—in a department chairman's office. Those days are over. Scientific misconduct, although still believed to be rare, is increasingly being pursued with the fervor once reserved for violent crimes."

176. It is possible to give a more benign interpretation of Aristotle's infamous discussion of natural slavery in *Politics* I.5–6, 1254a17–1255b15. He may be construed as merely making the point that, for some, education in the virtues can only go so far, given a nature rendering it difficult to cultivate virtuous habits in them (a similar point is made in *Ethics* X.9, 1179b20–30, but not in the context of slavery). In the nature/nurture debate, nurture can only go so far. That there are natural slaves, in this sense, seems defensible to me. However, if Aristotle is also saying that persons who are natural slaves ought to be enslaved and that it is right and just for this to be so, I would have to strongly disagree with him. That there are people who, through natural defects in character, fail to actualize what persons, for the most part, and with proper education in a healthy society, would fulfill, seems to be unremarkable to me.

5

Abolition of Legal Profession and Other Reforms

The lawyers, not the philosophers, are the clergy of liberalism. . . . Like other traditions, liberalism expresses itself socially through a particular kind of hierarchy. For in a society within which preferences, whether in the market or in politics or in private life, are assigned the place which they have in a liberal order, power lies with those who are able to determine what the alternatives are to be between which choices will be available. The consumer, the voter, and the individual in general are accorded the right of expressing their preferences for one or more out of the alternatives which they are offered, but the range of possible alternatives is controlled by an elite, and how they are presented is also so controlled. The ruling elites within liberalism are thus bound to value highly competence in the persuasive presentation of alternatives, that is, in the cosmetic arts.[1]

The notion that society is not a mere amalgamation of individuals held together through legal relationships does not mean that there is not an appropriate role for law as a constituent of the social order. Rather, the point is that an overemphasis on law is ultimately destructive of the very moral foundations of the social order that render natural social cooperation and accommodation possible at all.

Moreover, law itself cannot function justly without epieikeia, and epieikeia itself arises out of the natural bonds of community and not out of the legal order. To appreciate this fact is not to idealize the natural community, which itself can often behave unjustly. Rather, it is to recognize that some minimal level of natural sociability is absolutely necessary in order for justice to be at hand at all. While this natural sociability is not, in itself, sufficient for justice, ignoring this natural sociability in the name of legal justice is, indeed, the fundamental origin of legal injustice.

Accordingly, legal injustice originates in an intellectual and social moral vacuum, where the exclusive question is oriented toward the coherence of law and a legal system. While this reenforces the importance of maintaining a self-contained professional aristocracy of legal practitioners who alone are indoctrinated in this language game and who alone ultimately benefit from it, this preoccupation ultimately diverts attention from the real causes and solutions of injustice in a society. Indeed, Dworkin's so-called community of principle, which at least makes this elitism overt, is an essential and indispensable part of the industry of legal injustice. There are enough natural injustices in a society without the addition of legal injustices.

A person who exclusively focused on pharmacology as an answer to human health might serve the interests of pharmacists, physicians, and maybe even a few hypochondriacs very well. But anyone who focused on the question of what is a drug, as if that question had fundamental importance to human health, would be justly ridiculed by most persons.

Unfortunately, the same has not happened in the area of jurisprudence. Just as the health of the human body requires good diet, exercise, and rest, where drugs can help a generally healthy body that is temporarily sick but do little for a really sick person, so, too, does justice require something other than law. Epieikeia is an indication of what that something is, but it is far from a complete description of it. Rather, art, religion, the uses of leisure, the love of conversation, the love of one's children, the making of friendships, and liberality are among some of the intangibles associated with living together as friends in a social order in the same place. A society that places too high a premium on legal relationships is not a society that will ultimately place a high premium on such intangibles.

Indeed, whether in business or in government, it is perhaps telling that frequently, the most unjust and imbalanced persons rise to positions of leadership. Persons who ignore their children and view leisure time as the time to travel to some exotic clime and bask in the sun in a hotel environment often become chief executive officers in corporations, managing partners in law firms, colonels and generals, senators, and presidents. But persons living in their local community in the fullest sense of taking care of their children, becoming involved in the arts or with their neighbors or religious activities rarely have the time to become the persons who rise to the top of the business and governmental worlds. Accordingly, the persons who most often litigate legal issues, or most often legislate the laws or adjudicate them, often are not the persons leading social lives in the fullest sense—the latter simply believe that they do not have the time or interest for such intangible things. To believe that this has no deleterious effect on the nature of law and its relation, or lack thereof, to justice, requires an utter lack of imagination. An imbalance between the legal and natural social order will never be recognized as such or corrected, where a society's leaders lack the natural social virtues that can only arise from living a shared life with others.

The language of such elites is estranged from the language of ordinary persons, whose focus is their families and the communities they live in with other like-minded persons. In business, it is the language of selling off an unprofitable division, corporate restructurings, making decisions as if the corporation were a mere temporary guest in the local community. Global-ization of markets and international competitiveness are the buzzwords of this particular elite. In government, it is the language of taxing to pay for some grand design of benefit to certain groups at the expense of other groups, or of mandating certain groups to undertake some noble effort while hiding the cost of that effort from view.

Both language games involve the language of deception, manipulation, and power. And both are the predominant clients of the professionals who are the master inventors and manipulators of this language game of con-cealment (that is, the lawyers)—no one else has the time or resources to do this.

Certain rituals and pretenses are of particular importance to legal prac-tice in this environment. Changes in the tax laws are lobbied for and engi-neered in the name of fairness, a buzzword for complexity, special privileges, loopholes, and economic leveling for anyone not rich enough to hire a lob-byist-lawyer. In the adjudicative arena, the legal system purports to reserve fact finding to "impartial" juries, the composition of which is manipulated by the attorneys opposing each other on both sides of a dispute. Knowl-edgeable jurors are thought to be too knowledgeable to be impartial, and so are stricken from the jury, with the result that easily manipulated ignora-muses often are the result of pursuing this fictitious ideal of impartiality.

But the quest for a bogus impartiality suits very well the agenda of lawyers seeking to maximize the available levers of manipulation in the system. An-other example concerns the notion that certain rituals of procedural due process are great bulwarks against abuses of power by the government. But in reality, this merely means that an official desiring to abuse power must have good enough legal advice to commit an injustice using the appropri-ate procedures. It is inherent in our legal system that an official can cross all the t's and dot all the i's as far as procedural due process goes and still bring about, knowingly or unknowingly, the conviction of an innocent person or the absence of punishment for a person guilty of a violent, heinous crime.

For these reasons, the present chapter enumerates a variety of reforms, in varying degrees of effectiveness. Hopefully, readers will be charitable enough to recognize that the diagnosis of the problem outlined in the pre-ceding chapters does not automatically bring with it adequate solutions. A demonstration of the inadequacy of some or all of the reforms posed in this chapter should, from a logical standpoint, have no relevance to the validity or invalidity of my diagnosis of the problem, just as a physician may properly diagnose a particular disease without adequately prescribing the appropri-ate drug in the appropriate dosage.

Indeed, by the very premises of my analysis of legal injustices, the proposed reforms must be ultimately inadequate to the extent that they are merely legal reforms. The nonlegal reforms proposed in this chapter are, accordingly, more significant, though they are reforms in the same sense as the legal reforms are. The proposed reforms, indeed, may be criticized because they purport to be the natural end of a healthy social order and yet have not arisen naturally, thus raising questions as to how natural they really are. But the regulative idea of my exploration of legal injustices is that such conditions, at some point, may naturally arise, because man's natural sociability, even if it is repressed by the legal order, at some point has to surface.

Who would have thought that the Soviet empire would topple so quickly and spontaneously within, without much conscious design from some revolutionary elite? But that is, in fact, what happened. Likewise, it is contended that some of the reforms discussed in this chapter may, at some point, arise naturally, at a time when our system least expects it. The pervasiveness of the legal system and the legal industry in our society, at this point, is so overwhelming and growing at such a pace that many may despair of arresting it. But just when the Leviathan seems most invincible, it may overreach itself and implode.[2]

At this point, an attentive reader may have already inferred the root of the fundamental reforms to be proposed in this chapter. The language of jurisprudential legalism must be exposed for what it is, in the hope that the civic order will thenceforth dispense with such manipulations of language. This book itself is intended as a small step in the direction of this fundamental and essential reform.

1. Legal Reforms

One avenue to reform of the language of jurisprudence is the elimination of the special privileges attendant to the practice of the legal profession, hence, the elimination of the licensing of the legal profession. The bar may howl at such a proposal, claiming that it would encourage incompetents and dishonest ruffians to practice law. Yet in fact, the bar has not done a very good job of policing itself. Most persons cannot afford to use lawyers anyway, and, more important, the practice of law is too important a civic virtue to be left to professionals.[3] Arguing for the professionalization of law is like arguing that voting or military service should be professionalized by a certain group of persons interested in such activities. One of the fundamental conclusions of my examination into the nature and origins of legal injustices is that epieikeia cannot truly arise where the practice of law is confined to a professional group of lawyers. This finding is associated with the fact that the very notion of epieikeia has not retained its original meaning. Indeed, its original meaning is largely restricted and distorted when viewed as a component of the legal order that has been completely professionalized.

Those who emphasize the competence of lawyers in legal matters uncritically presuppose that the artificial separation of law, politics, and ethical inquiry has been beneficial. Attendant to this presupposition is a devaluing of epieikeia, since this intangible form of practical wisdom cannot be taught in law schools and cannot be reduced to a universalizable rule. But the test of law must not be its so-called fit with itself. Rather, its application must be tested against justice. And the justice against which the application of law ought to be continually tested is not legal justice, but natural justice. Such natural justice cannot take its content from the legal system in isolation from the political and ethical orders without thereby reducing itself to mere legal justice.

If one confines one's vision of legal justice to merely encompassing some sort of notion of coherence of the legal system within itself, legal injustices (in the broadened sense articulated in this analysis) will not be seen, precisely because they are coherent within this narrow framework. Only when this framework is opened to include coherence with the moral and social realms will such legal injustices be fully revealed. If one's notion of equity or epieikeia is confined to the language of appellate-court decisions discussing equity within a legal framework, one loses the vocabulary for expressing the broader meanings of epieikeia discussed in Chapter 4.

Similarly, if one views a business purely as having the goal of making profits and not as existing within a community for the purposes of serving that community, one will make decisions that will maximize profits in the short term for that business, even if this proves destructive to the community upon which that business relies in the long term. All of these confusions, in a sense, arise from the desire to deal with what are considered more objective and tangible constructs: the laws, a business's financial statements, and seeing a community as the organ of government. Rather, the appropriate way to deal with a community is to engage in the intangible yet real connections that we all feel and experience in our ordinary relationships. The language of law, government, business, and revolution is a language that conceals this basic experience from us, and ultimately, it confuses us if we allow it to.

The presupposition that knowledge of the positive law by itself, as a self-contained system with its own vocabulary, apart from any particular social context, is a competence that ought to be valued in a society to the same degree that the competence of a physician is recognized is far from unassailable. Indeed, knowledge of the law, in the sense of what is taught in law schools and tested on bar exams, is not knowledge of something valuable to society in the same sense as medicine is. This is not to say that knowledge of the law is of no value; rather, knowledge of the law has been overvalued as a social good, and this has worked to the interest of lawyers, as a professional group, at the expense of justice.

Knowledge of the law is, moreover, more analogous to the knowledge of a pharmacist than to that of a surgeon or physician. That is to say, knowledge of the law provides knowledge of a very limited tool with very limited uses in maintaining the social order. Just as we do not want pharmacists prescribing drugs or diagnosing diseases, we ought not let lawyers monopolize justice under the rubric of legal justice.

This leads to my second criticism of the notion of law as a competence worthy of professionalization: namely, the tendency of the legal profession to view justice achieved outside the legal system as always constituting unjust vigilantism. While vigilantism, particularly in perverse societies, is often unjust, legal justice, likewise, is unjust in perverse societies. The fact that an injustice is done within or outside the law does not make it unjust; rather, it is unjust because it is unjust. The notion that the presence or absence of law by itself makes an action just or unjust is merely part of the language of concealment that works so well to the advantage of monopolizing power in the organs of government and in the legal profession.

Most persons appear to achieve the expectations that society has of them. Where society has low expectations of a person, that person often will not achieve his or her full potential as a human being and may even become alienated and a criminal in that society. Conversely, where a society has high expectations of its citizens, these citizens will indeed behave closer to their full potential as human beings. For example, those who condemn the irrationality of modern juries often fail to note the role of the manipulations of lawyers and judges in keeping juries in the dark and in selecting the worst possible juries—all with legal pretexts that, on their face, lack credibility to any person familiar with the system.

Most, if not all of the modern law of evidence is precisely the articulation of a common law and codified rules of what may and may not be presented to juries. In addition, the mistrust of epieikeia by legal professionals reaches its complete apex in the modern practice of instructing juries that they do not have the power to disregard what they believe to be an unjust law in rendering their verdict. In fact, under the common-law doctrine of jury nullification, they do have that power.[4]

Part of the process of deprofessionalizing the legal system requires both the elimination of these rules of evidence and the informing of juries of their common-law right of jury nullification. Informed and educated juries would deliberate about what is relevant, rather than leaving this matter to the manipulations of lawyers. While empowering juries overnight (where citizens have been kept in the dark about a major component of civic virtue, namely, the practice of law) certainly has its dangers, there is a greater danger to the current pretense of an impartiality that does not exist. When a people are treated as slaves, they act like slaves. But treat people as important members of the process who must rise to the occasion because they have a stake in society's functioning fairly and justly, and it is possible to have just juries in the absence of the rules of evidence and the attendant manipulations by lawyers.

While the Lon Fuller school of jurisprudence might see value in the indirect, in circumlocution, in the artifice of the law, such concealment carries its price. And that price is the enserfment of a society's citizens. Accordingly, the abolition of the licensing of the legal profession and the empowerment of juries, along with full recognition of the doctrine of jury nullification, inevitably involve another reform: the abolition of the restriction of awarding judgeships only to persons trained as lawyers.

What justification exists for excluding the reasoning power of our greatest scientists, philosophers, and poets from the bench? There is no such justification, other than a legalistic one offered by lawyers who have a self-interest in retaining the prerogatives of a profession. Predictability (or fit) is perhaps the principal argument that might be credibly offered for such a view. But predictability is not a concern where epieikeia, rather than the law, reigns supreme. Predictability is, indeed, the legalistic counterweight to epieikeia. In fact, predictability becomes a rather weak counterweight to epieikeia when the number and complexity of laws expand, and the outcome is not predictable because of the administrative discretion of regulators and prosecutors, who are otherwise protected by sovereign immunity. It is, indeed, arguable that a minimalist legal system as envisioned here, where epieikeia is not suffocated by professionalized lawyers, will not be any less predictable than the current system because of its sheer complexity.

The practice of law is a species of the practice of citizenship, especially in contemporary society. A person is, arguably, not fully participating in the system as a "political animal" to the extent that he or she is not practicing law. Therefore, the professionalization of law is a form of limiting critical attributes of citizenship, in the fullest and most meaningful sense, to a very small, elite group of persons. Similarly, restricting the right to vote in the early nineteenth century was a form of effectively limiting a meaningful attribute of political participation.

Indeed, we are being a bit disingenuous and hypocritical when we smugly assume that our so-called democratic forms today are more democratic than those of the ancient Greeks on the mere basis of a universal right to vote and the absence of chattel slavery (even as the exploitation of wage slaves continues uncondemned). We seem to let the legal form or rhetorical label mask the true nature of many of our most fundamental relationships.

2. Political Reforms

Other reforms (here labeled political reforms, including legislative reforms) follow from what has already been asserted. The popular notion of term limits for legislators and Congress, already applicable to the top elected officials of the executive branch, ought also be applied to judges and prosecutors. Similarly, these positions ought to be rotated for a term among all intellectually competent citizens. When officials serving a limited term clearly understand that they, too, must spend a greater part of their days subject to the regime of other officials, their exercise of power might be more modest and humble.

Aristotle considered the idea of rotating offices to be more democratic than voting (which was considered oligarchical). Aristotle did not consider democracy to be the ideal form of government, but only the better of the perverse forms of government, a view quite different from current presuppositions. To the extent that one subscribes to the contemporary deference to democratic forms, Aristotle's characterization of voting as less democratic than rotating offices ought to make one reexamine the common prejudice favoring voting as somehow giving one democratic control over one's political choices. The alienation of most contemporary voters from the voting process may not be irrational and may, in fact, reflect their recognition that voting does not matter to them, to a certain degree. They are presented with the unacceptable choice of choosing between two or three persons, all of whom want the mandate to run the lives of everyone else.[5]

Voting magnifies the importance of government officials and the role of government in a society. A weak government that is selected through voting will, over time, grow into a stronger and larger government. A government in which officials serve limited terms and are rotated in the same manner as are potential jurors, with the same level of pay, is less likely to grow in size and power in a community.

The notion of sovereign immunity in all its forms should be eradicated from the legal system. Sovereign immunity insulates officials from accountability for their abuses of power (legal injustices). The very notion that some persons may be trusted with unlimited power in the legal system and that most other persons may not be trusted with any power in the legal system is at the very root of the corruption of the legal system.

A related and often proposed reform in the civil system would replace the American rule for legal fees with the English rule. In other words, the loser ought to pay the entire legal fees of both sides in civil litigation. Just as the elimination of sovereign immunity ought to put an end to frivolous prosecutions, by making a prosecutor liable for his or her misconduct, changing the bearer of the ultimate risk of loss in attorneys' fees would, likewise, limit the number of frivolous civil lawsuits that are currently entered only for their settlement value.

Finally, term limits also ought to apply to those high-level federal employees with adjudicative or enforcement powers over others (this clearly excludes from term limits most of the employees of the military, State Department, or similar functions, while term limits would encompass most of the high-level employees of the Departments of Justice, Treasury, Education, Housing and Urban Development, and so on). A professional civil service increases the power of this arm of the executive branch of government, at the expense of the other branches and of the citizenry at large. These high-level positions should, likewise, be rotated.

The legislative reforms should follow a similar tack to those of the executive and judicial branches of government. In addition to term limits, all offices would be filled through rotation rather than election. Moreover, legislative sessions would be limited to a small number of days a year (maybe two weeks), to minimize the amount of mischief that might otherwise be legislated. The idea would be that the role of government would be limited to providing internal and external security. All other areas would be left to the voluntary cooperation of private citizens.

Presumably, greater liberality would be fostered, and resources would go to private charity rather than being funneled to governmental bureaucracies. Accordingly, most laws would be reviewed and repealed, with a view to limiting the criminal law to laws against murder, robbery, and similar crimes.

Prison terms would be confined to violent criminals, who would all serve life terms. The income-tax and estate- and gift-tax systems would be abolished, with all revenue coming from consumption taxes.

Government and the laws would focus on a few priorities, so that the functions that the government had were done well. Thus, the punishing of murderers would be more adequately handled in a society where the focus of government exclusively was concerned with securing citizens from violence. (A government that regulates everything is not going to perform effectively this most basic function of stopping criminal violence. It will be much better at harassing nonviolent citizens.)

There are historical precedents for most of the reforms proposed in this chapter, in ancient Athens during the fifth and fourth centuries B.C.

1. In fourth-century B.C. Athens, the initiative for all political and legal actions or decisions resided exclusively with ordinary citizens and not elected political leaders, appointed judges, appointed administrators, public prosecutors, lobbyists, media leaders, or professional lawyers. That is, it was one of the few examples of a "direct" democracy, in which the people legislated and adjudicated their own laws, rather than being an "indirect" representative democracy, in which the people were limited to electing some of their decision makers. (Of course, the lifetime appointment of judges for unlimited terms is an oligarchical feature of our own system.)
2. All ordinary Athenian citizens had their turn in legislation, adjudication, or administration of the government, for limited terms, and most were selected by lot. This assured high levels of participation in the political process.
3. It was illegal to pay someone as an advocate in the law courts; rather, a party represented itself in any litigation. The Athenians regarded professionalism and democracy as contradictions.
4. In Athens, all prosecutions were by private citizens, as there were no persons given the extraordinary powers commonly given to state prosecutors today.
5. There was no notion of sovereign immunity in ancient democratic Athens. The absence of sovereign immunity manifested itself in many ways. For instance, private citizens could prosecute magistrates for abuses of power. In addition, citizens who were unsuccessful in prosecuting someone were personally liable for substantial sums of money in certain circumstances, thereby exacting a severe penalty for frivolous prosecutions. For example, such a penalty was exacted if they failed to convince at least one-fifth

of the jurors (usually more than five hundred persons, for public prosecutions). As a result, there was a great deal of scrutiny and accountability for all officials.[6]

There is another more recent historical precedent for some of the proposed reforms, provided by the ethnically and religiously diverse Swiss canton of Graubunden, formerly the Republic of the Three Leagues, in the sixteenth century.[7] The citizenry attained high levels of participation in legislating, as well as administering their own laws in a face-to-face, direct democracy. Most important decisions were local and subject to deliberation and ratification through the device of the referendum. For a time, drafting referendums requiring yea or nay votes was illegal, because the very nature of the referendum was a deliberative device to encourage participation in the drafting, and not mere ratification or veto of a proposed action. The government truly was of the people, to such an extent that only ministerial functions were delegated to most governmental officials, who were elected or selected by lot and rotated through their positions.[8] Vestiges of its roots in direct democratic practices remain in modern Switzerland, where many of the elected judges are not even lawyers.[9]

These examples are not intended to romanticize Athenian or Swiss democracy, but are offered to prompt just a smidgen of critical reflection on the part of those who would smugly dismiss as utopian fantasy any deviation from the present system.

3. Private Reforms

The above proposed reforms by themselves will not suffice if the large corporate institutions that have ostensibly arisen in the private market continue in their present form. Corporations are not exclusively the creations of the private market but are, in fact, the historical result of legislative enactment and privileges. The theory has been that capital formation is unlikely without establishing a limited-liability entity called a corporation to insulate the holders of property interests in the entity (the shareholders) from the ordinary legal risks that otherwise might cause an investor to think twice before investing his funds.

However, where legal risks are reduced by diminishing the power of government and lawyers, the rationale behind the current structure of corporate governance provided for under state laws might conceivably lose some of its force. Indeed, even under current corporate structures, creative lawyers and aggressive government regulators have devised new ways of "piercing the corporate veil" and legally seizing corporate assets. At any rate, the current approach of encouraging capital formation by limiting the liability of investors through the corporate structure is, conceivably, not the only way to establish organizations that effectively raise capital from private markets— provided one is satisfied with smaller levels of economic growth.[10] Conceivably, smaller levels of economic growth may not be such a disaster, in exchange for a more viable natural community. Economic growth that benefits a small segment of society loses some of its appeal, as that privileged strata becomes smaller and more insulated.

Indeed, the very idea of limited liability brings with it its own set of problems associated with global investors with little or no connection to a community, exerting considerable influence over whether that community retains a viable economy. In addition, with the exception of large institutional investors, most shareholders are so dispersed that the professional managers running corporations on a day-to-day basis are effectively insulated from accountability. This lack of accountability often results in inflated salaries for top management, even as decisions are made that have the effect of laying off the rank and file.

There is little difference between a fiduciary embezzling the corpus of a trust, a chief executive officer awarding himself excessive salaries and stock options, and a congressman awarding himself a salary and pension exceeding the wildest dreams of 90 percent of most Americans. Indeed, the only difference consists of a legal distinction: namely, the embezzlement by a fiduciary is illegal, whereas the acts of the CEO or congressman are legal.

However, all are lacking in epieikeia, something that is recognized when one expands into a contextual understanding of these actions, beyond the narrow confines of legality. This is another illustration of the ways in which the language of the law conceals and confuses, and it further illustrates the dangers of confining one's notions of justice to legal justice. Ordinary persons recognize all of these actions as being unjust, but only the embezzlement is legally unjust. For such CEOs to award themselves excessive salaries and fringe benefits while at the same time making decisions to lay off employees reveals the complete absence of any sense of natural justice or of any connection between corporate leadership and the surrounding communities.

Thus, the issue of private reform really comes down to individuals in the aggregate selecting certain ends for society that are worthy of being sustained, even at the price of reduced economic growth. The selection of these ends must arise naturally and not through legal or revolutionary reforms. The choices involve the aggregation of individual choices in a community and may be exemplified by its choosing to spend more time together as a community and less time pursuing purely economic goals. As the emptiness of the current corporate lifestyle wears down a significant number of persons, presumably this might lead some persons to choose different ends than the accumulation of wealth as their primary and sole reason for being on this Earth.

At some point, human nature being what it is, one would hope that the majority of people will tire of the pursuit of happiness and simply recognize that the attainment of happiness is not in the pursuit.[11] Anyone working as an employee in today's economy will recognize the exploitative attitudes of far too many corporate employers, which demand that employees sacrifice their local communities, children, and families to the corporation through excessive travel, excessive working hours, and periodic relocations to different communities. And, of course, this exploitation is possible because there are far too many employees ready to turn their corporate employer into a home to avoid their responsibilities in their real homes and communities. There often is a shallow attitude that values the tasks performed for remuneration over the care and education of children within the family, even as lip service is rendered by some to the importance of families and volunteerism in the community.[12]

No argument is being advanced here in favor of economic stagnation (recessions or depressions). However, the notion that short-term profit margins ought to be the exclusive ends of corporate structures is being challenged. Such ends ought also to include engaging in product research and development, marketing and delivering products and services to consumers, and providing employment to the community, all of which are the reasons why state legislatures established special advantages for corporate structures in the first place.

Emphasizing such long-term intangible ends, which are not quantifiable as profits but only as investments or costs on the current short-term balance sheet, often renders a company a takeover target. But ownership of a substantial number of shares of a company should not bring with it control over corporate governance. Indeed, the original theory behind affording limited liability to corporate shareholders was that because corporate governance was in the hands of boards of directors and corporate officers, the limited liability for stockholders ought to serve as a quid pro quo for giving up control over the management of the corporation.

Returning to the original concept behind the corporation, by imposing restrictions on the ability of shareholders to play any role whatsoever in the selection of corporate officers or boards of directors, is a conceivable reform. Why is it necessary for shareholders to vote? Let shareholders register their opinions by buying and selling shares in the market instead. In addition, the CEO and corporate-officer positions, as well as board-of-director positions, should be filled by rank-and-file workers and members of the community and should exclude any shareholders unless they also happen to be employees. These positions should be for limited terms and involve no extra pay. These reforms would not change the way small investors are treated by such corporations, but would only restrict the power of the large institutional investors who currently seem to have the only say in corporate governance.

These reforms are, arguably, more compatible with capitalism in the purest sense than is the current bureaucratic approach, which really makes the lack of accountability of those managing the private sector a mirror of the public sector. Nor would these reforms necessarily result in lower economic growth, in the long run. The short-term speculations and manipulations of the market by large institutional investors should not play any role whatsoever in the decision making of the company's board of directors and officers.

4. Gradual Timetable for Reforms

In reforming customs and the legal system, one does not want to make the very mistake criticized throughout my analysis of legal injustices: the mistake of emphasizing legal reforms at the expense of letting natural corrections of the current imbalances take their course. Accordingly, I recognize that the efficacy of the reforms proposed in this chapter may, in part, be affected by their manner of introduction, and that a gradual introduction of these reforms may be more efficacious than a sudden revolutionary change.

The thrust of all these reforms—of both government and the private sector—involves the displacement of relationships exclusively grounded in legal relationships by relationships in which the stake in the outcome is shared by those living together in the same community. This reveals probably the greatest constraint on all of the reforms mentioned thus far; elimination of the legal profession and greater democratization of society are unlikely to work where the society is too large and geographically dispersed. To be sure, the need to retain relationships between strangers who do not live together is not to be dismissed. Nevertheless, the current situation—in which even persons living together in the same geographic community are strangers to each other—is unacceptable. Moreover, evaluating our society purely in terms of economic growth plainly undervalues that which ultimately makes living in a society worthwhile.

Recognition of this state of affairs does not lead to conclusions in the form of the utopian designs of revolutionaries who would establish governments and legal systems to redistribute resources. The problem is how to return to the connectedness of the village from our present state of complex legal relationships without taking the route of Robespierre, Pol Pot, or the Shining Path. Displacing the coercion and violence of the legal system with revolutionary violence is clearly not a viable solution but will only make matters worse. The attempt to use the government peacefully (and yet not without coercion) to redistribute resources from one group to another is, ultimately, just a milder dose of the revolutionary package. Under this approach, we have seen the personification of the nation state and its organs of power, as if these constituted one's parents or village elders.[13]

The reforms proposed in this chapter attempt to dispense with both approaches, construing them as part of the problem. Without any assurance that these reforms, by themselves, are sufficient, it is clear that we have become too expansive as a society and that relationships with strangers continually intrude upon and attempt to overwhelm our more important relations with family and friends. A government and system of laws that expands to do what is envisioned by the leftist program ultimately erodes the basic functions of government. The task of protecting society (persons and possessions) from violent criminals cannot be carried out well when government does everything.

5. Final Reflections

Of course, one might try, somehow, to opt out of modern society altogether. But this avenue seems to be available only to the homeless and the insane. One cannot accumulate or hold on to any property earned through one's labor without filling out a myriad of forms and defending oneself against criminals who would seek to take away illegally the fruits of one's labor, on the one hand, and defending one's property against the government's efforts to diminish it or take it away for some ostensibly noble cause, on the other.

Perhaps, however, the problem lies in too great an expectation of justice. Living with some degree of natural injustices may well be better than adding to these even greater legal injustices. Indeed, perhaps we would evolve naturally back into village relationships if we took the first step of reducing the scope of governmental involvement in our lives and, with it, the role of professional lawyers. While such a step would not result in a greater degree of natural justice, it certainly could be argued that it would greatly diminish the realm of legal injustice.

None of what has been argued amounts to a contention to dispense with the notion of law. Instead, law would most likely prove more vital and respected when suitably limited and tempered by the epieikeia of the natural community. Indeed, it is conceivable that law would command greater respect and compliance in such a society than it currently does. In the contemporary United States, laws are exponentially generating new laws on a daily basis; governmental officials attempt to entrap and trick persons into violating the law; and persons can unknowingly violate laws, out of the sheer number and complexity of law's empire. More important, with the institution of the proposed reforms, government would focus its resources on what should be its top priority: internal and external security from violence, that is, protecting citizens from violent criminals and from aggression by foreign military invasions.[14]

The fact that we are not a small village does not render the present arrangement necessary. Rather, this unfortunate fact merely makes it more difficult to change and reform the status quo in the direction advanced by my examination into the causes of legal injustices. As intimated earlier, moreover, this assessment does not at all foreclose the possibility that the range of the law may become so pervasive that it ultimately is resisted and overcome in a new understanding and arrangement.

As inevitable and permanent as the current arrangement may seem, social arrangements have not always required professional lawyers and elaborate legal systems. At some point, the analogy of the Tower of Babel has to be seen as quite appropriate to a description of the present tendencies of our legal system. The danger persists that in the confusion of not reaching the heavens, ostensibly the goal of building the Tower of Babel in the first place, confusion itself becomes the established and accepted arrangement.

Indicating the confusion is, in itself, a reform, even if it does not, by itself, topple the tower of legalistic Babel. Understanding the origins of legal injustice may not eliminate legal injustices. Eliminating the legal profession and involving all citizens in the practice of law may not foster epieikeia in every human relationship. But these minimal reforms are a starting point, just as the expansion of voter suffrage has been a starting point. There is reason to hope that the exercise of civic virtues that encompass the practice of law (in effect, opening up such practice to all competent citizens) would result in a legal system with greater compliance levels and tempered with epieikeia.

To outline this rational hope is not to promise paradise, but it is no refutation of such reforms to point out that injustices will still arise. Rather, the point is that such reforms will, hopefully, reduce the quantity and magnitude of legal injustices, without necessarily eradicating them. The pagan priesthood of lawyers should no longer be allowed to intervene between the natural justice of citizens and the tempering of the harshness of the law with epieikeia.

The question of how to explain legal injustices, assuming that there is something called natural justice, is very much analogous to (and probably derivative from) the theodicical problem of explaining evil, assuming an all-powerful God who is good. A smaller subset of this broader question concerns whether epieikeia can exist in any form or degree, where less perfect friendships exist (and I submit that it does exist), and this question ultimately leads to the problem of how to make natural justice, in all its individuality and particularity, universal. Still another way of framing this latter question is to ask, simply, how is reform possible, given the perversity (to a greater or lesser extent) of all existing and past (and probably future) political regimes? The contemporary retort to this latter question ultimately challenges my very reason for even attempting this book, for it is, pointedly: What is the point of understanding the nature of legal injustice if one can not reform it?

My reply is that in the absence of such understanding, there are two very different risks. The first is that one may, someday, suffer or undergo some legal injustice (or see it inflicted on someone else with whom one is connected) and lack the small comfort that the possession of this understanding might provide. (Of course, I feel the pain of others to whom I am not connected other than by the bond of humanity, and this book enables me to attempt to share in their pain, however vicariously.) The second risk is that one may become a part of the growing industry of using the legal system to inflict injuries on others and sincerely believe oneself to be acting justly. (That is, one may become engaged in the all too common practice of doing wrong in the name of some good.)

Answering this retort presupposes, to some degree, the traditional Aristotelian question of whether leading a life as a virtuous person is compatible with being a good citizen in an imperfectly just, perverse polity (whether as an employee in a corporation or as a citizen in a nation state) in which the end of the polity has a weak connection (if any) to the well-being of its members. Accordingly, an understanding of the nature of legal injustices (and not necessarily their solutions) carries with it the choice of a quixotic en-

gagement (even if doomed to failure), in some small degree of reform, or
a resigned disengagement that permits one to more constructively redirect
one's attention to contemplation of broader, more fundamental questions.

There is some risk, however, that quixotic engagement can carry as its
price the prospect of becoming a part of the legal-injustice industry, whether
as a politician, lawyer, lobbyist, journalist, capitalist, or activist citizen. (But
maybe real reform has to come from the practices and customs of those who
are nonlawyers and nonpoliticians.) And implicit in this lies the contemporary preference for action, even if blind and misdirected, over contemplation.

As for the contemplative life, it is extremely hard to remain sufficiently
disengaged and remain a political animal (something that comes naturally
to being human), so some level of engagement within one's immediate network of associations inevitably insinuates one to some level of compromise
with the life of action. But for me, the ideal of the contemplative life retains
considerable appeal. At least its broader questions carry less risk of actively
abetting harm. As much as I have disparaged metaphysical attempts to solve
ethical and legal problems (as attempted by Kant), maybe the complete solution, rather than the partial solution offered in this book, requires some
sort of return to metaphysics.[15]

Jurisprudence, shorn of its theological roots, maybe has lost its way in the
dark wood. But then, some of the most central religious symbols have been
built upon a notion of justice that I find repellant: the idea that the sacrifice
of an innocent to expiate the crimes of a community is part of some incomprehensible divine plan that is somehow the essence of justice. But this
metaphor seems to work in many forms across many cultures and religions,
which makes the difficulties of the task of making the notion of justice advanced herein more comprehensible to me. It is difficult to understand particulars (and especially a notion of justice as emphasizing the particular)
without some notion of the universal,[16] and, as a result, the easy tendency, in
my view, is to completely obliterate the particular in the envelope of some
universal. And so I am compelled to close this present inquiry by acknowledging failure.

And yet, if one reconsiders the historical metaphor of the so-called Tower
of Babel myth, one might recognize in my presumed "failure" something
analogous to that moment of recognition in the myth when those engaged
in the doomed building project ceased their construction efforts. While the
failure to complete the Tower of Babel was, in one sense, a testament to their
failure, in another sense, this very mythic failure opened man up to a diversity of languages and a recognition of man's natural limitations. And the

various languages became an incomprehensible Babel only for the purposes of continuation of that misconceived enterprise of building the tower and all that such an enterprise represented.

It is in this latter sense that my failure to join in the debate about the blueprint for the Tower of Babel comprising our legal system is only a failure if one believes that we ought to continue the expansion of the present legal system as a means of addressing every possible defect in natural justice. As imperfect as humans naturally are, we might find it easier to live with each other to the extent that we moderate the range of law's empire, to use a Dworkian metaphor. And the sooner we recognize that the Dworkian enterprise is doomed, with due apologies to his Herculean judge, the sooner we can cease imputing great philosophic weight to the rhetorical arguments of hired guns and maybe give as much credence to law schools as most lawyers currently give to theological seminaries.

But such a recognition will only arise when persons are empowered to acknowledge what they grasp when they perceive what is just or unjust, whether or not that recognition is something easily articulated within the verbal formulas constituting the law. When men acknowledge that the wrench they feel in their gut when they encounter an injustice is as real as something they apprehend through sight, then the empty verbal formulations of the law will cease to have a greater reality than does justice.

Galileo is reported to have challenged those relying upon textual authority to deny the reality of his astronomical observations to simply look through the telescope and believe the testimony of their eyes.[17] I, likewise, challenge those who question the workings of epieikeia and natural justice to open themselves up to the evidence revealed by their souls.

Notes

1. Alasdair MacIntyre, *Whose Justice? Which Rationality?* (Notre Dame: University of Notre Dame Press, 1988), 344–45.

2. Of course, the fact remains that there has been no such implosion, and the legal elites have such a stranglehold on society that it is still unthinkable for most people to even contemplate life without professional lawyers—and this fact may be viewed by some as the ultimate refutation of the theory of this study.

3. See Milton Friedman's classic economic arguments exposing the hypocrisy underlying occupational licensure laws for lawyers, barbers, and physicians, in *Capitalism and Freedom* (Chicago: University of Chicago Press, 1962), 137–60.

4. Jeffrey Abramson's book makes a detailed case for empowering juries, by allowing informed persons to sit as juries rather than excluding them in the name of impartiality, and by recognizing the legitimacy of jury nullification. Jeffrey Abramson, *We, the Jury: The Jury System and the Ideal of Democracy* (New York: Basic Books, 1994).

5. A classic examination of the futility of voting and the absence of meaningful choice in

many voting patterns and procedures (that are not corrupt) is contained in Kenneth J. Arrow's *Social Choice and Individual Values* (New Haven: Yale University Press, 1963).

6. Mogens Herman Hansen, *The Athenian Democracy in the Age of Demosthenes* (Oxford: Blackwell, 1991), 314: "Every fourth adult male Athenian citizen could say, 'I have been for twenty-four hours President of Athens'—but no Athenian citizen could ever boast of having been so for more than twenty-four hours."

7. The canton consists of Germans, Italians, and Romansch, as well as Protestants and Catholics in fairly balanced proportions.

8. See Benjamin Barber, *The Death of Communal Liberty: A History of Freedom in a Swiss Mountain Canton* (Princeton: Princeton University Press, 1974). Jurisdictional fragmentation assured that the locus of most decisions such as those currently undertaken at the national level in the United States, including those involving most taxes, adjudication, and even foreign policy, were local. The right to bear arms and defend the republic was also central to the republic's notions of civic participation, in circumstances where every other European nation used professional armies or mercenaries.

9. See, for example, Freda Adler's speculative discussion as to why Switzerland enjoys very low violent crime and imprisonment rates, an index (for me) of the effectiveness of a society's legal system, in *Nations Not Obsessed With Crime*, 15–23.

10. Is an unstable but growing economy preferable to a slower-paced economy with more stable social structures in place?

11. See Christopher McMahon's well-reasoned argument for more corporate democracy, and his criticism of the inadequacy of grounding the legitimacy of current corporate forms exclusively on economic growth, in *Authority and Democracy: A General Theory of Government and Management* (Princeton: Princeton University Press, 1994).

12. Arlie Russell Hochschild, *The Time Bind: When Work Becomes Home and Home Becomes Work* (Metropolitan Books, 1997); Dana Mack, *The Assault on Parenthood: How Our Culture Undermines the Family* (New York: Simon and Schuster, 1997).

13. The confusion of language that speaks of the government as if it were one's parents or family or community, and of the legal system as if this (like revolution) would remedy all natural injustices, is the same kind of confusion as that which reduces all justice to legal justice and all morality to mere conformity with the laws. The leftists' confusion of what is community is just as problematic as is the positivists' confusion of justice with mere legality.

A community in which community is the government is not a community at all. Justice in which all justice is legal is the grounding of all legal injustice. Both stem from a failure to conceive of a contextual understanding of community or justice, a context that must step outside of political theory and examine these notions from the ordinary experiences of those who live together.

14. There is no other justification for government or legal coercion.

15. And while, in some respects, Hegel's shadow (and its resurgence in some communitarians) has silently loomed over significant components of my project, it ought to be fairly apparent that the laws, the corporate associations or "civil society," and impartial civil servants of the Rechsstaat are not analogues to the interplay between friendship and natural justice within Aristotle's political community.

16. It is an unfortunate fact that some (if not most) persons are all too often unable to discern the justice or injustice of their own actions without the intervention of some appeal to an abstract universal principle.

In the biblical account in Samuel II of David and Bathsheba, King David did not recognize the injustice of his own actions in taking from the herds of a poor neighbor (rather than his own) to entertain a guest, until the prophet Nathan told him a story about a rich man who did the same, prompting David's response: "The man that hath done this thing shall surely die." And to David's surprise, Nathan replied, "Thou art the man."

I would like to thank Hadley Arkes for pointing out this example to me as a serious consideration that might temper my overall argument. Incidentally, King David reminds me of some modern "liberal" tax attorneys who favor the progressive income tax in the name of "fairness" and at the same time advise wealthy clients on how to shelter their incomes.

17. Ludovico Geymonat, *Galileo Galilei: A Biography and Inquiry into His Philosophy of Science* (New York: McGraw-Hill, 1965), 35–45.

Bibliography

Primary Sources

Aristotle. *The Complete Works of Aristotle.* Ed. Jonathan Barnes. Princeton: Princeton University Press, 1984.

Dworkin, Ronald. *A Matter of Principle.* Cambridge: Harvard University Press, 1985.

———. *Law's Empire.* Cambridge: Harvard University Press, 1986.

———. "Liberal Community." *California Law Review* 77 (1989): 479–504.

———. *Life's Dominion: An Argument About Abortion, Euthanasia, and Individual Freedom.* New York: Alfred A. Knopf, 1993.

———. "Natural Law Revisited. *University of Florida Law Review* 34 (1982): 165.

———. *Taking Rights Seriously.* London: Duckworth, 1977.

———. "Unenumerated Rights: Whether and How *Roe* Should Be Overruled." *University of Chicago Law Review* 59 (1992): 381–432.

———. "What Is Equality? Part 3: The Place of Liberty." *Iowa Law Review* 73 (1987): 1–60.

———. "What Is Equality? Part 4: Political Equality." *University of San Francisco Law Review* 22 (1987): 1–40.

———. "Will Clinton's Plan Be Fair?" *New York Review of Books,* 13 January 1994, 20–25.

———. "Reply to Critics." 26 May 1994, 52–53.

———. "Women and Pornography." *New York Review of Books,* 21 October 1993, 37–42.

———. "Reply to Catherine MacKinnon." *New York Review of Books,* 3 March 1994, 48.

Kant, Immanuel. *Critique of Practical Reason.* Trans. L. W. Beck. Indianapolis: Bobbs-Merrill, 1956. Originally published as *Kritik der praktischen Vernunft* (Berlin: Konigliche Preussiche Akademie der Wissenschaften, 1913).

———. *Grounding for the Metaphysics of Morals.* Trans. James W. Ellington. Indianapolis: Hackett, 1993. Originally published as *Grundlegung zur Metaphysik der Sitten* (Berlin: Konigliche Preussiche Akademie der Wissenschaften, 1913).

———. *Lectures on Ethics.* Trans. Louis Infield. Indianapolis: Hackett, 1963.

———. *On a Supposed Right to Lie Because of Philanthropic Concerns.* Trans. James W. Ellington. Indianapolis: Hackett, 1993.

———. *The Metaphysical Elements of Justice.* Trans. John Ladd. Indianapolis: Bobbs-Merrill, 1965. Originally published as *Metaphysik der Sitten* (Berlin: Konigliche Preussiche Akademie der Wissenschaften, 1914).

Secondary Sources

Abramson, Jeffrey. *We, the Jury: The Jury System and the Ideal of Democracy.* New York: Basic Books, 1994.

Addis, Adeno. "Individualism, Communitarianism, and the Rights of Ethnic Minorities." *Notre Dame Law Review* 67 (1991): 615–76.

Adler, Freda. *Nations Not Obsessed with Crime.* Littleton, Colo.: Rothman, 1983.

Alexander, Larry. "Striking Back at the Empire: A Brief Survey of Problems in Dworkin's Theory of Law." *Law and Philosophy* 6 (1987): 419–38.

Arendt, Hannah. *Eichmann in Jerusalem: A Report on the Banality of Evil.* New York: Viking Press, 1963.

Arkes, Hadley. *First Things.* Princeton: Princeton University Press, 1986.

Arrow, Kenneth J. *Social Choice and Individual Values.* New Haven: Yale University Press, 1963.

Augustine, Saint. *On Free Choice of the Will.* Trans. Anna S. Benjamin and L. H. Hackstaff. New York: Library of Liberal Arts, 1964.

Austin, John. *The Province of Jurisprudence Determined.* Ed. H. L. A. Hart. New York: Humanities Press, 1965.

Austin, W. Timothy. "Crime and Custom in an Orderly Society: The Singapore Prototype" *Criminology* 25 (1987): 279–92.

Axelrod, Robert. *The Evolution of Cooperation.* New York: Basic Books, 1981.

Banfield, Edward C. "Welfare: A Crisis Without 'Solutions.'" *Public Interest* 16 (Summer 1969): 89–101.

Barber, Benjamin. *The Death of Communal Liberty: A History of Freedom in a Swiss Mountain Canton.* Princeton: Princeton University Press, 1974.

Beck, Lewis White. *A Commentary on Kant's Critique of Practical Reason.* Chicago: University of Chicago Press, 1960.

Bentham, Jeremy. *A Comment on the Commentaries and a Fragment on Government.* Eds. J. H. Burns and H. L. A. Hart. London, 1977.

———. *A Fragment on Government.* Ed. F. C. Montague. Oxford: Oxford University Press, 1891.

———. *An Introduction to the Principles of Morals and Legislation.* Eds. J. H. Burns and H. L. A. Hart. London: Oxford University Press, 1970.

———. *Of Laws in General.* Ed. H. L. A. Hart. London: Athlone Press, 1970.

Berle, Adolphe A., Jr. "Corporate Powers as Powers in Trust." *Harvard Law Review* 44 (1931): 1049–74.

———. "For Whom Are Corporate Managers Trustees? A Note." *Harvard Law Review* 45 (1932): 1365–72.

Bernstein, Richard. *Dictatorship of Virtue.* New York: St. Martin's Press, 1994.

Blum, Lawrence. *Friendship, Altruism, and Morality.* New York: Routledge and Kegan Paul, 1980.

Bovard, James. *Lost Rights: The Destruction of American Liberty.* New York: St. Martin's Press, 1994.

Butler, Henry N. "The Contractual Theory of the Corporation." *George Mason University Law Review* 11 (Summer 1989): 99–123.

Chansky, James D. "Reflections on *After Virtue* After Auschwitz." *Philosophy Today* (Fall 1993): 247–56.

Cicero, Marcus Tullius. *Laws.* Trans. C. W. Keyes. Cambridge: Harvard University Press, 1928.

Cooper, John. "Aristotle on Friendship." In *Essays on Aristotle's Ethics.* Ed. A. O. Rorty. Berkeley and Los Angeles: University of California Press, 1980.

Cover, Robert. *Narrative, Violence, and the Law: Essays of Robert Cover.* Ed. Martha Minow, Michael Ryan, and Austin Sarat. Ann Arbor: University of Michigan Press, 1992.

de Tocqueville, Alexis. *Democracy in America.* Trans. Henry Reeve. New York: Alfred A. Knopf, 1980.

———. "Memoir on Pauperism." Trans. Seymour Drescher. *Public Interest* 70 (Winter 1983): 102.

Dodd, E. Merrick. "For Whom Are Corporate Managers Trustees?" *Harvard Law Review* 45 (1932): 1145–63.

Ellickson, Robert C. *Order Without Law: How Neighbors Settle Disputes.* Cambridge: Harvard University Press, 1991.

Epstein, Richard. *Simple Rules for a Complex World.* Cambridge: Harvard University Press, 1995.

Farnsworth, E. Allan. *Contracts.* Boston: Little, Brown, 1982.

Finnis, John. *Natural Law and Natural Rights.* Oxford: Oxford University Press, 1980.

———. "On Reason and Authority in *Law's Empire.*" *Law and Philosophy* 6 (1987): 357–80.

Frank, Jerome. *Law and the Modern Mind.* New York: Brentano's, 1930.

Friedman, Lawrence M. *Total Justice.* New York: Russell Sage Foundation, 1994.

Friedman, Milton. *Capitalism and Freedom.* Chicago: University of Chicago Press, 1962.

Fuller, Lon L. *The Morality of Law.* New Haven: Yale University Press, 1964.

Funk, T. Markus. "Gun Control and Economic Discrimination: The Melting-Point Case-In-Point." *Journal of Criminal Law and Criminology* 85 (1995): 764–806.

Geymonat, Ludovico. *Gallileo Galilei: A Biography and Inquiry into His Philosophy of Science.* New York: McGraw-Hill, 1965.

George, Robert. *Making Men Moral.* Oxford: Oxford University Press, 1993.

Glendon, Mary Ann. *Abortion and Divorce in Western Law: American Failures, European Challenges.* Cambridge: Harvard University Press, 1987.

Guest, Stephen. *Ronald Dworkin.* Stanford: Stanford University Press, 1991.

Hanson, Thomas L., Irwin Garfinkel, Sara S. McLanahan, and Cynthia K. Miller. "Trends in Child Support Outcomes," in *Demography.* Washington, D.C.: November 1996.

Hart, H. L. A. "Positivism and the Separation of Law and Morals," in *Essays in Jurisprudence and Philosophy.* Oxford: Oxford University Press, 1983.

———. *The Concept of Law.* Oxford: Oxford University Press, 1961.

Hayden, Mary. "Rediscovering Eudaimonistic Teleology." *Monist* 75 (January 1992).

Hegel, Georg Wilhelm Friedrich. *Philosophy of Right.* Trans. T. M. Knox. Oxford: Clarendon, 1967.

Hobbes, Thomas. *Leviathan.* London: Penguin, 1968.

Hochschild, Arlie Russell. *The Time Bind: When Work Becomes Home and Home Becomes Work.* Metropolitan Books, 1997.

Holmes, Oliver Wendell, Jr. *Holmes-Pollock Letters* 36. Ed. Mark DeWolfe Howe, 1961.

———. "The Path of the Law." *Harvard Law Review* 10 (1896).

Howard, Philip K. *The Death of Common Sense.* New York: Random House, 1995.

Hoy, David Couzens. "Dworkin's Constructive Optimism v. Deconstructive Legal Nihilism." *Law and Philosophy* 6 (1987): 321–56.

Hume, David. *A Treatise of Human Nature.* Oxford: Oxford University Press, 1978.

———. *Essays: Moral, Political and Literary.* Oxford: Oxford University Press, 1963.

Hyde, Henry. *Forfeiting Our Property Rights.* Washington, D.C.: Cato, 1995.

Jenkins, Iredell. *Social Order and the Limits of Law.* Princeton: Princeton University Press, 1980.

Kahn, Paul. "Community in Contemporary Constitutional Theory." *Yale Law Journal* 99 (1989): 1–96.

Kelsen, Hans. *Pure Theory of Law.* Trans. Max Knight. Berkeley and Los Angeles: University of California Press, 1978.

Keyt, David. "Three Basic Theorems in Aristotle's *Politics.*" In *A Companion to Aristo-*

tle's Politics. Eds. David Keyt and Fred D. Miller Jr. Cambridge: Basil Blackwell, 1991, 118–41.

Langton, Rae. "Duty and Desolation." *Philosophy* 67 (1992): 481–505.

Levin, Nora. *The Holocaust: The Destruction of European Jewry, 1933–1945.* New York: Schocken Books, 1973.

Leyden, W. von. *Aristotle on Equality and Justice.* New York: St. Martin's Press, 1985.

Locke, John. *Two Treatises on Government.* Ed. Peter Laslett. Cambridge: Cambridge University Press, 1988.

Long, Roderick T. "Aristsotle's Conception of Freedom. *Review of Metaphysics* 49 (1996): 801–2.

MacIntyre, Alasdair. *After Virtue,* 2d. ed. Notre Dame: University of Notre Dame Press, 1984.

———. "The Privatization of Good." *Review of Politics* (1990): 344–61.

———. *Whose Justice? Which Rationality?* Notre Dame: University of Notre Dame Press, 1988.

MacCormick, Neil. *Legal Reasoning and Legal Theory.* Oxford: Oxford University Press, 1978.

Mack, Dana. *The Assault on Parenthood: How Our Culture Undermines the Family.* New York: Simon and Schuster, 1997.

McMahon, Christopher. *Authority and Democracy: A General Theory of Government and Management.* Princeton: Princeton University Press, 1994.

Miller, Fred. D., Jr. "Aristotle and the Origins of Natural Rights." *Review of Metaphysics* 49 (June 1996): 877–78.

———. "Aristotle on Natural Law and Justice." In *A Companion to Aristotle's Politics.* Eds. David Keyt and Fred D. Miller Jr. Cambridge: Basil Blackwell, 1991, 279–306.

———. *Nature, Justice, and Rights in Aristotle's Politics.* Oxford: Oxford University Press, 1995.

Mitchell, Lawrence E., ed. *Progressive Corporate Law.* Boulder, Colo.: Westview, 1995.

Mogens, Herman Hansen. *The Athenian Democracy in the Age of Demosthenes.* Oxford: Blackwell, 1991.

Montesquieu. *The Spirit of the Laws.* Trans. Thomas Nugent. New York: Hafner Press, 1949.

Morawetz, Thomas. "Understanding Disagreement, the Root Issue of Jurisprudence: Applying Wittgenstein to Positivism, Critical Theory, and Judging." *University of Pennsylvania Law Review* 141 (1992): 371–456.

Murphy, James Bernard. "Nature, Custom, and Stipulation in Law and Jurisprudence." *Review of Metaphysics* 43 (1990): 751–90.

O'Hare, William P. "A New Look at Poverty in America," in *Population Bulletin.* Washington, D.C.: September 1996.

O'Neill, Onora. "Universal Laws and Ends-in-Themselves." *Monist* 72 (1989): 341–63.

Posner, Richard A. *Overcoming Law.* Cambridge: Harvard University Press, 1995.

———. *The Economic Analysis of Law,* 2d ed. Boston, 1977.

Postema, Gerald J. *Bentham and the Common Law Tradition.* Oxford: Oxford University Press, 1986.

Pound, Roscoe. *An Introduction to the Philosophy of Law.* New Haven: Yale University Press, 1922.

Rasmussen, Douglas B., and Douglas J. Den Uyl. *Liberty and Nature, An Aristotelian Defense of Liberal Order.* La Salle, Ill.: Open Court, 1991.

Rawls, John. *A Theory of Justice.* Cambridge: Harvard University Press, 1971.

Robinson, Daniel N., and Rom Harre. "The Demography of the Kingdom of Ends." *Philosophy* 69 (1994): 5–19.

Ryle, Gilbert. "Categories." *Proceedings of Aristotelian Society* 38 (1937–38).

Sandel, Michael. "Liberalism and the Claims of Community: The Case of Affirmative Action." In *Ronald Dworkin and Contemporary Jurisprudence*. Ed. Marshall Cohen. Totowa, New Jersey: Rowman and Allanheld, 1984.

Sarat, Austin, and Thomas R. Kearns. "Making Peace with Violence: Robert Cover on Law and Legal Theory." In *Law's Violence*. Ed. Austin Sarat and Thomas R. Kearns. Ann Arbor: University of Michigan Press, 1992.

Schmitt, Carl. *Political Theology*. Trans. George Schwabb. Cambridge: MIT Press, 1988.

Selznick, Philip. "Dworkin's Unfinished Task." *California Law Review* 77 (1989): 505.

Sherman, Nancy. *The Fabric of Character: Aristotle's Theory of Virtue*. Oxford: Oxford University Press, 1989.

Shiner, Roger A. "Aristotle's Theory of Equity." In *Justice, Law, and Method in Plato and Aristotle*. Ed. Spiro Panagiotou. Edmonton, Canada: Academic Printing and Publishing, 1987: 173–91.

Sowell, Thomas. *Markets and Minorities*. New York: Basic Books, 1981.

Stern, Robert L., Eugene Gressman, Stephen M. Shapiro, Kenneth S. Geller. *Supreme Court Practice*, 7th ed. Washington, D.C.: Bureau of National Affairs, 1993.

Strauss, Leo. *Natural Right and History*. Chicago: University of Chicago Press, 1953.

Sullivan, Roger J. "The Kantian Critique of Aristotle's Moral Philosophy: An Appraisal." *Review of Metaphysics* 28 (1974): 24–53.

Taylor, Charles. "The Nature and Scope of Distributive Justice." In *Philosophical Papers*, vol. 2. Cambridge: Cambridge University Press, 1983.

Thomas Aquinas, Saint. *Summa Theologica*. Trans. Fathers of the English Dominican Province. New York: Benzinger Brothers, 1947.

Unger, Roberto Mangabeira. *Knowledge and Politics*. New York: Free Press, 1975.

———. *The Critical Legal Studies Movement*. Cambridge: Harvard University Press, 1983.

Waterlow, Sarah. *Nature, Change, and Agency in Aristotle's Physics*. Oxford: Oxford University Press, 1982.

Williams, Bernard. "Dworkin on Community and Critical Interests." *California Law Review* 77 (1989): 515.

Wolgast, Elizabeth. *The Grammar of Justice*. Ithaca: Cornell University Press, 1987.

Yack, Bernard. *The Problems of a Political Animal: Community, Justice, and Conflict in Aristotelian Political Thought*. Berkeley and Los Angeles: University of California Press, 1993.

Zacharias, Fred C. "Specificity in Professional Responsibility Codes: Theory, Practice, and the Paradigm of Prosecutorial Ethics. *Notre Dame Law Review* 69 (1993): 223–309.

Public Record

American Bar Association Model Rules for Professional Responsibility.

Statutes, Debates, and Hearings

Title 18, Federal Sentencing Guidelines (1995).

21 U.S.C. Sections 853(e) and 881(e).

28 U.S.C. Sections 991 et. seq.

28 U.S.C. Sections 1251, 1254, 1257, 1291 and 1292.

42 U.S.C. Section 5106a.

138 Cong. Rec. S17603 (8 Oct. 1992).

H. Conf. Rep. No. 103–711, 1994 U.S. Code Cong. and Admin. News: 1856.
H. Conf., Rep. No. 103–711, 1994 U.S. Code Cong. and Admin. News: 1856.
Sen. Hrg. No. 105–190, Hearings Before the Senate Finance Committee, *Practices and Procedures of the Internal Revenue Service*. Washington, D.C., 1997.
Sen. Hrg. No. 104–799, Hearings Before the Subcommittee on Terrorism, Technology, and Government Information of the Senate Judiciary Committee, *The Federal Raid On Ruby Ridge, ID*. Washington, D.C., 1997.

Regulations

58 Fed. Reg. 51266 (1 Oct. 1993). EEOC Proposed Regulations on Religious Harassment.
ABA Model Rules 7.2, 7.3, and 8.4; ABA Code DR 1–102.

Cases

Batson v. Kentucky, 476 U.S. 79 (1986).
Belle Terre v. Borass, 416 U.S. 1 (1974).
Bennis v. Michigan, 116 S.Ct. 994 (1996).
Board of Education of Kiryas Joel Village School District v. Grumet, 129 L.Ed.2d 546 (1994).
Buhl v. Kavanagh, 118 F.2d 315 (6th Cir. 1941).
Burns v. Reed, 11 S.Ct. 1934 (1991).
Capital Square Review and Advisory Bd. v. Knights of the Ku Klux Klan, 132 L.Ed.2d 650 (1995).
Carrie Buck Buck v. J. H. Bell, 274 U.S. 200 (1927).
Century Indemnity Co. v. Kofsky, 161 A. 101 (Conn. 1932).
Claussen, 502 N.W.2d 649 (Mich. 1993).
Commonwealth v. Amirault, 677 N.E.2d 652, 665, 424 Mass. 618 (1997).
Commonwealth v. Lindsay, 489 N.E.2d 666 (Mass. 1986).
Concrete Pipe and Products, Inc., v. Construction Laborers Pension Trust, 113 S.Ct. 2264 (1993).
Corcoran v. United Healthcare, Inc., 15 E.B.C. 1793 (5th Cir. 1992).
Davis v. Carothers, 335 S.W.2d 631 (Tex. Civ. App., Waco, 1969).
Dred Scott v. Sandford, 60 U.S. (19 How.) 393 (1856).
Escobedo v. Illinois, 378 U.S. 478 (1964).
Firestone v. Bruch, 489 U.S. 101 (1989).
Gitlow v. New York, 268 U.S. 652 (1925).
Harris v. Forklift Systems, Inc., 126 L.Ed.2d 295 (1993).
Harmelin v. Michigan, 115 L.Ed.2d 836 (1991).
Hughes v. Commonwealth, 16 Va.App. 576, 431 S.E.2d 906 (1993).; *rehearing en banc*, 18 Va.App. 510, 446 S.E.2d 451 (1994).
Hurley v. Irish-American Gay, Lesbian, and Bisexual Group of Boston, 132 L.Ed.2d 487 (1995).
Imbler v. Pachtman, 95 S.Ct. 984 (1976).
Jacobson v. United States, 112 S.Ct. 1525 (1992).
Jones v. U.S. Drug Enforcement Administration, 1993 U.S.Dist. LEXIS 5409 (Apr. 23, 1993).
Lee v. Weisman, 112 S.Ct. 2649 (1992).
LTV Steel Co. v. Shalala, No. 93 CIV. 0554 (JSM). (S.D.N.Y. Dec. 14, 1993).
Maccabees v. City of Ashland, 109 S.W.2d 29 (Ky. 1937).
McCummings v. New York City Transit Authority, 81 N.Y.2d 923, 613 N.E.2d 559 (1993).

Meritor Savings Bank, FSB v. Vinson, 447 U.S. 57 (1986).
Mertens v. Hewitt Association, 113 S.Ct. 2063 (1993).
Michaels v. New Jersey, 625 A.2d 489 (N.J.Super.A.D. 1993).
Mikels v. Cowie Cut Stone Co., 171 N.E. 251 (Ohio App. 1929).
Miranda v. Arizona, 384 U.S. 436 (1966).
Mordt v. Robinson, 156 So. 535 (Fla. 1934).
Nash v. Gardner, 101 S.E.2d 283 (S.C. 1957).
Pearcy v. Citizens Bank and Trust Co. of Bloomington, 96 N.E.2d 918 (Ind. 1951).
People v. Gilbert, 63 Cal.2d 690, 408 P.2d 365 (1965).
People v. Peete, 28 Cal.2d 306 (1946).
People v. Purvis, 52 Cal.2d 871, 346 P.2d 22 (1959).
Piscataway Township Board of Education v. Taxman, 91 F.3d 1597 (3d Cir. 1996).
Price v. Price, 7 S.E.2d 510 (W.Va. 1940).
R. A. V. v. City of St. Paul, Minnesota, 505 U.S. 377 (1992).
Rich v. Stephens, 11 P.2d 295 (Utah 1932).
Roe v. Wade, 410 U.S. 113 (1973).
Shepherd v. Dougan, 76 P.2d 442 (Idaho 1953).
Smith v. Whitman, 189 A.2d 15 (N.J. 1963).
Terminiello v. Chicago, 337 U.S. 1 (1948).
Underwood v. Phillips Petroleum Co., 155 F.2d 372 (10th Cir. 1946).
United States v. Carolene Products Co., 304 U.S. 144 (1938).
United States v. D'Amato, 39 F.3d 1249 (2d Cir. 1994).
United States v. Jennifer Skarie, No. 91–50007, 1992 U.S.App. LEXIS 16884 (9th Cir., July 28, 1992).
United Wire, Metal and Mach. Health and Welfare Fund v. Morristown Memorial Hospital, 995 F.2d 1179 (3d Cir. 1993).
Wasson v. Pledger, 96 S.W.2d 8 (Ark. 1936).
Williams Bros. Lumber Co. v. Anderson, 78 S.E.2d 612 (Ga. 1953).
Woodlawn Federal Savings and Loan Association v. Williams, 187 So. 177 (Ala. 1939).
Young v. American Mini Theatres, 427 U.S. 50 (1976).
Zabolotny v. Commissioner, 97 T.C. 385 (1991), *affirmed in part, reversed in part,* 7 F.3d 774 (8th Cir. 1993).

General Reference

Cleary, Edward W., Kenneth S. Brown, George E. Dix, Ernest Gellhorn, D. H. Kaye, Robert Meisenholder, E. F. Roberts, and John W. Strong, *McCormick on Evidence,* 3d ed. St. Paul, Minn.: West Publishing Co., 1984).
The Holy Bible, Authorized (King James) Version. Cleveland: World Publishing.
30A *Corpus Juris Secundum.* St. Paul, Minn.: West Publ. Co., 1992.

Newspapers, Magazines, Television

Adler, Stephen J. "Lawyer's Poker: Stacking the Marcos Jury." *Wall Street Journal,* 14 September 1994, B1, B12.
Allen, George. "Justice and the Criminals." *Washington Times,* 7 November 1994, A23.
Anders, George, and Laurie McGinley. "Surgical Strike, A New Brand of Crime Now Stirs the Feds: Health-Care Fraud." *Wall Street Journal,* 6 May 1997, A1.

Arkes, Hadley. "Anti-Abortion, but Politically Smart." *Wall Street Journal,* 28 March 1995, A26.

Associated Press. "Cleared of Child Abuse, He Sues." *New York Times,* 8 September 1994, A21.

Berstein, Richard. "The Case of Order v. Disorder in the Court." *New York Times,* 10 May 1995, C19.

"Bill Clinton and the ADA." *Wall Street Journal,* 20 May 1994, A10.

Bovard, James. "Disabilities Law, Health Hazard." *Wall Street Journal,* 23 March 1994, A14.

———. "The Latest EEOC Quota Madness." *Wall Street Journal,* 27 April 1995, A14.

Burnham, David. "Punish or Perish at IRS: Will the Taxman's Quotas Catch You on April 15?" *Washington Post,* 13 March 1988, C1, C2.

Cannon, Lou. "Another Casualty of the Rodney King Case; The Stereotyping of Stacey Koon." *Washington Post,* 31 December 1995, C7.

Carlson, Peter. "The Magazine Reader: Murder in the First Degree." *Washington Post,* 16 September 1997, E1, E8.

Cooper, Kenneth J. "House Seeks to Delete Death Penalty Bias Provision." *Washington Post,* 17 June 1994, A10.

Crenshaw, Albert B. "Beleagered IRS Anounces Steps to Curb Abuses." *Washington Post,* 26 September 1997, A13.

Davis, David Brion. "At the Heart of Slavery." *New York Review of Books,* 17 October 1996, 51.

Duncan, Richard F. "A Speech Code for Lawyers." *Wall Street Journal,* 3 February 1994, A14.

Farney, Dennis. "Shaky Ground: Gay Rights Confront Determined Resistance from Some Moderates." *Wall Street Journal,* 7 October 1994, A1.

Fields, Suzanne. "Even Among Academics, Bad Taste Is Not a Crime." *Washington Times,* 17 October 1994, A19.

———. "The Sexual Revolution in the White House." *Washington Times,* 9 May 1994, A21.

Flaherty, Mary Pat, and Joan Biskupic. "Rules Often Impose Toughest Penalties on Poor, Minorities: Justice by the Numbers." *Washington Post,* 9 October 1996, A1, A27–28.

Francis, Samuel. "The News You Won't Be Hearing from the Anti-Gun Lobby." *Washington Times,* 1 November 1994, A19.

Friedman, Milton. "Why a Flat Tax Is Not Politically Feasible," *Wall Street Journal,* 30 March 1995, A14.

Gardner, Richard A. "Modern Witch Hunt: Child Abuse Charges." *Wall Street Journal,* 22 February 1993, A10.

Glassman, James K. "Buying Off Justice." *Washington Post,* 25 November 1997, A19.

Goldstein, Avram. "Lawmakers Rethink Managed Care Appeals Process." *Washington Post,* 6 December 1997, B4.

Green, John. "Cann ed: When a Beer Company Executive Tried to Discuss a Racy 'Seinfeld' Episode with a Female Co-Worker, He Was Fired. But He Got the Last Laugh." *Washington Post,* 5 October 1997, F1.

Greenfield, Meg. "Right and Wrong in Washington: Why Do Our Officials Need Specialists to Tell the Difference?" *Washington Post,* 6 February 1995, A19.

———. "Sexual Harasser?" *Washington Post,* 30 September 1996, A23.

Gugliotta, Guy. "Deciphering a Code that is Mostly Just Taxing." *Washington Post,* 25 October 1994, A15.

Gimbel, Peter. "A Swiss Who Bent Rules to Save Jews Is Refused a Pardon: Treatment of Paul Grueninger Reflects Europe's Turmoil over World War II Legacy." *Wall Street Journal,* 3 June 1994, A1.

Hamilton, William. "Crimes of Passion Spark Intense Debate." *Washington Post,* 14 August 1994, A3.

Harris, John F. "One Day After Retiring, Navy Admiral Assails Sen. Murray on Harassment Issue." *Washington Post,* 3 November 1994, A6.

Hays, Laurie. "A Matter of Time: Widow Sues IBM over Death Benefits." *Wall Street Journal,* 6 July 1995, A1.

Henthoff, Nat. "A Zero for Jesus in a Public School." *Washington Post,* 26 January 1996, A23.

———. "'I Would Prefer Not To': The Man Who Refused to Go to Sexual-Harassment Prevention Class." *Washington Post,* 24 September 1994, A27.

———. "The AIDS Establishment's Conspiracy of Silence." *Washington Post,* 1 October 1994, A23.

Hirsh, Michael. "Inside the IRS: Lawless, Abusive, and Out of Control." *Newsweek,* 13 October 1997, 33–39.

"Homicide: A Special Report." *Newsweek,* 15 August 1994, 20–49.

Horwatt, Sally. "The Freudian Referral Slip." *Washington Post,* 25 July 1993, C3.

Ingersoll, Bruce. "Old Order: GOP's Plans to Curtail Government Benefits Bring No Pain to Amish." *Wall Street Journal,* 22 December 1995, A1.

Jenkins, Holman W., Jr. "Who's Scamming Whom?" *Wall Street Journal,* 5 August 1997, A19.

Jennings, Marianne M. "Trendy Causes Are No Substitute for Ethics." *Wall Street Journal,* 1 December 1997, A22.

Kamman, Bob. "Tax Czars vs. the Poor." *Wall Street Journal,* 17 January 1997, A12.

Kristol, Irving. "The Tragic Error of Affirmative Action." *Wall Street Journal,* 1 August 1994, A20.

Lambert, Wade. "Title IX Costs Black Men, Lawyer Says." *Wall Street Journal,* 12 June 1994, B7.

Larry King Live television interview of Mike Gibson and John Walsh, CNN, 16 November 1994.

Lempres, Michael T. "In Kobe, the Looting That Wasn't." *Washington Times,* 31 January 1995, A17.

MacDonald, Heather. "Free Housing Yes, Free Speech No." *Wall Street Journal,* 8 August 1994, A12.

Macey, Jonathan R. "The '80s Villain, Vindicated." *Wall Street Journal,* 18 July 1995, A12.

Mack, Dana. "Child Abuse Noose: Turning Parents into Perpetrators?" *Washington Post,* 30 January 1994, C3: "A Florida couple was convicted of abuse for restricting a foster child's television viewing."

Mauro, Tony. "Court Rules Against Jewish School District." *USA Today,* 28 June 1994, A3.

Martin, Stefan. "The Crucible, Part II: The Witches of Fairfax." *Washington Post,* 25 July 1993, C3: "In the zeal to find abusers, have we gone too far?"

McGee, Jim. "Misconduct Cases Rise at Justice Department. *Washington Post,* 23 April 1996, A15.

Meyer, Eugene L. "Poisoned Memories: Danny Smith Was Tried for Child Abuse. Then His Daughter Had Second Thoughts." *Washington Post,* 27 May 1994, D1.

Neuhaus, Richard John. "Don't Cross This Threshold." *Wall Street Journal,* 27 October 1994, A20.

"Not So Stupid." *Wall Street Journal,* 3 November 1994, A18.

Novak, Robert D. "Billionaire's Tax Break" *Washington Post,* 16 February 1995, A23.

Packwood, Bob. "Bill and Me." *Wall Street Journal,* 13 May 1994, A10.

Postrel, Virginia I. "Reawakening to Waco: Does the Federal Government Understand the Message It's Sending?" *Washington Post,* 30 April 1995, C3.

Rabinowitz, Dorothy. "An Army of Schindlers from Italy." *Wall Street Journal,* 7 December 1993, A14.

———. "Kelly Michael's Orwellian Ordeal." *Wall Street Journal,* 15 March 1993, A14.

Rabkin, Jeremy. "New Checks on Campus Sexual-Harassment Cops." *Wall Street Journal,* 19 October 1994, A21.

Roman, Nancy E. "Unmarried Couple Lose Rental Case." *Washington Times,* 3 June 1994, A1, A9.

Samuelson, Robert J. "Whitewater: The Law as a Pit Bull." *Washington Post,* 5 July 1994, A16.

Schmitt, Richard B. "EEOC May Pit Church vs. State at Work." *Wall Street Journal,* 8 June 1994, B8.

Seigle, Greg. "D.C. Man Convicted in Hill Aide's Murder: Jury in 2d Trial Takes Just 3 1/2 Hours." *Washington Times,* 7 September 1994, A1, A10.

Selz, Michael. "Family Businesses Organize to Seek Estate-Tax Deferral." *Wall Street Journal,* 18 May 1994, B2.

Shellenberger, Sue. "Child Care Crunch Puts Parents Between the Kids and the Boss." *Wall Street Journal,* 12 October 1994, B1.

———. "Family-Friendly Firms Often Leave Father Out of the Picture." *Wall Street Journal,* 2 November 1994, B1.

Suro, Roberto. "Town Faults Law, Not Boy, in Sex Case," *Washington Post,* 11 May 1997, A1.

Thomas-Lester, Avis. "Abduction Suspect Paroled in '79 Case: Kidnapped Boy's Mother Questions Role of Judicial System, D.C. Police." *Washington Post,* 3 October 1994, A1.

Tolman, Jonathan. "A Sign of the Times." *Wall Street Journal,* 20 September 1994, A22.

Toothman, John W. "Real Reform." *ABA Journal,* September 1995, 80–81.

Trescolt, Jacqueline. "Honeymoon's Over: Legislators Threaten Arts Agency Again." *Washington Post,* 22 June 1994, D1, D8.

Vobejda, Barbara, and Judith Havemann, "Welfare Clients Already Work Off the Books." *Washington Post,* 3 November 1997, A1.

Walsh, Edward. "Illinois Court Backs Biological Parents." *Washington Post,* 14 July 1994, A3.

Weiss, Rick. "Proposed Shifts in Misconduct Reviews Unsettle Many Scientists." *Washington Post,* 30 June 1996, A6.

Index

JOHN C. ANDERSON holds a law degree and a doctoral degree in philosophy from The Catholic University of America, and practiced law for five years in Washington, D.C. An independent scholar, he now works for the Army.